This

... is an authorized facsimile made from the master copy of the original book. Further unauthorized copying is prohibited.

Books on Demand is a publishing service of UMI. The program offers xerographic reprints of more than 136,000 books that are no longer in print.

The primary focus of Books on Demand is academic and professional resource materials originally published by university presses, academic societies, and trade book publishers worldwide.

UMI
BOOKS ON DEMAND™

UMI
A Bell & Howell Company
300 North Zeeb Road ❧ PO Box 1346
Ann Arbor, Michigan 48106-1346
800-521-0600 ❧ 313-761-4700

Printed in 1996 by xerographic process on acid-free paper

Crisis in Costa Rica
The 1948 Revolution

Latin American Monographs, No. 24
Institute of Latin American Studies
The University of Texas at Austin

CRISIS
in Costa Rica

The 1948 Revolution

by JOHN PATRICK BELL

PUBLISHED FOR THE INSTITUTE OF LATIN AMERICAN STUDIES
BY THE UNIVERSITY OF TEXAS PRESS, AUSTIN AND LONDON

International Standard Book Number 0-292-70147-0
Library of Congress Catalog Card Number 77-165920
© 1971 by John Patrick Bell
All Rights Reserved
Type set by G&S Typesetters, Austin
Printed by Capital Printing Company, Austin
Bound by Universal Bookbinders, Inc., San Antonio

CONTENTS

Preface xi

Chapter 1. Introduction and Background 3

Chapter 2. The Social Question 19

Chapter 3. The Issue of Communism 41

Chapter 4. Fiscal Corruption and Mismanagement . . 62

Chapter 5. Conspiracy, Rebellion, and the Second
Republic 81

Chapter 6. The Electoral Question 106

Chapter 7. Revolution and Negotiated Peace . . . 131

Chapter 8. Epilogue 155

Selected Bibliography 163

Index 177

PREFACE

Although several general works on Latin American, Central American, and Costa Rican history mention the Costa Rican revolution of 1948, a full and objective account is needed. Many works in Spanish tell a part of the story, but almost always in a partisan manner. The few works in English which devote significant attention to Costa Rica in 1948 are based on the same five or six works written by supporters of the National Liberation movement.

The very fact of a successful armed uprising occurring in that generally stable and pacific nation intrigued me. Many works indicated that prior to this upheaval, Costa Rica's political system had degenerated, almost overnight, from an exemplary democracy to a cruel tyranny. Determining whether or not such a decline had actually taken place was a topic that appeared to be a fascinating one for further inquiry. If this deterioration had occurred, what were the underlying causes? If it had not, what had happened to persuade so many scholars, journalists, and others to accept that interpretation?

Since the event was contemporary, it was possible to interview many who had participated in the insurrection. Approximately two hundred personal interviews were conducted in Costa Rica with men who had fought or otherwise been involved in the revolution and with the events which led up to it. The interviews yielded new insights and gave access to invaluable primary source material, not available through more customary channels, such as public and institutional libraries. Although there is presently a wealth of research material in Costa Rica, future years will surely bring new sources when the men who made the revolution write about their roles in the conflict. Perhaps this narrative will prompt some of them to offer new interpretations of the revolt. Such a reaction would in itself justify this study. A comprehensive account by José Figueres would be of particular benefit to all interested in Costa Rica and Latin America in general.

My own interpretation of the revolution as the culmination of an extended period of social tension determined to a large degree the structure of this work. The first chapter provides introduction and background; the second through the sixth deal with the same time frame, each chapter beginning in 1940 and covering the years up to the revolt. They are organized topically. Chapters two, three, four, and six each deal with a major issue of the period, while chapter five focuses on the organization and activities of the revolutionaries from 1940 to 1948. The months immediately preceding the uprising and the revolution itself are treated in chapter seven. Chapter eight then investigates the performance of the revolutionaries after they had come to power.

I wish to express my gratitude to the many people who generously aided me in the preparation of this study. It would be impossible to acknowledge adequately their many kindnesses and impractical to mention each individually. I, however, would be truly derelict not to at least indicate to the reader those deserving special recognition. William J. Griffith directed the progress of this research with infinite care and precision without intruding himself directly into the study. He, therefore, bears no responsibility for its shortcomings but much of the credit for whatever contribution the study makes to an understanding of Costa Rican history. Thomas L. Karnes shared his invaluable knowledge of the subject acquired through his own research in Central America. For their always proficient and often inspired proofreading and for their careful typing of the manuscript, I am grateful to my wife Dora Inés and our good friend Athleen Reddy.

In Costa Rica, many encouraged and supported the study by

spending long patient hours answering my inquiries, opening their private collections to my scrutiny, and introducing me to yet others, equally willing to assist. Outstanding in this connection were Ricardo Fernández Peralta, Rafael Obregón Loría, Enrique Guier, Virginia Zúñiga, José Figueres Ferrer, Rafael Angel Calderón Guardia, Carlos Meléndez, Maximiliano Koberg Bolandi, Máximo Quesada, Fernando Valverde, Carlos Luis Fallas, Alberto Martén, Alexander Murray, Jorge Arturo Montero, José Albertazzi, Eugenio Rodríguez Vega, Edgar Cardona, and Salvador Avila.

I also appreciate the cooperation and assistance given by several institutions. The following libraries and archives contributed significantly: Biblioteca Nacional de Costa Rica, Latin American Library (Tulane University), Biblioteca de la Universidad de Costa Rica, Archivo Nacional de Costa Rica, and the Earl Gregg Swem Library (College of William and Mary). A fellowship from the Social Science Research Council made it possible for me to do research for a full year in Costa Rica; two summer grants from the Danforth Foundation greatly accelerated the progress of the work.

Crisis in Costa Rica
The 1948 Revolution

CHAPTER 1

Introduction and Background

Costa Rica has long enjoyed the distinction of being a living exception to the generalization that republican government is appropriate neither to the tropics nor to Hispanic peoples.[1] She cherishes a historical tradition of a stable society, a high rate of literacy, democratic institutions, and peaceful transfer of power from constitutional president to constitutional

[1] Most books on Costa Rica emphasize her orderly development and adherence to political democracy. Of particular note are Chester Lloyd Jones, *Costa Rica and Civilization in the Caribbean*, the classic account in English; Carlos Monge Alfaro, *Geografía social y humana de Costa Rica*, and *Historia de Costa Rica*. A pro-Liberación Nacional interpretation is found in Hugo Navarro Bolandi, *La generación del 48*, pp. 15–118, in which Liberación Nacional perfects Costa Rican democracy. Eugenio Rodríguez Vega provides a sociological interpretation in his *Apuntes para una sociología costarricense*. A view of Costa Rican democracy at the beginning of our period is given by John Gunther in his article "Costa Rica: A True Democracy," *Current History*, December 24, 1940, pp. 11–12.

president. Her pride in this rich heritage is shared by her less favored sister nations of Hispanic America who see in her orderly and peaceful development a hopeful prognosis for their own futures. Hispanic Americans in times of turmoil in their native lands have frequently sought refuge in hospitable and encouraging Costa Rica.

This pacific tradition was broken in 1948 by revolution.[2] The only prior twentieth-century deviation from the pattern of peaceful transfer of power had occurred on January 27, 1917, when President Alfredo González Flores (1914–1917) fell to a bloodless coup d'état led by his minister of war, Federico Tinoco Granados. The revolution of 1948 differed sharply from the coup d'état of 1917. It sought to solve quickly the multiple dysfunctions in Costa Rican society[3] and to bring a new group to power rather than to defend the status quo as had Tinoco. The revolution of 1948 occasioned a bloody forty-day conflict which nearly led to civil war.

The revolution climaxed an extended search for a viable government in a nation whose society had grown beyond its traditional institutional structure. This search accelerated during the 1940's as competing political groups proposed solutions which they tried to persuade the nation to follow.

Costa Rican society evolved in isolation from its neighbors. At first for geographic reasons and later by choice, it remained on the

---

[2] "Revolution" as used throughout this work simply means an armed uprising undertaken to seize the government and thus political power. This broad definition includes, then, a typical coup d'état as well as a mass movement undertaken to overthrow the power of a ruling class. Other qualified uses of the word are also employed. "Social revolution" can be armed, or not, as long as it brings a rapid change that alters basic social relationships. Another term used, "myth of revolution," has a more subjective meaning. It consists of a set of ideas that forms a belief system in response to the wishes for transcendent change by a group of dissenters. The "myth of revolution" is a means by which rebellious individuals justify their advocacy of revolution and channel their actions into attempts to fit their nation to a specific theoretical framework. "Rebellion" as used here means a group act of defiance directed against the state of affairs and therefore against those thought to be responsible for the state of affairs.

[3] For a discussion of multiple dysfunction as the cause of revolution see Chalmers Johnson, *Revolution and the Social System*, p. 22.

margin of Central American and other international affairs. Spaniards who settled as agricultural colonists in the sixteenth century came not to gain quick wealth and return to Spain, but to create a permanent community. As early as the seventeenth century there was a notable "absence of an aristocracy and of a class that enjoyed prestige and privilege because of its status."[4] There were no feudal or semifeudal serfs as there were in the rest of Central America.

Through the first approximately three hundred years of its existence, Costa Rica practiced a form of agrarian democracy. Most families lived isolated one from the other and earned a rather sparse living by their own work on their own land. There were those who prospered more than others but, in general, a sense of equality and frugality reigned. In his *Incidents of Travel in Central America, Chiapas, and Yucatán,* John Lloyd Stephens noted that the people of Costa Rica lived at a materially higher level than those in the rest of Central America, that they lived in harmony, and that their industry produced sufficiency but not plenty.[5]

In such a society the Costa Rican developed a sense of individualism and equality that was still characteristic in the twentieth century, despite the appearance of a well-defined and recognized elite. Mario Sancho made this comment about the upper classes in the nineteenth century: "First we must say that in Costa Rica there has never really been an aristocracy . . . all came from Spain without great fortunes and none managed to acquire one here. . . . Those who did achieve riches in the nineteenth century had a strong and better cultivated sense of social cooperation [than those of today]."[6]

The upper class began to form with the advent of coffee production on a large scale, roughly in the period from 1830 to 1890. It was a working class whose initiative, drive, and understanding of the mechanisms of capitalism, especially as applied to commercial farming, brought to Costa Rica the largest measure of prosperity

---

[4] Preston James, *Latin America,* pp. 723–724.

[5] John Lloyd Stephens, *Incidents of Travel in Central America, Chiapas, and Yucatán,* I, 282–290.

[6] Mario Sancho, *Costa Rica: Suiza Centroamericana,* p. 9. [Pamphlet.]

that she had known. "To work for a living was never looked down on in Costa Rica."[7] New lands were brought into cultivation and old lands improved. The advantages these men reaped as a result of their knowledge and techniques gave them an ever-increasing ascendency over their fellows. By the 1920's this advantage no longer depended on the personal qualities exemplified by the progenitors but on the simple accumulation of capital.[8]

Along with progress, this new class brought a concentration of wealth which Costa Rica had not known. The nation of small farmers, within a generation, became a nation of large capitalistic farmers, who employed many farm laborers. Some small farmers remained in possession of their land but were unable to live by its fruits, and they along with their families worked for wages on the big estates.

The small holding persisted and persists today to such a degree that statistics on the average-size farm in Costa Rica are quite misleading. There were indeed many small proprietors but no more than 5 percent of the coffee growers owned more than 50 percent of the coffee production.[9] The smaller producers tended to become dependent on the large producers who controlled the *beneficios*, where the beans were prepared for market.

The large-sized holding predominated in banana farming and cattle-raising to an even greater extent than in coffee cultivation, but these developments occurred at a later period, in areas outside the *meseta central*. Although relevant to the problem of dysfunctioning in Costa Rican society, these later patterns are of only

[7] James, *Latin America*, p. 724.

[8] Gunnar Myrdal stresses the point throughout his *Economic Theory and Underdeveloped Regions* that in a laissez-faire environment, in which unguided market forces determine resource allocation, cumulative movements in income inequalities are established. In Costa Rica these cumulative movements worked to the advantage of the coffee growers even though they no longer fulfilled the entrepreneurial roles of their fathers and grandfathers.

[9] Stacy May, *Costa Rica: A Study in Economic Development*, p. 43. Seventy-five percent of the coffee growers cultivate fewer than three and one-half acres each (William S. Stokes, *Latin American Politics*, p. 178).

peripheral significance in the development of the dominant social group.

Much of the wealth accumulated during the period of rapid growth in coffee production went into the material progress of the nation. Reinvestment helped expand the coffee industry and provide the economic infrastructure needed to market it. The new entrepreneurial class, however, also availed itself of the opportunity afforded by prosperity to break out of the traditional isolation of Costa Rican life. By travel and study abroad, this group further differentiated itself from the mass of Costa Rican countrymen. As Eugenio Rodríguez Vega expressed it: ". . . higher education was within the main reach only of the rich, who used to travel to Europe to earn doctors' degrees."[10]

From this class emerged the Generation of 1889 which established universal education and the democratic practices that made Costa Rica an exemplary nation in Latin America. Mario Sancho noted, however, that by 1935 the descendants of the upper class had atrophied in contrast with their progenitors in that they no longer cooperated for the common welfare.[11]

This elite was made up of coffee growers, bankers, large commercial interests often allied to or representing foreign capital, and a few very successful professionals. It lacked organization and coherence. As Rodríguez Vega remarked, "Its components are, after all, sons of Costa Rica and therefore lacking in the organizational ability necessary to constitute itself for a common cause."[12]

After the drive and initiative this class had originally shown, it now appeared exhausted. Composed of circles of friends, the elite, acting almost as by accord on national affairs, tried to maintain a status quo, socially and economically. Paradoxically, it attempted to maintain its position without relinquishing traditions of education and democracy, which by their very nature threatened the

[10] "La educación solo estaba al alcance de los ricos, lo que viajaban a doctorarse en Europa" (Rodríguez Vega, *Apuntes*, p. 113).

[11] Sancho, *Costa Rica*, p. 9.

[12] Rodríguez Vega, *Apuntes*, p. 114.

status quo. On one hand, it remained a working elite that knew its farms and seldom practiced absenteeism; but, on the other, it failed by refusing to continue the progressive policies of previous generations which had consistently sought new frontiers for economic development.

The descendants of these innovators chose, rather, to live contentedly with the profits from their favorably situated coffee farms and to allow the economy to stagnate. Not only did they fail to bring new techniques, products, and enterprises to Costa Rica, but, by taking title to lands which they often had never seen and seldom thought of exploiting, they also hindered the continued extension of one of the few actively expanding agricultural frontiers in Latin America. The titles were patrimony or "money in the bank" for future generations; not for all Costa Ricans, however, but for their own respective families.

Development came to be largely the concern of other groups. Foreign capitalists and immigrants, socially acceptable to the elite, mainly devoted themselves to founding large-scale farms, commercial enterprises, and some manufacturing concerns. Restless small farmers and farm laborers, who simply sought out and occupied uncultivated land on the agricultural frontier, added important increments of production. They cultivated new lands without affirmation by the state of their right to do so. Their numbers reached sufficient proportions to earn them recognition as a distinct social group, the members of which were disparagingly called parasites.[13]

A rigid division of classes never existed in Costa Rica even after

---

[13] The "Ley de parásitos" enacted by Calderón Guardia, provided for a form of land redistribution. A Costa Rican farmer could occupy and till any uncultivated piece of land and it became his property. If the particular property was registered in someone else's name, the former owner received compensation from the state. The law did not provide an organic solution to the agrarian problem but it had several immediate advantages. It brought uncultivated land into cultivation, it provided a safety valve for population pressure on the *meseta central*, it required little planning or new bureaucratic machinery, and it added to the number of small independent farmers who were considered to be essential to the strength of Costa Rican democracy.

the advent of the elite based on coffee production. Class there, much as in the United States, was based on economic status.

The middle class in Costa Rica differed radically from that in other Central American countries. It began to emerge simultaneously with the formation of an elite. It developed chiefly in urban areas and was composed of professionals, white-collar workers in government and commerce, skilled workers, and small businessmen, but it also included farmers who owned middle-sized holdings or who produced crops largely for domestic consumption. After educational reform made primary education free and obligatory, the middle class grew continuously in size, and its values tended to be accepted as the national norm.

Costa Rica was also an exception to the class pattern characteristic of much of Latin America. In most of her sister states, the middle class of the cities was a mere extension of the landowning oligarchy, sharing its values and aspirations and almost invariably allying with it against the "pretensions" and aspirations of the lower classes.[14] The Costa Rican middle class traditionally has been strong and numerous, and it has possessed a sense of identity distinct from the oligarchy toward which it has often been antagonistic.

Costa Rican democracy, as postulated and later developed by the Generation of 1889, implied a continual renewal and extension of popular participation in political decision-making if the society were to remain in functional condition.[15] One goal of popular edu-

---

14 K. B. Griffin, "Reflections on Latin American Development," *Oxford Economic Papers*, 18 (April, 1966), 17–18. Griffin continues: "This coalition then has been able to fragment the lower classes by granting partial concessions which are not distributed evenly." In Costa Rica the coalition existed briefly in 1948 for the election and revolution and greatly reduced the power of the organized lower groups. However, the middle class then overtly began to swell its numbers by additions from the lower classes through positive action on the part of the state.

15 The two outstanding figures of the Generation of 1889 are three-time President Ricardo Jiménez Oreamuno and two-time President Cleto González Víquez. Hugo Navarro Bolandi devotes three chapters of *La generación del 48* (pp. 31–46) to an interpretation of the effects of this generation on Costa Rican political life.

cation was to prepare people for participation in the governmental process. A robust free press stimulated popular interest in political developments. In short, political concern and expression of public opinion through elections, with encouragement from the elite, became real factors in Costa Rican life. This is not to assert that all elections were completely fair, and that organized political parties eclipsed *personalismo*. Political life was characterized, however, by strong resistance to dictatorships, great concern by citizens on national issues, and a manifest desire to elect honest men and to ensure the constitutional subordination of the executive to the judicial and the legislative authorities within their spheres. The oligarchy allowed democratic traditions to persist and, in the political realm, gradually extended the suffrage and stimulated active participation of the electorate in national decision making. The ever-widening social and economic gap between the oligarchy and the middle and lower classes contrasted sharply with the democratic tradition which the elite defended and to a certain degree extended. The contrast was somewhat blurred in practice, for the small farmers and agricultural workers generally voted as directed by the local political caudillo or their patrón.[16]

The highly articulate middle groups produced by the internal development of Costa Rica after 1850, however, were largely denied effective voice in national life. Because of the opportunities for education provided after 1880 and the consequent high literacy rate, these middle groups maintained a relatively high level of aspiration, but limited economic opportunity kept them impecunious.[17]

Nascent urbanization in the twentieth century increased the numbers of this economically poor but well-defined and self-conscious middle class. City voters of all classes by the 1920's manifested a marked inclination to vote their personal interests or consciences. These "nontraditional" voters searched for a means of political expression which would be responsive to their needs.

[16] Mario Sancho, *Memorias*, p. 244, has an account of this practice in operation.

[17] Sancho, *Costa Rica*, p. 8.

The ease with which the progressive government of President Alfredo González Flores fell in the coup d'état of 1917 made it evident that the current for change in Costa Rica had yet to attain any real strength or cohesion. This desire for change was first strongly expressed in the 1920's by General Jorge Volio's Reform party, which exerted an influence and suffered a demise similar to that of the Populist party in late nineteenth-century United States.

General Volio added both color and an acute social conscience to Costa Rican politics. He gave up the priestly life for one of intense public activity. The Reform party was above all interested in the solution of the social problems which beset the nation.[18] General Volio was his party's candidate in the election of 1924, and, when the inconclusive results of the voting left the decision to Congress, he threw the support of his party to Ricardo Jiménez of the National Republican party.[19]

The banner of modernization and reform passed from the Reform party of the 1920's to the Communist party, the Bloque de Obreros y Campesinos (Workers' and Peasants' Block), established by Manuel Mora Valverde in 1930.[20] In the period 1930–1940, the Costa Rican Communists organized segments of public opinion in the cities of the *meseta central* and among the workers of the coasts.

The elite felt menaced by the reforms of President González Flores and by those proposed by the Reform party. It was horror-struck by the possibility that the Bloque de Obreros y Campesinos might grow to a position of influence in Costa Rica. However, the elite, as a group, seemed unable to develop a persuasive alternative. The Communists' emphasis on reform alarmed the upper class, but, by and large, the party was considered a legitimate political group of purely Costa Rican extraction. During this period

[18] Ricardo Blanco Segura, *Monseñor Sanabria*, p. 80.

[19] Navarro Bolandi describes the election in these terms: "None of the three received the absolute majority prescribed by law. . . . Don Ricardo Jiménez had to make a pact with the party of the people and thanks to the agreement, he became President for the second time" (*La generación*, p. 64). Also, see Ricardo Fernández Guardia, *Cartilla histórica de Costa Rica*, p. 140, which indicates that the procedure used by Congress was of questionable legality.

[20] At the time he was a twenty-year-old law student.

the term *comunismo criollo* came into general use. In 1934, the Communists were active in organizing and conducting a strike in the banana plantations on the Atlantic coast. The violence displayed on this occasion further upset the elite and provided evidence that the press used to discredit the Communists.[21]

León Cortés Castro, candidate of the National Republican party, became the champion of anticommunism in the electoral campaign of 1935–1936. He presented communism to the electorate as an insidious and deceptive international conspiracy which intended to foment international revolution. Within Costa Rica, he alleged, the objective was to be attained by means of the Bloque de Obreros y Campesinos. Communism was a threat to all that was most sacred to Costa Rica: the family, religion, and political institutions. At this level the program and potential of *comunismo criollo* bore little objective relation to the communism Cortés presented to the electorate.

The Communist threat was the chief issue exploited in the Cortés campaign. Typical of his electoral propaganda was a full-page advertisement which, in two-inch letters, charged:

> To Vote for Octavio Beeche
> is
> To Vote for Communism
> and
> To Vote for Communism
> is
> To Go against the Republic
> To Go against Our institutions
> To Go against Our Religion[22]

Cortés' offer to protect the nation from the "red hordes," elicited wide, popular support, particularly among the religiously oriented *campesinos*. He succeeded, among his followers, in giving "Communism" a sinister connotation, representing it as something far more significant than an interpretation of history, a theory of social

---

[21] For a brief discussion of the strike see Rafael Obregón Loría, *Conflictos militares y políticos de Costa Rica*, p. 114.

[22] *La Tribuna*, February 6, 1936, p. 6.

organization, or a program of social and economic reform; instead it connoted a mysterious and malevolent power. The campaign, however, seemed not to discredit Manuel Mora or his followers; they were too familiar to be considered part of the "red hordes." Cortés' attack did, however, cast distrust by way of association. International communism was widely accepted as a menace, but the familiar *comunismo criollo* was, at best, only partially and unconvincingly identified as forming a part of that threat.

The advent of the Bloque de Obreros y Campesinos led indirectly to some deviations from tradition. In their anxiety to diminish the influence of the Communists, Presidents Ricardo Jiménez Oreamuno (1932–1936) and León Cortés Castro (1936–1940) introduced the mechanism of suffrage into the political arena. President Jiménez responded to pressure to outlaw the Bloque by promulgating a compromise measure which permitted the party to present candidates, but denied it representation in the supervision of the polling places that was accorded other political parties. His measure, making voting obligatory, served to counter the vote of city workers with votes from the countryside.[23] In the 1938 Congressional election, Cortés arbitrarily set aside the election of the Bloque candidate, Professor Carlos Luis Sáenz, overriding the protests of the Electoral Council and despite the resignation, en masse, of that body.[24]

Under the competent and respected leadership of Mora, the Communists attained considerable strength by the mid-1930's. In the province of San José they elected Mora to the Congress, and they provided the major issue on which León Cortés Castro won the presidency. During the Cortés administration, the Communists firmly established themselves as the nation's ideological party. They were a relatively small but militant group with a national organization and enjoyed considerable status among intellectuals and political leaders.

By 1940, three political groups in Costa Rica advocated positive

---

[23] Sancho, *Memorias*, pp. 326–327.

[24] The president of the Council was the noted historian Ricardo Fernández Guardia.

governmental action to bring about social and economic reform. In addition to the Bloque de Obreros y Campesinos, there were the Centro para el Estudio de los Problemas Nacionales (Centro), and a segment of the traditional National Republican party organized around the figure of the presidential candidate, Dr. Rafael Angel Calderón Guardia. The Centro championed a mixed economy in contrast to the Communists' advocacy of state ownership of all productive facilities. All three groups postulated the necessity for more effective democracy in political, social, and economic life, but there were important differences in the means by which they proposed to reach their goal.

The Centro was founded by young professionals, students, and white-collar workers in early 1940 by expanding an association of law students.[25] The membership of the Centro was almost exclusively middle and upper class. Its members were from the ranks of those highly favored few who reached the last years of secondary school and from the even more restricted group who were able to pursue university studies.

The *centristas* (the members of the Centro) had a high degree of social cohesiveness. They were almost exclusively from the *meseta central*, and similar in age and experience. They entered the organization because it was an "in group" and because of discontent with the current state of affairs.

The Centro became the directing force among university students. After a student political demonstration on May 15, 1943, in protest against proposed changes in electoral procedures, members of the Centro were reinforced by great numbers of secondary students.[26] Youth, idealism, and ambitions would make the Centro a

[25] *Surco*, No. 49 (September, 1944), p. 2. Two favorable treatments of the Center for the Study of National Problems occur in Alberto Cañas, *Los ocho años*, pp. 43–49, and in Navarro Bolandi, *La generación del 48*, pp. 104–114. Cañas traces the origins of the Centro to the Asociación Cultural de Estudiantes de Derecho, founded in 1937, and to the impulse given to the recently formed Federación by the return of Professor Roberto Brenes Mesén who retired from Northwestern University in 1939 to return to his native Costa Rica.

[26] Cañas, *Los ocho años*, p. 47.

most desirable supplement for any political movement that could manage to direct it.

In the 1940 election, ex-President Jiménez opposed the National Republican candidate, Calderón Guardia. Mora entered into the Alianza Democrática (Democratic Alliance), which backed the candidacy of Jiménez in opposition to the official candidate. This electoral alliance, although backed by Mora, was dominated by non-Communists who seated seven of nine representatives on the executive committee of the coalition. Among the non-Communists who supported the Alianza were such dedicated democrats as Otilio Ulate, Fernando Valverde, Dr. Antonio Peña Chavarría, and Tomás Soley Güell.[27]

In the electoral campaign of 1939 and 1940, President Cortés deviated from the electoral ideal by intervening against the candidacy of Jiménez. He used anticommunism as justification for his action. Attempts by Jiménez' supporters to organize were broken up forcefully by police, using the flat edges of their swords.[28] Jiménez withdrew his candidacy and the race became virtually uncontested. Persecution by President Cortés caused almost complete abandonment of the Alianza for the 1940 election, but remnants worked with Mora in 1940 and again in 1942 to achieve democratic ends.

President Cortés' reputation as an authoritarian ruler, gained by his interventions in the elections of 1938 and 1940, worked to increase popular acceptance of the Bloque de Obreros y Campesinos. Mora and his followers actively opposed the President's methods and, in the press and in Congress, energetically campaigned for electoral probity and courageously championed the democratic practices in which Costa Ricans had traditionally believed. The Communists capitalized on popular concern for electoral probity to build influence and respect for their party and to heighten their *power capability*.[29] After the encroachments by Cortés on freedom

---

[27] Manuel Mora Valverde, *Dos discursos en defensa de Vanguardia Popular*, p. 14. [Pamphlet.]

[28] *La Tribuna*, September 2, 1944, p. 1.

[29] Political capability in this context means "a property of a group or individ-

of the ballot, liberals and conservatives alike joined in supporting the cause of effective suffrage. The Communists, however, carried the banner. They made electoral reform a major point in their program and eventually allied themselves, politically, with the National Republicans.

Calderón Guardia enjoyed great personal popularity. It was generally believed that he was strong enough to carry the election without Cortés' intervention against the coalition which opposed him.[30] In response to public outcry against such tactics, and despite the implied criticism of his own party, Calderón Guardia pledged himself to support electoral reform and thus bring an end to coercion and chicanery at the polls.[31]

Calderón Guardia was elected President in February, 1940, at what appeared to be a propitious moment for Costa Rican democracy. He received a vast majority of the popular vote, and, in his inaugural address, he promised the nation that he would effect change with continuity under a program of social and economic development which he characterized as social-Christian. Continuity would be provided by his affiliation with the National Republican party, his devout Catholicity, and his adherence to the capitalistic system. Social change would be rapid, he promised, but consistent with Costa Rican tradition, for it would be based on the social teachings of the Catholic church.[32]

Circumstances in Costa Rica appeared to favor the success of Calderón Guardia's program. The fiscal situation of the country was sound as a consequence of the austere administration of León Cortés Castro. The Catholic church had already manifested its

---

ual that enables it to be politically influential, in other words, a political resource. Possession of a *power capability* is the price of admission to the political arena. Those who possess significant power capabilities will 'be taken into account' when political decisions are made" (Charles W. Anderson, *Politics and Economic Change in Latin America*, p. 91).

[30] Calderón Guardia was elected with one of the greatest majorities in Costa Rican history. He received nearly 93,000 of more than 102,000 votes cast (*La Tribuna*, February 12, 1940, p. 1).

[31] *La Prensa Libre*, February 12, 1940, p. 1.

[32] Juan Rojas Suárez, *Costa Rica en la Segunda Guerra Mundial*, p. 273.

concern for the betterment of Costa Rican social conditions. The archbishop of San José, Monseñor Víctor Manuel Sanabria Martínez, a man of the people and a close friend of Calderón Guardia, openly and fervently espoused reform and progress and exhorted his clergy and the faithful to do likewise.

Despite the seemingly propitious circumstances for social reform at the initiation of Calderón Guardia's administration, his program almost immediately came under fire. The Communists attacked it as insincere and politically motivated, a charge which the Centro later strongly echoed. Both the Communists and the Centro questioned Calderón Guardia's program on ideological grounds.

By 1940, organized labor and a substantial number of professionals, university students, and white-collar workers were prepared to assert their right to a voice in their nation's affairs. They hoped to achieve an extensive reorientation of the economy, a step which they believed to be a prerequisite toward obtaining an acceptable standard of living and toward establishing such bases for economic development as to make the attainment of a higher level of material existence possible. This does not mean to imply that they were unconcerned about the cultural level of society. With sufficient reason, they believed that, given her economic bases, Costa Rica had made remarkable progress in cultural affairs.

When Calderón Guardia assumed the presidency in 1940, he faced a difficult task. If he was to succeed in maintaining social equilibrium, he had to exceed the bounds of a traditional Costa Rican chief executive.[33] He confronted a situation in which violent social discord was at all times possible. From a long-term point of view, he decided that he could save Costa Rica from armed conflict on a large scale only by a determined effort to solve basic questions.

The disequilibrium in Costa Rican society centered around four major issues. But the social question was the core issue—failure to solve it was tantamount to an invitation to violence. The second most basic problem was the electoral question. People had begun to doubt the efficacy of the vote and the electoral process. The issue

[33] Lawrence and Sylvia Martin, "Four Strongmen and a President," *Harper's*, 185 (September 1942): 424–427.

of communism further complicated both of these fundamental issues. The determination of the elite to thwart the participation of the Communists in the democratic process and the Communists' consequent effort to reveal all the accumulated defects in the system of exercising suffrage had the net effect of undermining the citizens' belief in their part in the decision-making process. The fourth major issue was that of fiscal corruption and mismanagement which further compounded the task of maintaining Costa Rica's accustomed tranquility.

The *calderonistas* properly focused their program and risked the prestige of their leader on the solution of the key problem, the social question,[34] but their political opponents emphasized the other three major issues during the eight-year period from 1940 through 1948.

[34] Daniel Oduber writing in *La Nación* (March 31, 1965, p. 12, "Tarea inaplazable de los costarricenses") in fact refers to the movement for social reform, the affirmation of democratic institutions, and structural changes for a new orientation for economic development as the salient characteristics of the past twenty-five years. He thus indicates a continuum which included the administrations of Calderón Guardia and Picado.

CHAPTER **2**

The Social Question

Costa Rica in the 1940's suffered many of the social maladjustments that have come to be associated with underdeveloped nations. It was an agrarian society clinging to its traditional way of life in a rapidly changing world. It was drawn toward modernization, however, by the desire to share the benefits of industrialization, its products, values, and ideas.[1]

Costa Ricans generally suffered from poverty and its related ills. Neither the public nor the private sectors of the economy, however, commanded capital for investment in sufficient volume to break the self-perpetuating poverty cycle. Housing was inadequate and transportation was deficient. Unemployment and underem-

[1] Three good sources on the social question in Costa Rica are Dr. Rafael Angel Calderón Guardia, *El gobernante y el hombre frente al problema social costarricense* [Pamphlet]; John and Mavis Biesanz, *Costa Rican Life*; and Eugenio Rodríguez Vega, *Apuntes para una sociología costarricense.*

ployment restricted earning power. Endemic diseases shortened the
average life span of the Costa Rican and burdened many an individual with a significant measure of misery. Malnutrition and the
resulting diseases afflicted many, particularly children. Each form
of distress and want reinforced the persistence of the others and
seemed to doom the nation to perpetual underdevelopment. Tancredo Pinochet, a Chilean journalist commenting on the purportedly
equitable distribution of land in Costa Rica, put it neatly: "What is
well distributed in Costa Rica is poverty."[2]

Poverty was real in Costa Rica but it was only relative. Costa
Ricans often minimized the problem by a too facile comparison
with their sister nations of Central America; they did indeed live
better than their Central American neighbors and, for that matter,
better than most of the other peoples of Latin America. Economic
conditions were really bad only on the coasts, in Guanacaste, and
among the Amerindians of the Talamanca area. But even in the
meseta central, great numbers, probably the majority, of the lower
classes lived far below the level of their expectations, and the urban
middle groups felt the pinch of inflation and the lack of opportunity.

No group in society took a Social Darwinist view of poverty; all
lamented it, but most of the upper and middle classes generally
managed to ignore the situation and to convince each other that.
after all, everyone lived pretty well in Costa Rica. By 1940, however, the extent of poverty in the nation had become a political issue, doggedly impressed on the conscience of the nation by the
Communists.

The social problems were made acute by the growth rate of the
population. The number of inhabitants climbed steadily from
colonial times, almost entirely from natural increase rather than

[2] Mario Sancho, *Memorias*, p. 284. Sancho notes that the Chilean journalist
Tancredo Pinochet, whom he had taken to see for himself the conditions in
which the small proprietors lived in the province of Cartago, caused a scandal
that evening in Cartago by a remark to the effect "que contra lo que . . . había
dicho el ministro . . . de que la propiedad estaba muy bien dividida en Costa
Rica, el paseo a Orosi lo había convencido de que lo que estaba realmente bien
dividida en este país era la pobreza."

from immigration, until the last decades of the nineteenth century when immigration began to contribute significantly to population growth. At the time of independence (1821) there were an estimated 60,000 inhabitants;[3] by 1927, there were 472,000,[4] of whom nearly 9.4 percent were foreign born.[5] (Although few in number, immigrants received a hospitable welcome in Costa Rica, and all opportunities afforded by the country were open to them.)[6] Between 1930 and 1940 population increased 27 percent;[7] by 1950, the annual rate of increase had reached 4 percent.[8] Most of the population—the percentage stood at 70 as late as 1950—lived in the *meseta central*, one of the few zones of concentrated rural settlement in Hispanic America.

If population pressure was a major dimension of the social problem on the national level, it was even more pronounced in the capital. Necessary services could not be expanded rapidly enough, and much of the population found the facilities afforded by the capital greatly lacking.

One of the most acute inadequacies suffered by the nation was in housing. All the groups in Costa Rica preoccupied with social problems were concerned with this shortage and studied both its causes and its remedies. One of the most effective graphic presentations which drew attention to the situation was a two-page study printed in the *Diario de Costa Rica*. In words and pictures it portrayed the urban poor crowded into grossly inadequate and unsanitary *barrios* (neighborhoods) in and around the capital.[9] It noted the absence of hygienic conditions and the consequent prevalence of tuberculosis,

[3] Chester Lloyd Jones, *Costa Rica and Civilization in the Caribbean*, p. 35. For population data on Costa Rican population in the nineteenth century, see Bernardo Augusto Thiel, "Monografía de la población de la república de Costa Rica en el siglo XIX," pp. 1–52 of *Revista de Costa Rica en el siglo XIX*.

[4] Robin A. Humphreys, *The Evolution of Modern Latin America*, p. 160.

[5] Jones, *Costa Rica and Civilization*, pp. 36–37. The foreign born were chiefly Europeans, other Latin Americans, and Jamaicans. Also see fn. 23, this chapter.

[6] Presidents Cortés, Picado, Figueres, and Orlich were all sons of immigrants.

[7] *Time*, January 1, 1945, p. 32. Sumner Welles gave the growth rate as 26 percent per decade (*An Intelligent American's Guide to the Peace*, p. 194).

[8] Hubert Herring, *A History of Latin America*, p. 827.

[9] *Diario de Costa Rica*, May 28, 1944, pp. 12–13.

intestinal parasites, and other health hazards. The article cited the example of the Pasaje Racia in which seventy *turgios* (shacks) and three hundred inhabitants were crowded into "an area the size of the patio of a middle-income home." The study showed that the structures in these neighborhoods harbored an average of five, and as many as eight, persons per room. It pointed out the prevalence of "all social vices" in these areas and the consequent "great weight on the honorable poor."[10] The Junta Nacional de la Habitación estimated that San José alone needed at least three thousand additional houses without taking into consideration the increase resulting from the upward trend in population.[11]

Although housing deficiencies were most acute among the urban poor, they also keenly affected the middle class and added to its potential for revolution. War conditions increased the scarcity and the price of housing for the "middle and salaried classes,"[12] particularly in San José. The Centro's analysis held that the public works of Calderón Guardia made building materials and labor costly; the increasing bureaucracy attracted rural and provincial workers; and inflation decreased the real wages of the middle class. The presence of citizens of the United States, "both military and civilian" intensified the problems.[13] They came to Costa Rica during World War II to assist in the defense of the Western Hemisphere.

There are no studies for rural areas comparable to those made of the urban slums. Mario Sancho in his *Costa Rica: Suiza Centroamericana*, however, depicted the inhabitants of much of the countryside as living in squalor. According to his account, farm laborers

10 The use of the term "honorable poor" is indicative of the middle- and upper-class origins of the youths of the Centro who prepared the study. It implies the existence of a dishonorable poor and one wonders if the authors would have made a similar breakdown within other economic groups and on similar bases. Another assertion, farther on in the article, indicated that, although shocked and dismayed at the conditions, they did not necessarily believe that those who endured them were victims of society, since "most seemed unconcerned about how they lived."

11 *Diario de Costa Rica*, May 28, 1944, p. 13.

12 *Surco*, no. 47 (May–June, 1944), p. 44.

13 Ibid., pp. 44–45.

and small farmers lived with their large families in one-room dwellings without any sort of sanitary facilities.[14] In *La huelga de brazos caídos*, Roberto Fernández Durán in more literary fashion described some of the deficiencies of housing in the countryside: "Incessantly the rain poured on the broken tile roof of an unheated rural house. A thin stream of clear water fell into the sleeping area."[15]

Despite the needs of a growing population the nation did not make effective use of the national territory. Out of a total area of approximately 23,000 square miles, the cultivated area about 1945 was estimated to be only 2,000 square miles. The uncultivated area included 10,200 square miles of unoccupied grassland and 10,000 square miles of uncleared forests.[16]

The failure to advance the frontier signaled the loss of the old Costa Rican spirit of entrepreneurship and adventure, once among the salient characteristics of its elite coffee planters.[17] Complacency coupled with a high birth rate placed unnecessary pressure on the already settled areas of the nation. It was incumbent on those who held the accumulated capital of the society to carry out this essential task of fomenting development in order to relieve the pressure on the land of the *meseta central*.[18] By default the task largely fell to the so-called parasites who, on their own initiative and without titles, squatted on the land and opened new areas to cultivation.

Despite Costa Rica's relatively high standard of living, her inhabitants suffered from deficiencies in nutrition. Prior to World War II she ranked below nine American nations in three important

[14] Mario Sancho, *Costa Rica: Suiza Centroamericana*, p. 16. [Pamphlet.]

[15] Roberto Fernández Durán, *La huelga de brazos caídos*, p. 7. [Pamphlet.]

[16] Welles, *An Intelligent American's Guide*, p. 194.

[17] Sancho charges that they not only had ceased to extend the frontier but also were losing out to German, English, and United States capital in the settled areas (*Memorias*, p. 221).

[18] K. B. Griffin, "Reflections on Latin American Development," *Oxford Economic Papers*, 18 (April, 1966), pp. 21–22, contains a discussion of the effects of this phenomenon on Latin American agriculture in general.

per capita consumption categories: total calories, grams of protein per day, and kilograms of milk per year.[19] An effective remedy to this situation required economic development and the resolution of the entire social problem. It also required that the populace change its concept of the composition of a good diet. Dr. Antonio Peña Chavarría, the superintendent of the San Juan de Dios hospital and a long-time proponent of social justice, considered malnutrition to be "the national disease."[20]

The social question in Costa Rica can be segmented for purposes of discussion, but the problem was basically a single one—that of a society in which those who exerted the greatest influence had allowed the nation to fall behind others. The deprived elements of this society, recognizing their disadvantage within their own nation and contrasting the level of their own domestic welfare with that achieved by the advanced industrial nations, sought to establish a new social order. They urged amelioration of immediate wrongs through positive action by the state.

During the era when the Communist party rose to political stature in the banana-producing areas, the social problem there had had especially poignant qualities. The United Fruit Company was a power unto itself, and its area was in every sense, except by formal definition, a colony where many of the characteristics of United States imperialism, on which Communist propaganda often dwells, were exemplified. The company's use of its political, economic, and social power was arbitrary and authoritarian. The workers, unorganized until the great strike of 1934, suffered daily injustice and hardship.[21] Racial discrimination and discrimination

---

[19] Lawrence Duggan, *The Americas: The Search for Hemisphere Security*, p. 27. The nine countries were Argentina (which ranked above the United States in all three), Cuba, Uruguay, Paraguay, Brazil, Chile, the Dominican Republic, Peru, and Honduras.

[20] *Acción Demócrata*, July 29, 1944, p. 3.

[21] For a semiautobiographic treatment of the politics of the period outside the *meseta central*, the conditions of the workers in the banana zone, and the organization of the strike see Carlos Luis Fallas' novel, *Mamita Yunai*, pp. 45–80. See also Rafael Obregón Loría, *Conflictos militares y políticos de Costa Rica*, p. 114, for a brief discussion of the course of the strike, and Carlos Luis Fallas, *La*

by national origin were the order of the day, with the most desirable positions reserved for white foreigners. The living conditions were harsh, and summary dismissal was a constant threat for the workers. To many of the workers living in the unhealthful and alien conditions of the camps, the Communist interpretation of the class struggle made unusually good sense and, consequently, the movement flourished.

A congressional commission named in 1934 to survey the banana zone published a critical report on the conditions it observed. The findings left the commission with no doubt as to the "inhuman, unhealthful, and careless treatment" to which the United Fruit Company subjected its agricultural laborers.[22]

The banana areas in so many respects resembled foreign colonies that the bulk of the population of the *meseta central* scarcely thought of the banana zone as forming part of the national territory, or of its inhabitants as Costa Ricans, which quite often they were not.[23] Although the inhabitants of the *meseta central* looked sometimes with scorn and sometimes with pity on the workers from the coasts, they nearly always regarded them as outsiders. Not only were the workers of a different color, but, accustomed to a different climate, they also dressed inappropriately for the higher altitudes. Alberto Cañas Escalante makes clear this ambivalent attitude in his description of the participation of *mariachis*, individuals brought to the capital from the coast, in the events associated with an attempted general strike: "The *mariachis*, gloomy, dark, and fearless, have returned from the coasts. They slowly traverse the

---

gran huelga bananera del Atlántico de 1934 [Pamphlet], for a more ample but also partisan view.

[22] Sancho, *Memorias*, p. 257.

[23] A high percentage of the workers, other than the English-speaking Negroes descended from workers brought in by Minor Keith to build the railroad, were not Costa Rican. This ratio was partly due to the Costa Rican's general aversion to work on the hot coasts and also because the Fruit Company could thus deal more arbitrarily with the workers (*La Nación*, Sept. 14, 1948). An example of such arbitrary treatment came after the 1948 revolution when many Nicaraguan workers on the Pacific coast plantations were simply deported because they had supported Calderón Guardia (Fallas, *La gran huelga*, pp. 16–17). Similar events also had occurred previously, following the strike of 1934.

city with their rifles on one shoulder and their blankets on the other, bewildered by day, shivering at night, always menacing."[24] The phenomenon was perhaps more clearly expressed in a newspaper account that described the hilarity with which citizens of San José observed "Negroes and Communist stevedores," some without shoes or shirts, presuming to guard the streets of the capital as though they were citizens with something to defend.[25] They were regarded as something other than full-fledged Costa Ricans.

Outside the banana zone, the Costa Rican social structure did not exemplify the Marxian dichotomy of exploited and exploiter. There were, indeed, isolated instances of exploiters and exploited, but this pattern was not characteristic of the entire society. On the contrary, Costa Ricans developed widespread social consciousness throughout the twentieth century.

The direct effects of World War II intensified the social problems of Costa Rica. The nation was cut off from normal sources of imports; its domestic production was taxed by the greater demands of a growing population and by pressure to increase exports to Panama and the Canal Zone—its contribution to the allied cause. Shortages of capital goods and manufactured articles and a scarcity of foodstuffs brought inflation. The war resulted in an unaccustomed intervention by the central government in the national life; it regulated prices, initiated projects to create employment, inaugurated public works, constructed the Pan American Highway, and augmented military activities. These unusual wartime functions, combined with certain innovations under the social reform program, gave many the impression that the government was guilty of a massive "invasion" into private affairs. This attitude among the people further complicated the always difficult task of fostering social change.

By 1940, significant segments of the population felt the need for change, but the sense of urgency on the issue was scarcely great enough to lead to revolt.[26] Politically articulate groups postulated

[24] Alberto Cañas, *Los ocho años*, p. 119.
[25] *Diario de Costa Rica*, July 25, 1947, p. 1.
[26] In the early 1940's Costa Ricans who lived in small towns tended to see

programs of reform and revolution that attracted the support of deprived elements within society. Many individuals, the Catholic church, the nascent labor movement, and agencies of the national government directed their best efforts toward a search for the means of breaking the poverty cycle. Through these groups the disadvantaged segments of the population hoped to attain equality of access to the formal institutions of society. They particularly hoped to influence in their favor such factors underlying social mobility as education, occupation, place of residence, and medical care. In short, they sought the extension of power, both political and economic, to a larger proportion of the total community.

Calderón Guardia responded to the demand for reform when he assumed the presidency in 1940, and, in so doing, he offered the electorate a viable alternative to the Communist solutions to social questions. His inaugural address outlined measures by which his government proposed to foment the social, cultural, and economic development of the nation. He promised particular attention to the less well developed areas of Costa Rica, such as Guanacaste and the Atlantic region which had been largely abandoned by the United Fruit Company. He pledged himself to a revision of the entire system of taxation on the just basis of capacity to contribute. He promised to give a new impulse to rural credit, to provide for a program of land distribution through the National Bank, and to initiate a program of low-cost housing. He proposed to found a national university that would orient public opinion on social questions and promote the general progress of the republic. As a contribution to the welfare of all, he promised to institute a modern system of social security, such as was found in the more advanced nations of South America and in Mexico.[27]

Calderón Guardia's program,[28] in contrast to that of the Bloque

misery as their lot and evidenced a marked tendency to interpret their lives in economic terms. However, they looked to electoral political action as the means for bringing about the necessary changes. See Irvin L. Child, "The Background of Public Opinion in Costa Rica." *Public Opinion Quarterly*, 7 (1943): 242–257.

[27] Juan Rojas Suárez, *Costa Rica en la Segunda Guerra Mundial*, p. 274.

[28] "La nueva administración sustenta, en lo político, la doctrina del cristianismo social, tal como lo exponen las admirables enciclicas de León XIII y Pio

de Obreros y Campesinos, promised not to involve the government
in any economic activity that could be realized by private capital.
In fact, it would endeavor to provide new incentives for private
enterprise through tax credits and foreign exchange privileges for
new industries.

Calderón Guardia promised a virtual social revolution without
violence. A significant and far-reaching program of reform was to
be carried out by an enlightened group from within the "civil
oligarchy," the so-called men of forty years of age or the *ricos progresistas* (progressive men of wealth). Both of the latter terms were
employed by his opponents in subsequent years in a pejorative
sense.

The administration enacted a series of laws which lessened the
problem. It limited the rights of the property holder by freezing
rents and by making it far more difficult to evict a tenant who paid
his rent; in 1942 it had created low-cost housing cooperatives, and
in 1943 it authorized the National Bank of Securities to invest in
housing construction. The results were good; the Centro faulted
Calderón Guardia mainly for not having created an autonomous
institution to solve the problem.[29]

Many aspects of the problem intensified during World War II,
and Calderón Guardia, chiefly for political reasons, accelerated the
pace of reform. His haste, at least in part, was a response to the
threat that the Communists might draw popular support away
from the more traditional political leadership. In 1940, there was
little doubt that pressure for political, social, and economic change
was largely identified with the Communists, not with the National
Republicans. Calderón Guardia was also motivated to act promptly
in order to offset the loss of support from the political right occasioned by the defection in 1941 of ex-President Cortés from the
National Republican party to form the Democratic party. Cortés'

XI y como lo sintetizara el Cardenal Mercier en su *Esbozo de una síntesis
social*" (Calderón Guardia, *La Tribuna*, May 9, 1950).

[29] *Surco*, no. 47 (May–June, 1944), p. 46. The National Liberation party
founded such an institute during the administration of Figueres, INVU (Instituto Nacional de Vivienda y Urbanismo).

party attracted the majority of the elite which came to fear either the nature or the rapid enactment of the President's program.

In spite of the exigencies of war, the Calderón Guardia government realized prodigious advances for the nation. It sponsored comprehensive programs that included, among others, the Law for New Industries to encourage diversification of the economy; the creation of the Social Security System and enactment of the Labor Code; the pragmatic Land Law, the so-called Law of the Parasites, which allowed the landless to acquire title to land on the promise of cultivating it; and a simple but effective program of distributing free shoes to needy children in the first grade to protect their feet against parasites and to help abate the feelings of inferiority produced by the lack of such a basic item.[30] These and other measures were sponsored by Calderón Guardia to build the infrastructure of a socially oriented national economy and to deal, simultaneously and directly, with the pressing needs of the most deprived members of the Costa Rican family.

Calderón Guardia also requested constitutional changes to grant authority for measures necessary to solve the agrarian problem. He proposed to give primary emphasis to the development of the small farm, "the base of our social peace and of the tranquility established by our forefathers."[31] He reaffirmed the right of private property, but he proposed to modify Article 29 of the constitution to allow Congress, by a two-thirds vote with just indemnification, to impose limitations in the interest of society on the use of private property.[32]

The three elements of the Calderón Guardia program that were

---

[30] Three good sources generally favorable to Calderón Guardia are José Albertazzi Avendaño, *La tragedia de Costa Rica: La obra social del Presidente Calderón Guardia*; and Rojas Suárez, *Costa Rica en la Segunda Guerra Mundial*. *Surco* reports critically on the progress of his program but, in general, presents fairly objective accounts.

[31] "El Sr. Oduber no puede alzar una bandera en la que jamás ha creído" (Calderón Guardia as quoted by Rogelio Ramos Valverde, *La Nación*, January 21, 1965, p. 20).

[32] Rojas Suárez, *Costa Rica*, has the text of the reformed article as it was later passed by Congress and that affirms the social function of land (p. 93).

most important in establishing a greater degree of social justice in
Costa Rica were social security provisions, labor legislation, and
the constitutional amendments. The amendments contained social
guarantees which could provide the legal base for future reforms.

Chronologically, the first of these measures was the establishment, in 1941, of the Social Security System, the first in Central
America, adapted from the Chilean program with the help of experts from that country.[33] The insurance was made compulsory for
all persons under sixty years of age serving as industrial or agricultural workers, as self-employed artisans working at home, and
as domestic employees, including maids. The money accumulated
from the payment of assessments was to be invested under the
supervision of a board consisting of the secretary of state for the
treasury and the managers of the National Bank of Costa Rica and
the National Insurance Bank. The employee, the employer, and
the state all made compulsory contributions to the insurance fund.
The law called for gradual extension of the system geographically
until it should cover the whole nation.[34]

The most basic of Calderón Guardia's reforms was the amending
of the constitution to include social guarantees and to assert the
social function of property. The President submitted to Congress
his projected chapter on "Social Guarantees" on May 16, 1942.[35]
He reaffirmed his Christian outlook and based his proposals on the
doctrines set forth by Pope Leo XIII and Pope Pius XI in their
respective encyclicals *Rerum Novarum* and *Quadregesimo Anno*.
The sixteen articles of the "Social Guarantees" expressed an ideal
toward which he believed Costa Rican society should work.

The proposed amendments, in themselves, had no legal force, but
rather stated basic principles in a fashion similar to the Bill of
Rights which was added to the Constitution of the United States of
America. The amendments made explicit the social rights previ-

[33] Ibid., p. 274. Its principal author, Oscar Barahona, later was invited by the
newly elected President of Guatemala, Juan José Arévalo, to draw up a similar
measure for that country.

[34] *La Gaceta*, November 14, 1941.

[35] *International Labour Review* 46 (November, 1942): 587.

ously considered implicit, but their substance was to be defined by Congress and their interpretation by the courts. The "Social Guarantees" included the right to establish cooperatives, to set up a Social Security System, to regulate working conditions, to establish a minimum living wage, and to bargain collectively in labor disputes. They upheld the right of equal opportunity for urban and rural laborers, the right to establish labor courts, and the right to preferential treatment in hiring practices for the Costa Rican worker as opposed to those of other nationalities.[36]

A more immediate and direct blow to what the elite considered its sacrosanct prerogatives came in August, 1943, with the promulgation of the Labor Code. This comprehensive enactment in 628 sections replaced, consolidated, and complemented a number of social measures previously in force and gave specific expression to some of the principles enunciated in the social guarantees. The law was thoroughly democratic and capitalistic.[37]

The Labor Code provided for the establishment of a Labor Ministry, made collective bargaining mandatory in disputes between labor and management, guaranteed the right of labor to organize, and assured the essential dignity of the individual worker by affording protection against arbitrary dismissal. The law created labor courts to which the worker could take his grievances rather than to his employer, who might present him with the unsavory alternatives of surrendering either his dignity or his livelihood. The code gave labor specific rights within society around which it could form a collective conscience short of the concept of class warfare.

Several other administration measures sought by various means to alleviate the misery of the poor and to minister to the needs of the unfortunate. The National Bank began to extend its operations into the less densely populated areas of Costa Rica in order to provide the small farmers and businessmen of the interior an easier

---

[36] *Ibid.*, pp. 587–588, has a complete list of the provisions of the amendment.
[37] "Cuales conquistas sociales posteriores a 1948 son más importantes que las anteriores a ese año?" (Fernando Trejos Escalante, *La Nación*, January 18, 1965, p. 17).

access to capital. It established a new section which, through extension of credit and provision of expert advice and counsel, promoted the organization of cooperatives and financed low-cost housing. The Caja Costarricense del Seguro Social supplemented the activities of the bank in the low-cost housing area.[38] These government-operated, capital-lending institutions thus made available some of the scarce credit resources of the nation in the form of conventional loans in geographic areas and in fields of endeavor which previously had been neglected.

One cooperative which the National Bank sponsored was La Victoria, described as "the first Costa Rican Cooperative of Agricultural-Industrial Production." For years the small farmers in the area of Grecia had sought governmental aid in establishing a cooperative sugar refinery which would liberate them from the widely fluctuating prices paid for semirefined cane sugar and enable them to produce refined sugar which sold at a stable price. Using as a nucleus the *finca* and refinery La Victoria, expropriated as a "German" property from the Niehaus family during World War II, the National Bank helped the farmers to set up a producers' cooperative.[39]

Calderón Guardia also attempted to build up the Pacific fishing industry. Primarily he was concerned with helping people to obtain a more adequate diet, but he also hoped to accelerate economic growth in the Puntarenas area. By means of an advertising campaign, he sought to encourage the people of the *meseta central* to eat fish to help remedy nutritional deficiencies, particularly the lack of protein. This, like many of the programs, was slow to develop, for the people did not readily change their traditional diet. The idea was derided by much of the press and even by the Centro,

[38] Albertazzi, *La tragedia*, p. 12. Low-cost houses with long-term financing under the Caja Costarricense del Seguro Social were constructed by the hundreds in and around San José, Heredia, and Cartago. Those houses which I visited in 1964–1965 remained comfortable dwelling places well adapted to the climate of the *meseta central*. The many-faceted approach of the *calderonistas* was supplanted subsequently under Liberación Nacional by an autonomous entity, INVU (Instituto Nacional de Vivienda y Urbanismo).

[39] Rojas Suárez, *Costa Rica*, pp. 178–182.

yet twenty years later some far-reaching results could be seen in the inexpensive and varied seafood offered in the markets of the capital, at least in part attributable to his program.

The estimated three thousand Amerindians, perhaps the most long-suffering and ignored inhabitants of the nation, were recognized by the Law for the Protection of the Indian. This measure established means for providing medical service, potable water, and access roads for their region.[40]

The National University, with its site in San José, was formed by bringing together the several colleges then in existence and creating others. It afforded opportunities for domestic study to those who could not afford to go abroad, and it also served the nation as a general force for modernization. This act was of tremendous importance—until this time Costa Rica lacked even a single university.

The positive program of social reform proposed by the *calderonistas* from within the elite made them anathema to most of their class. To much of the oligarchy, Calderón Guardia and his followers were indistinguishable from the Communists. The movement, however, was essentially capitalistic and probably would have expanded their class without drastically changing its composition. *Calderonismo* applied the principles attributed by Arthur Schlesinger, Jr., to President John F. Kennedy when, some twenty years later, he formed the Alliance for Progress: "The men of wealth and power in poor nations. . . . 'must lead the fight for those basic reforms which alone can preserve the fabric of their own societies.' "[41]

Calderón Guardia thought he had achieved consensus on his program of reform, but the resistance of the elite to change proved deeper than he had anticipated. The determined recalcitrance of some of the middle class came as a surprise, for it was from members of that class that strong vocal demands for change had come. The most vociferous opponents of the *calderonista* program, organized as the Social Democratic party by 1945, objected not so much

[40] Albertazzi, *La tragedia*, p. 20.
[41] Arthur M. Schlesinger, Jr., *A Thousand Days*, p. 722.

to change itself as to the changes proposed by the party in power and the auspices under which they were to be accomplished. The members of the Centro and Acción Demócrata, forerunners of the Social Democrats, opposed Calderón Guardia's program on ideological grounds, but they seem to have been motivated more by personal aversion to Calderón Guardia than by ideological difference.

The National Republicans' program for social reform enunciated by Calderón Guardia had to compete for support with other proposals ostensibly designed to attain the same ends. More or less complete plans were put forth by the Communists' Bloque de Obreros y Campesinos, which changed its name to the Vanguardia Popular in 1943, and by the Centro. To combat the program announced by Calderón Guardia, ex-President Cortés founded the rightist Democratic party.

From its foundation until 1945, the Centro presented itself to public opinion as an apolitical group interested in studying and seeking solutions to the difficult problems which faced the Costa Rican nation. Rodrigo Facio, a recognized leader of the group, shocked by the insinuation that the members were indeed involved in politics, asserted: "It is well known, by virtue of our declaration of electoral neutrality, that our only political concerns are the welfare and progress of Costa Rica."[42] The Centro proposed to stand off from active politics in order to view the milieu with detachment and objectivity. Then, with the studies complete, it could decide what should be done for Costa Rica.

The members of the Centro did not, however, remain aloof from Costa Rican politics. Their publication, *Surco*, took on a discernible antigovernment bias; by 1943, they were thinking in terms of founding a political party through which they intended to redirect the destinies of the nation.[43] In *La Hora* and *Diario de Costa Rica*, they gave their "prognosis" of what ailed Costa Rica. Their writ-

---

42 Rodrigo Facio, *El Centro ante las garantías sociales*, p. 9. [Pamphlet.]
43 John and Mavis Biesanz, *Costa Rican Life*, p. 241.

ings indicated utter dissatisfaction with the treatment prescribed by Dr. Calderón Guardia.[44]

The Centro quickly made its mark in Costa Rica. Older politicians saw it as a potential means for combatting the regime and as a force of some consequence in national life. The studies made by its members generally were serious and to the point. They lodged their most telling protests not against those who had shown little initiative in solving the graver of national problems but against those in power who had undertaken that arduous task, in a manner which the Centro considered "unscientific."

The Centro prided itself on its "advanced" thought. It tended to scorn the old Costa Rican and the "politicians" whom, together with the money interests of Costa Rica, it identified as the "civil oligarchy." It began to postulate a series of panaceas for the nation, the sum of which was the ideology of the group. Since socialism was "advanced," the *centristas* referred to themselves as socialists. Their socialism, at least at this juncture, might better be described as a social conscience, or as a sensitivity to the sufferings and privations of the lower classes.

A sociologist from the United States described the Centro as the most alive organization in Costa Rica.[45] The social cohesiveness of its members made it easy for them to understand each other and to postulate solutions for national problems which they could espouse as a group.[46] Their youth perhaps excuses them for the pretension of thinking that such a narrowly based group could speak for the nation. They largely justified their pretension by applying Ortega y Gasset's concept of a generation and later referred to themselves as the "Generation of Forty-eight."[47]

[44] The most comprehensive example is Rodrigo Facio, *El Centro ante las garantías sociales*. He does not limit himself to a rather harsh criticism of the social legislation but attacks almost every aspect of the administration.

[45] Biesanz, *Costa Rican Life*, p. 169.

[46] Hugo Navarro Bolandi notes this "homegeneity" in *La generacion del 48*, p. 109.

[47] Eugenio Rodríguez Vega, *Apuntes para una Sociología Costarricense*, pp. 82–84 and Navarro Bolandi, *La generación*.

Despite their studies of national problems, the narrow composition of their group made it difficult for the youths of the Centro to understand and interpret the programs and tactics of the government.[48] Their lack of understanding led them to dismiss the social reform program of the *calderonistas* as "politics," and their wholesale condemnation of proposed measures made them susceptible to an alliance with reactionary elements seeking to oppose Calderón Guardia.

Ideologically the Centro differed from most of the opposition in that it favored a positive governmental program to foster economic and social development, a contrast to the classical liberal program of Cortés's followers. Socially they were close to the elite, understood it, shared its values, and enjoyed its confidence.[49]

The Centro's importance transcended its role as an independent political force. It provided the nucleus for the Social Democratic party, founded in 1945. In that year it joined with Acción Demócrata, a group of young activists within the ranks of Cortés' Democratic party.[50] Unlike the Centro, Acción Demócrata was more concerned with political contests per se and with the issue of fiscal responsibility than with the social question.

Acción Demócrata established itself as a separate political party shortly after the 1944 election.[51] To state its position in Costa Rican politics it established a weekly newspaper, *Acción Demócrata*, the first issue of which appeared on February 26, 1944, under the direc-

[48] *Surco*, no. 47 (May–June, 1943), p. 84.

[49] An indication that their favored position in society did not escape the pro government forces with their strong lower class following is evident in the epithets which they applied to the youths of the Centro: *Niños bien* and *glostoras*. Glostora was a brand of hair lotion which was widely known and widely used by those to whom the epithet was applied. See Arturo Castro Esquivel, *José Figueres Ferrer*, p. 61.

[50] Cañas, *Los ochos años*, p. 69. Also see *La Nación*, September 11, 1949, p. 10. concerning the organization of Acción Demócrata.

[51] *Acción Demócrata*, February 26, 1944, p. 1, notes that the party of the same name had begun its independent life but did not give the precise date. It stated that the party's foundation came after the defeat of Cortés (February 13), so it was founded between February 13 and 26, 1944.

tion of Alberto Martén, a close friend of José Figueres Ferrer, to whose political fortunes it devoted considerable space.

Figueres achieved some fame in Costa Rica as an uncompromising opponent of Calderón Guardia and as the only Costa Rican political exile since the days of the Tinocos. On July 8, 1942, Figueres, a coffee and *cabuya* grower, had made a particularly harsh radio speech against the President on personal, ideological, and practical grounds. Figueres attacked him as a demagogue who was leading the nation to financial, economic, and social disaster. He particularly criticized him for his increasingly close relations with the Communists and for the administration's conduct of the war. The speech resulted in Figueres' exile. From outside the country and after his return, he became one of the most determined opponents of the National Republicans.[52]

It was the Centro's orientation on social reform which prevailed in the Social Democratic party. The formation of the Social Democratic party brought the Centro into active involvement in electoral politics. The Social Democrats in turn became the catalyst in holding together the various elements opposed to Calderón Guardia. This political coalition organized in 1945 was known simply as the Opposition,[53] a united force; the opposition to the National Republicans had lacked cohesion until that time.

The Centro charged Calderón Guardia with having "put the cart before the horse" in the enactment of a Social Security Law. It approved the purpose of the measure but held the President responsible for technical imperfections which might result from drafting

[52] For a more detailed treatment of Figueres and his role in Costa Rican politics during his exile, see Chapter 5.

[53] In this work "the Opposition" refers to the electoral coalition established to oppose the National Republicans and Vanguardia Popular. The Opposition formed in 1945 in order to confront the anticipated candidacy of Calderón Guardia in 1948 for a second term. The three major parties were the Unión Nacional, personalistic party formed around Otilio Ulate, the publisher of the *Diario de Costa Rica*; the Democratic party, the political vehicle of León Cortés, formed in 1941 after he broke with the National Republican party; and the Social Democratic party.

the law without first conducting a statistical or technical study as the Centro would have done. It accused the President of pure demagoguery in rushing into law a measure he had not properly studied.[54] The Centro, whether by inadvertence or by purpose, seems to have disregarded the evidence that resistance by the elite made enactment of the law of utmost importance even if its initial application was less than optimal.[55]

The Centro likewise opposed the government's role in the creation of the cooperative, La Victoria—the idea for which had originated with the Centro. Even though the central government was the only agency capable of setting up the proposed cooperative, *Surco* found it unbelievable and somehow improper that Calderón Guardia should have carried out the Centro's suggestion. The implication that the government had "stolen" their plan accurately reflected the attitude of the young men of the Centro toward Calderón Guardia. They considered him to be unoriginal and therefore unworthy of their esteem. Moreover, they wanted revolutionary accomplishments free of the taint of compromise and political expediency with which they charged the "corrupt politicians" and the representatives of the "civil oligarchy" who composed the administration.

Calderón Guardia's Labor Code also met with immediate opposition from employers and antigovernment forces. Widespread dismissals of workers preceded the formal signing of the measure into law, and many employers, both industrial and agricultural, increased their financial support of the candidacy of ex-President Cortés. Opponents charged that the code was defective and that it was politically motivated; they denounced it as communistic and called for its repeal. The basis for the latter contention was not the law itself, but the open and militant support given it by Vanguardia Popular.

[54] The system, with modifications, continues to expand and provide greater and more comprehensive service for Costa Rica, including an integrated system of hospitals, clinics, and mobile health units.

[55] *Surco*, no. 47 (May–June, 1944), pp. 38–39, discusses the system and its success as well as the alleged political aims of Calderón Guardia. Also, see *La obra social*, p. 15.

The varied and, in some respects, too elemental programs initiated by Calderón Guardia occasioned derision largely because they were directed toward the needs of the more underprivileged of the Costa Rican family. They were criticized for being politically motivated.

The urban middle sectors also needed relief, but they enjoyed little benefit from the programs. The long-range results were to prove beneficial to the entire nation, but the immediate ameliorative features and the brave new hope for the future were felt chiefly by the most needy members of the society. The absence of measures to meet the needs of the middle sectors led many to view Calderón Guardia's program as a sham. This defect partially offset the favorable overall effects of the measures and had serious political repercussions.

The business circles increased their support of various opposition forces and thereby weakened the *calderonistas*. Political polarization, however, was far from complete in the 1944 election. The opposition to Calderón Guardia was vigorous, even to the point of an armed uprising plot, but it did not in 1944, as it did in 1948, achieve the full support of the right.

Calderón Guardia headed a traditional party which included elements from all segments of society, and he attracted a following among the masses of society such as no previous political figure had achieved. The leadership of the party, however, remained with men who had served in the governments of Cortés and Jiménez, professional politicians identified with the "civil oligarchy." The combination of elements appeared supple enough to withstand political turmoil and to see the new social orientation through to execution and to at least tacit acceptance without violent discord.

From 1940 forward, the various contestants in the political arena could not disregard Calderón Guardia's functioning program with its sharp focus on social issues. He was determined, even if it entailed intimidation, to carry out his plans. His program and the methods he used to put it into effect therefore became inextricable parts of the social issue. His work of reform challenged the domination of the elite, which consequently became politically more active, aware, and cohesive. While the political program of the elite stressed a number of issues, its major interest was to maintain itself as the director of society and to forestall, at least, a program of social reform. An even more significant challenge to Calderón Guardia's program came from elements of the middle sectors who organized the Social Democratic party; although not opposed to social reform per se, they developed different approaches from those of Calderón Guardia. The political alliance of the majority of the elite and the Social Democrats against Calderón Guardia and the National Republicans underlay the revolution of 1948.

CHAPTER 3

The Issue of Communism

COMMUNISM WAS A SIGNIFICANT FORCE in shaping the revolution of 1948. It was one of the major issues that led up to the armed insurrection, and during the course of hostilities it was *the* one of crucial importance. The issue was posed at several levels. On the theoretical level, the problem was whether or not the Communist solution would remedy the dysfunctional conditions of Costa Rican society. On the level of practical politics, the question centered on the degree of influence and power achieved by Vanguardia Popular, the Communist party. Of particular interest in this regard was its role as an indigenously organized and developed political party, with international ties, which found it expedient between 1942 and 1948 to collaborate with the National Republicans. On yet another level, the question arose about the use of the term "Communism" as a scare label, synonymous with a demonic and insidious force threatening the life of the republic. Calderón Guardia opened himself to attack on this issue by accepting political collaboration from Mora's Communist party.

At first the Costa Rican Communists had opposed Calderón Guardia's administration. Indeed, during the first two years of his term Calderón Guardia frequently presented his reform program as a means of counteracting the growing power and influence of Manuel Mora and the Communists. He appealed to all classes to support his reform measures, not only because they were essential to national well being but because they also combatted communism.

Calderón Guardia, challenged on the right by Cortés and on the left by Mora, later proved receptive to an offer of political support from the Communists. Mora promised to assist the government politically if Calderón Guardia would quicken the pace of reform. The Communists did not formally enter the government in the sense that they received no ministerial positions in exchange for their support, but their representatives in Congress adhered to Calderón Guardia's program, and their political propaganda rather abruptly shifted from opposing to backing the administration. Their assistance, however, was selective; they defended measures for social reform and exhorted Calderón Guardia to make even greater efforts on behalf of the working classes.

Calderón Guardia decided to risk loss of support on the right in order to see through his program of social and economic reform. The assistance of the Communists strengthened his political position by changing that element of opposition into an ally and by the addition of the militant organization which Mora had built up.

The Communists made the most effective use of their minority role from 1942 to 1948. With their support, much of the program of reform they had long espoused was enacted by the National Republicans. The objective conditions following the 1942 election made political collaboration desirable to both the Communists and the National Republicans, in spite of their ideological differences. For the Communists it was an opportunity to assist in the enactment of measures to ameliorate the conditions of the lower classes;

it also provided opportunity for some members of the party to participate in lower-level government work.

Coming as it did at a time when the Soviet Union fought as an ally of the Western democracies, the alliance was portrayed by its architects as consistent with the united war effort against Nazi Germany. International communism in fact encouraged national Communist parties to collaborate with democratic governments during World War II. United States representatives in Costa Rica also seemed to look favorably on the alliance.[1]

The Bloque de Obreros y Campesinos and its successor, Vanguardia Popular, advocated realistic programs of reform realizable within the democratic process. In 1943, Archbishop Sanabria stated publicly that he found nothing in the program of Vanguardia Popular which would exclude a practicing Catholic from participation and membership in that party.[2] In fact, he said, it was the only party in the nation which offered workers opportunity to air grievances which called for redress.[3] The position taken by the archbishop further indicated the degree to which the Communists in Costa Rica had achieved respectability at the time of their political alliance with the National Republicans.

The seeming inconsistency of Calderón Guardia's acceptance of support from Communists for his program to combat communism was reconciled, at least in part, by Mora's dissolution of the Bloque in 1943. Mora immediately formed the Vanguardia Popular, however, which ostensibly accepted the social-Christian program of

1 An indication of this approbation was the active participation of the chief of the U.S. Military Mission, Col. R. E. Jones, alongside Communist leaders in the antifascist demonstrations in San José on July 4, 1942. Col. Jones served as head of mission from February 5 to July 24, 1942. See Daniel Oduber and Luis Alberto Monge, "Dictaduras, imperialismo y democracia," *Combate*, 9 (March–April, 1960): 14, for a discussion of the participation of officials of the United States government in the demonstration of July 4, 1942.

2 *International Labour Review* 50 (1944): 257; Ricardo Blanco Segura, *Monseñor Sanabria*, p. 89.

3 *La Tribuna*, June 20, 1943, p. 1. Also see Víctor M. Sanabria, *Palabra dirigida al venerable clero de la arquidiócesis de San José*, p. 25. *Acción Demócrata*, April 7, 1944, p. 1, commenting in a different vein, agreed with Sanabria's appraisal of Vanguardia Popular as the only workers' party.

Calderón Guardia.[4] It appears that Mora followed the international Communist line throughout the period, but in the context of the early 1940's he could do so without bringing into question the indigenous quality of his party.

Calderón Guardia arrived at his decision to accept support from Mora for pragmatic political reasons. The constitution denied him a second consecutive term as president, and his party recognized the serious challenge which Cortés' candidacy represented to completion of its reform program.

Teodoro Picado, the National Republican candidate, lacked the charisma of the three caudillos, Cortés, Mora, and Calderón Guardia. The sectional strength of the Communists among the voters of both coasts would prove useful to the *calderonistas* in the crucial 1944 election.[5]

After 1942, the Communists suffered as well as benefited from their political alliance with the government. They lost appeal because Calderón Guardia, from the presidency, offered solutions to Costa Rican problems which conformed more closely to the idiosyncrasies of the people and had greater promise of fulfillment than did those of the Communists. They also suffered the consequences of being close enough to power to be expected to deliver on their promises and to be associated with the faults as well as the successes of the regime; they were no longer able to pontificate from without as a party of protest. They were tainted by association with the fiscal corruption, the financial difficulties, and the electoral abuses of the administration. This situation contrasted significantly with the position of prestige and the image of responsibility that the Communists enjoyed prior to 1942 when Mora and his party could in justice be portrayed as the victims of undemocratic acts.

Vanguardia Popular's support of Picado allowed Cortés with greater appearance of reason to repeat his electoral tactics of 1936. The terms *caldero-comunismo* or *picado-comunismo*, given the strength of Mora's following and his open support, carried some semblance of validity. The charge, however, that the leadership

[4] *Bulletin of the Pan American Union* 78 (September, 1944): 526–528.
[5] See chapter 5 for a discussion of the reasons for strength on the coasts.

of the National Republican party was Communist or was composed of Communist-sympathizers was vacuous and vicious propaganda.

Picado won the 1944 election, but he immediately faced a unified resistance that endeavored by all possible means to discredit his government and to avert a second presidential term for Calderón Guardia.[6] The political alliance between the National Republicans and Vanguardia Popular afforded its opponents a most effective basis for attack. The Opposition was able to form and to operate a terrorist organization without general condemnation largely because the populace had become accustomed to such tactics and accepted terrorism as an almost legitimate form of political activity against an allegedly unjust regime. The cadres formed by the Social Democratic party and the violence they perpetrated seemed to be a logical response to the violence of the Vanguardia Popular goon-squads[7] and their participation in the intimidation practiced by the *calderonistas* in the 1944 presidential election.

The Opposition skillfully avoided the wholesale application of the Communist label to the National Republican party and its leadership. It realized that individuals so characterized would be known well enough by citizens in a very small nation that the validity of such a charge would probably be immediately challenged. Its strategists therefore concentrated on Calderón Guardia whose great personal popularity among the lower classes constituted the principal obstacle to defeating the National Republicans.

During the period 1945 to 1948 a new international factor improved the political fortunes of the Opposition. The West, and particularly the United States, became acutely aware of the threat of communism. The traditional Costa Rican affinity toward the United States had grown even closer during World War II, and when relations between the United States and the Soviet Union

[6] Calderón Guardia remained the leading figure in the National Republican party and the most prominent political leader in the nation. He did not run for the presidency in 1944 because the Constitution prohibited consecutive terms. However the Opposition and his own National Republican Party presumed that he would run for a second term in 1948.

[7] The term used in the Spanish original was *brigadas de choque*, which means "storm troops" but was quite an inaccurate description of the groups in question.

became strained during the postwar years, that state of affairs affected the issue of communism in Costa Rica. The Communist newspaper, *Trabajo*, continued to feature stories from Communist nations on such topics as the exploits of a Soviet soccer team, but in the postwar context these innocuous accounts took on a sinister aspect as they clearly identified Vanguardia Popular with the "official enemy."[8] The use made by Vanguardia Popular's ideological opponent, the Social Democrats, in their newspaper of feature stories of opposite tenor, such as the preparation of Blair House in Washington, D.C., for use as a guest house by visiting dignitaries, tended to align the two parties in juxtaposition analogous to the postures assumed by their great power ideological mentors.

Any contention or assertion couched in terms of anticommunism during the postwar period in Costa Rica benefited from a multiplier effect. This state of affairs strongly affected the individualistic and conservative *campesino*. The Costa Rican way of life had been that of the countryside; communism threatened it. In fact, any form of modernization and industrialization threatened it. That the traditional way of life had been in decline since the advent of large-scale commercial farming made the rural areas of the nation no less vulnerable to hysterical anticommunism. The decrease in relative importance of the small independent farmer made him especially susceptible to political appeals that included the promise to protect his way of life from any alleged threat. He knew and believed that the countryside was dwindling in importance to the nation. This conviction may have predisposed him to accept an interpretation which attributed this decline to a powerful, malevolent, and foreign force.

The important change had not taken place within Costa Rica but rather in the relationships of the great world powers. As the foreign policy of the Soviet Union moved toward a state of mutual antagonism with the United States, the tendency in Costa Rica was to follow the lead of the latter. The Costa Rican, rich and poor,

---

[8] "The Cold War has already begun. Now the official enemy of the western democracies is Communism" (Alberto Cañas, *Los ocho años*, p. 90).

urban and rural, conservative and liberal, was in general favorably disposed toward the United States.[9] This trust and belief in the United States as a nation persisted despite the antipathy of important segments of the population toward certain practices of the United Fruit Company and other American enterprises in Costa Rica and in Latin America in general. The Costa Rican kept these practices in proper perspective; he generally held the United States in high esteem and looked to it for leadership in international affairs.

The United States clearly identified Russia and communism as the enemy and moved closer to adoption of a "get tough" policy.[10] The average citizen of the United States, in the atmosphere of rivalry and distrust which prevailed between his nation and Russia, "now regarded the Soviet Union, and the ideology for which it stood, as a definite menace to everything for which he stood."[11] The change was perceptible in 1945 and by 1948 had assumed the state of open discord.

Mora's party was a major issue in the Costa Rican electoral campaigns of 1936, 1940, 1944, and 1948. Opposing parties in each of these campaigns represented communism to the electorate as a movement alien in inspiration and in ultimate leadership. Specifically, they charged that it presented a challenge to the nation's heritage of stability, order, and peaceful solution to conflicts, and also to the Catholic religion of which the majority of Costa Ricans were practicing devotees.[12]

The initial political success achieved by the Communists in 1934 had inspired that government to employ tactics intended to limit the impact of the new party, Bloque de Obreros y Campesinos. The anticommunism it inaugurated became a characteristic of all subsequent elections. Identification of a party or candidate with Mora

[9] Irvin L. Child, "The Background of Public Opinion in Costa Rica," *Public Opinion Quarterly* 7 (1943): 244.

[10] Oscar T. Barck, Jr., *A History of the United States since 1945*, p. 105.

[11] Ibid., p. 106.

[12] Mario Sancho, *Memorias*, pp. 36–37.

proved, with one possible exception. to be a political detriment. (The exception occurred in 1944 when León Cortés suffered defeat despite his warning against the "red hordes" of Mora and Picado.)

The Opposition attempted to make political capital of the growing breach between the two major world powers. In the 1946 off-year election, with an eye directed toward the 1948 presidential election, it endeavored internationally as well as nationally. to affix the epithet "Communist" to Calderón Guardia.

The National Republicans realized the plight in which their alliance with Vanguardia Popular placed them for the crucial 1948 elections, but they were unable to extricate themselves with honor. Vanguardia Popular fulfilled the political pact and pragmatically assisted in the realization of a program of social reform which did not conform to its Communist ideology. The National Republicans felt bound to carry through their program. which could be accomplished only within the framework of their political alliance with the Vanguardia Popular, faced as the National Republicans were with the relentless obstructionism of the Opposition.

A detailed treatment of the organization and development of the Communist movement in Costa Rica is neither essential nor appropriate to this discussion. Several aspects of that development, however, were of crucial importance to an understanding of why Costa Rica forsook her tradition of orderly transfer of power and settled the issue by force of arms following the election of 1948. The most important aspects of its development may be traced to the consistent participation of Communist candidates in elections, the indigenous organization and orientation of the party, the capable leadership it enjoyed. the role it played in the organization of the local labor movement and in the education and general uplift of the workers,[13] the political alliance it formed with the National

---

[13] The cultural and educational enterprises of Vanguardia Popular were varied. Their programs included language instruction, boy scouts, musical events, book clubs, sports instruction and competition, as well as instruction in Marxist-Leninism and world and national events. These are only a few of the activities which were regularly announced in *Trabajo*.

Republicans, and finally, the impact of the Cold War and its role in national life.

The majority of the leadership of the movement worked among the laborers of the *meseta central* and the coasts; Carlos Luis Fallas was outstanding in this regard.[14] Fallas, himself, had risen from the ranks of labor; a shoemaker and worker in the banana plantations, he eventually obtained a position of leadership in the Costa Rican Labor Federation and in Vanguardia Popular. The leaders helped organize segments of the working classes so that they could effectively seek immediate amelioration of their condition within the democratic and capitalistic society which then existed. They devoted themselves not only to the implementation of the social revolution, which they believed would inevitably bring the proletariat to power, but to educating and preparing the future victors for their exercise of power. Mario Sancho in his *Memorias* observed that "there in their cells, the catacombs of a new political religion, they [the workers] began to develop a passion for reading. . . . Communism . . . realized a determined task in education. . . . [It has] changed the workers' style of life."[15] This educational work had the net effect of bringing segments of the lower classes into the favored portion of Costa Rican society that forms public opinion and, hence, they could affect decision making on the national level.[16]

To a great extent and contrary to the teachings of its theorists, the Communist party in Costa Rica prospered under the personalistic leadership of Manuel Mora. It was Mora's party, and he was the caudillo, in the Costa Rican civil tradition, of the rank and file. He dedicated his life to his people with the devotion of a Las Casas. An article in the *Christian Science Monitor Magazine* in 1942 de-

[14] Other outstanding leaders of Mora's party were Carmen Lyra, the educator and writer; Fabián Dobles, the novelist; Alfredo Picado, the labor leader; Jaime Cerdas; Arnoldo Ferreto; and Carlos Luis Sáenz.

[15] Sancho, *Memorias*, pp. 249–250.

[16] Victor Alba discusses the crucial importance of this advance for any group in Latin America, for it is only within this sector that the economic situation has progressed in the last decades (*Parásitos, mitos y sordomudos*, p. 19).

scribes Mora as one of the most active and respected members of the Congress. He was appraised as a healthful influence accepted by responsible citizens, and as a "watchdog for injustice."[17]

In part, Mora's prestige and that of the other Communist leaders, notably Fallas, was a result of their dedication and personal integrity. Also of importance, however, was the domestic origin and orientation of the party. This characteristic generally saved the members from being burdened with a foreign-agent identity, at least until the events of 1945–1948 polarized public opinion and obscured the subtlety of the relationship. Costa Ricans still draw a distinction between communism before and after the revolution. Even the staunchest opponents of the pre–1948 communism refer to it as *comunismo criollo*, thus distinguishing it from the less independent and clandestine party that operated subsequently.[18]

In the generally accepted view of Navarro Bolandi, *comunismo criollo* grew out of the unsuccessful democratic movement attempted by Volio.[19] *Comunismo criollo* was "conceived by native-born minds and directed by the native borns." They accepted the Communist banner as a means to seek the social and economic advances which they had failed to achieve under Reformism.[20] In the early days of Mora's party even Otilio Ulate, who later became an uncompromising anti-Communist, defended the party's participation in Costa Rican life.[21] *Acción Demócrata* in an editorial explained Ulate's position and that of many other responsible citizens, who had earlier defended the Communists:

During the first years of their life as a group . . . "the comrades" . . . took several attitudes which earned them national prestige. They joined many honorable battles; they denounced electoral frauds; they combatted unjust contracts with banana and electrical companies. . . . Their efforts attracted to them the sympathy of part of those healthy

[17] Lawrence and Sylvia Martin, "Five Wise Men of Costa Rica," *Christian Science Monitor Monthly Magazine*, April, 1942, p. 5.

[18] Hugo Navarro Bolandi, *La generación del 48*, p. 89.

[19] Of interest is the fact that General Volio, in the closing days of the revolution, identified himself with the defense of the government.

[20] Navarro Bolandi, *La generación*, p. 89.

[21] *Acción Demócrata*, April 26, 1947, p. 3.

sectors which without sharing their ideology . . . came to the conclusions that it was necessary to help the Communists in their campaigns and they contributed their votes to keep Manuel Mora in Congress.[22]

The party defended the electoral rights of all citizens, and, in particular, attempted to safeguard the rights of labor and of the peasants.[23] These causes along with the caliber of its leadership won it acceptance among responsible Costa Ricans.

International communism followed the strategy of the Popular Front only from 1935 until 1939; the party in Costa Rica consistently pursued such a policy until 1948. The term Popular Front perhaps does not accurately describe Mora's position, since at no time did he or his comrades actually participate in a government. They did, however, collaborate with democratic parties in the various electoral struggles and from 1942 to 1948 supported and contributed to the sweeping social-Christian reform program of the National Republicans.

Although their rhetoric generally followed the Marxist-Leninist line, Mora's followers, prior to the election of 1944, did not engage in violence or intimidation. At no point did they attempt to seize the government by force. Mora took the position that violent revolution was not necessary or called for in Costa Rica, because the Communists participated in the democratic institutions of the nation and could thus impel a peaceful transformation of "systems and institutions."[24]

The off-year elections in February, 1946, were unusually fair. Predictably, the Communists slipped badly; their decline was due as much to their association with the government as to the identification of Vanguardia Popular with communism, which was now defined as an international movement hostile to the Western democracies. They found their prospective support lessened by international events just when their actual influence had, at least in the opinion of Arnoldo Ferreto, a leading Vanguardia Popular

[22] Ibid., April 26, 1947, p. 4.

[23] John and Mavis Biesanz, *Costa Rican Life*, p. 227.

[24] Manuel Mora Valverde, *Por la afirmación de nuestra democracia: por el progreso y bienestar de nuestra nación*, p. 7. [Pamphlet.]

theoretician, reached a new high.[25] Their alliance with the government was of utmost importance to them.

After the 1944 election, the Opposition resolved to abstain from attendance in Congress. The ostensible motive for this action was to protest alleged fraud in electoral procedures; actually, it was to embarrass the government. The boycott by the Opposition deputies had the effect of forcing the National Republicans to continue the alliance with Vanguardia Popular. Without the assistance of the *vanguardistas* at Congress, the government would be paralyzed by a semipermanent lack of quorum. The Opposition thus helped to keep the National Republicans in alliance with the Communists and to preserve a major issue for the proximate presidential campaign.

The issue had an equal or greater effect internationally. *El Social Demócrata*[26] and to a lesser extent *El Diario de Costa Rica* published open letters to the "foreign colony resident in Costa Rica," to the United States ambassador, or to the American people warning them of the serious Communist threat in Costa Rica.[27] These items were always quick to state that the last thing the authors wanted was foreign intervention in their domestic affairs; they simply wanted the world to be aware of the danger.

In July, 1946, *Acción Demócrata* began to employ the rhetoric of the Cold War in its columns. It utilized most of the distortions and oversimplifications that maintain the division of the world into two segments. The good people consisted of the United States and its allies; the bad people, the Russians and their allies, including the various Communist parties in the West. *Acción Demócrata* actually employed the words *good* and *bad* and equated the international situation to the national situation. The "good" people nationally were those who supported the Opposition; the "bad" people were those who did not. It was not in that journal's view a time when one

[25] Arnoldo Ferreto, *Los principios de organización del Partido Vanguardia Popular*, p. 6. [Pamphlet.]

[26] *El Social Demócrata* succeeded *Acción Demócrata* as the party organ for the Social Democratic party in May, 1947.

[27] *Acción Demócrata*, March 16, 1946, p. 2.

could be neutral; it was a time to stand up and be counted against the "bad" both internationally and nationally. It was time to stand up and be counted in opposition to *caldero-comunismo*, the purported Costa Rican counterpart of the Soviet Union and its allies.

In the distorted and moralistic view of *Acción Demócrata*, Costa Rican democratic institutions did not apply to the "reds." Those "bad Costa Ricans" had lost any rights which they had previously shared with their fellow citizens. It referred to Picado as a puppet president unworthy of respect because he was managed by the "comrades." The worst among the "bad" were the *vanguardistas*, who "must be treated as totalitarians and not with reason or with decency."[28]

As the election of 1948 drew near, the Social Democrats carried to the United States itself the propaganda campaign to identify the National Republicans with communism. With the financial help of "private United States citizens," they published articles condemning the purported Communist infiltration and control of the Costa Rican government. They organized picketing in New York and Washington to let the world know that there was imminent danger of a Russian beachhead being established in the heart of the Americas, next door to the Panama Canal.[29] A key figure in the campaign to discredit his government in the United States was Gonzalo Facio, a Social Democrat who later served as Minister of Justice and still later as Costa Rican ambassador to the United States.[30]

In the context of the last days of the electoral campaign, *El Social Demócrata* pinpointed its position toward Communists with the explicit statement that "the Communists are not Costa Ricans" even though they were native citizens.[31]

[28] Ibid., August 5, 1944, p. 1.

[29] *La Nación*, May 4, 1948, p. 6.

[30] In the private collection of Professor Carlos Meléndez Ch. of the University of Costa Rica, there is a photograph of Facio among other anti-Communist pickets. Also, see *La Gaceta*, January 19, 1950, which indicates that the costs of this protest were later paid for by the nation when the Junta Fundadora de la Segunda República in October, 1948, reimbursed the Costa Rican League against Communist Domination.

[31] *El Social Demócrata*, February 2, 1948, p. 2.

It appears that both the domestic and the international campaigns had some effect on United States policy makers. The United States ambassador, Howlett Johnson, considered favorable to Calderón Guardia, was hastily called to Washington for consultation in March, 1947.[32] He returned to San José only to put his affairs in order and departed on May 16. His replacement, Walter J. Donnelly, arrived in June.[33] In his first press conference, Donnelly discussed communism as he saw it—a threat to all the peoples of America which it was necessary for all governments to combat.[34]

Donnelly, in turn, was replaced in November by Nathaniel Davis, a career diplomat, whose previous and subsequent appointments suggest that San José was an unusual duty station. He was serving in Russia at the time of his appointment to Costa Rica, and at the termination of his tour of duty there in May, 1949, he was appointed ambassador to Hungary.[35] Among the attentions that Costa Rica received from the United States during that period was the assignment of an ambassador expert in Communist affairs.

Mora had difficulty, despite his pragmatism, devising a program for his party in the circumstances that prevailed during the first years of the Cold War. The change in the international situation also weakened the Communists. They lost the prestige that they had enjoyed as a result of the alliance of the Soviet Union with the Western democracies. Mora recognized the strength of Calderón Guardia among the workers and the possibility that support for the Communists could be diminished as much by the charisma of Vanguardia Popular's ally as by onslaught from open adversaries.[36]

The renewed international activity of the Soviet Union tended to

[32] *Diario de Costa Rica*, May 18, 1947, p. 1.

[33] After his short period as ambassador in Costa Rica, Donnelly went to Bogotá, Colombia, as part of the U.S. delegation to the Ninth International Conference of American States (March 30, 1948), and later served as Ambassador to Venezuela. Milton Eisenhower in *The Wine is Bitter*, p. 163, identified Donnelly as "Walter J. Donnelly, Vice-President of United States Steel, living in Venezuela, a former United States Ambassador, and favorably known throughout the hemisphere."

[34] *La Nación*, June 27, 1947, p. 1.

[35] Ibid., May 28, 1949, p. 1.

[36] *Trabajo*, March 8, 1947, p. 1.

make Mora's position less tenable. He laid his party open to successful attack by the Opposition by organizing demonstrations against
U.S. aid to Greece and Turkey.[37] His disregard for the effect such
stands might have on public opinion during a crucial political campaign indicated that the alliance with Calderón Guardia was secondary to his international commitments. The Cold War was
changing *comunismo criollo*. As *La Nación* succinctly pointed out,
communism in Costa Rica would sooner or later fall by weight of its
foreign ways.[38]

Picado considered the possibility of a break with Vanguardia
Popular "in exchange for the support of the capitalistic sector
affected by the social legislation, a powerful force which had opposed him."[39] When he failed to arrive at what he considered a
reasonable agreement, he chose to accept continued collaboration
with Vanguardia Popular.[40]

The Communists played into the hands of the Social Democratic
party by notoriously claiming that they dominated the administration.[41] By this pretense they hoped to escape the plateau of political
power that they had reached in 1942 but subsequently had not been
able to ascend. Despite its alliance with the National Republicans,
Vanguardia Popular was not a political force of the first order.[42]

As a radical reform party within a democracy, Vanguardia
Popular found itself with a militant but limited membership and
with little possibility of achieving power. Its successes were limited
to influencing national politics and seeing some of its program
enacted by the National Republicans, a more broadly based traditional party. It achieved some of its goals in much the same way as
did "third parties" in the United States during the Populist and
Progressive eras; that is, through a major party.

The Social Democrats openly courted the support of the United

[37] *La Nación*, October 22, 1947, p. 1.
[38] Ibid., September 28, 1947, p. 1.
[39] Ricardo Fernández Guardia, *Cartilla histórica de Costa Rica*, p. 149.
[40] Ibid., p. 149.
[41] Arnoldo Ferreto, *Los principios de organización del Partido Vanguardia*, p.
6. [Pamphlet.]
[42] Robin A. Humphreys, *The Evolution of Modern Latin America*, p. 147.

States in their campaign against communism. This courtship served the immediate aim of the Opposition to discredit the government and, of equal importance, it also served to identify the Social Democrats as the political group in Costa Rica most fully aware of the "menace of communism." Not only did the Social Democrats recognize the national, continental, and global threat of communism, as did the United States, but they also conveniently placed their political adversary, the National Republicans, as party to the threat.

The Social Democratic party's strategy was surely calculated to appeal to the United States, which suffered some shock on discovering that the post–Second World War world did not readily follow its direction.[43] The *calderonistas* did not respond to the United States' appraisal of the threat but continued to treat Vanguardia Popular as the minor force that it actually was in national politics. The full thrust of the Social Democratic party's strategy can be appreciated only in the light of the consternation felt by the United States as it discovered the complexity and difficulty of dealing with the Soviet Union and the reluctance of non-Communist nations to follow its policy changes. Denis W. Brogan, one of Britain's most sensitive and sympathetic commentators on America, summed up this aspect of the Cold War in the following manner: ". . . it was far more of a shock to find that a great many peoples and a great many governments that were not Communist, including some that were determinedly anti-Communist, did not . . . throw themselves into the arms of the United States and accept, without questioning, American leadership."[44]

The *calderonistas* did not find it hard to choose sides in the Cold War. They, like the vast majority of Costa Ricans, were almost habitually partisans of the United States, but they simply could not see that Mora's party, given its small membership and its recent lack of growth, could constitute a grave threat to anyone. The social reform program of Calderón Guardia had largely taken away its thunder. Concern about a Communist takeover was unrealistic.

Politically, however, the danger proved to be entirely real. The

[43] Denis W. Brogan, *The Price of Revolution*, p. 220.
[44] Ibid., pp. 220–221.

immense anti-Communist propaganda effort of the United States worked to Calderón Guardia's disadvantage. The Opposition was able to convince many Costa Ricans and some citizens of the United States of the truth of the simple but false assertion made by its full-page advertisements that "Calderón es comunista."

In February, March, and April of 1947, the *Diario de Costa Rica*, property of the Opposition candidate, Otilio Ulate, carried on an intense campaign to label Calderón Guardia "Communist." There were articles which told Costa Rica to take part in' the crusade against Marxist "infiltration" and photographs and articles which showed Calderón Guardia working with the *vanguardistas* in the period of his first administration. A political cartoon of April 3, 1947, showed a *campesino* speaking in dialect to a kindly Uncle Sam, revealing to him the "truth" that Costa Rica was in Communist hands.[45]

Although backed by the Opposition, Ulate headed the ticket of the Partido Unión Nacional (National Union party). His party was founded in the post-1944 period for the purpose of backing his candidacy. He was chosen as the Opposition's presidential candidate in February, 1947.[46] As the owner of the *Diario de Costa Rica*, he had a ready instrument to advance his political fortunes.

Civic and other groups published their allegiance to the Opposition cause in the *Diario de Costa Rica*. Frequently they opposed Calderón Guardia and Vanguardia Popular as being part of the international threat of communism. A good example of these attacks is a two-page spread published by the white-collar workers, foremen, and lower-level executives of the United Fruit Company in the *Diario de Costa Rica* on June 20, 1947. In bold letters it proclaimed their stand: "For the salvation of Costa Rica"; "Calderón is a Communist" and "The Opposition will arrive to Power."[47]

Calderón Guardia tried to counter the attack by every means open to him. He declared himself anti-Communist and reminded the electorate of the sympathy accorded Mora and his party in the

45 *Diario de Costa Rica*, April 3, 1947, p. 1.
46 See chapter 6 for a discussion of the nomination of Ulate.
47 Original in Spanish. This and all other translations by the author.

past by the leading Opposition figures, including Ulate. Calderón
Guardia categorically stated that he was not, never had been, and
never would be a Communist.[48] He had, however, accepted indirect
help from the now "official enemy" and therein was the predica-
ment from which he could not extricate himself.

The National Republicans and Vanguardia Popular had not renewed their electoral alliance in the 1947–1948 presidential campaign. The official party, however, continued to enjoy the general
support of the six *vanguardistas* in Congress and the parties were
identified in the popular imagination.

By September, Calderón Guardia had adopted a more subtle approach to the Communist issue than his usual personal denial, and
in doing so he attempted to discredit Ulate as well. He tried to
persuade the nation that Ulate was most unwise to seek intervention by the United States and that, by constantly repeating the
charge that the nation was controlled by Moscow, Ulate served to
create doubt outside the country as to the position of the nation in
the new international confrontation. He countered such propaganda ploys as the publication in *La Nación* of a manifesto of
solidarity with the Democratic nations, by the Opposition deputies,[49]
by sounding a nationalistic note—it was a Costa Rican election;
Costa Ricans would decide their own fate; and Manuel Mora was
Costa Rican.[50]

La Nación, then a recently established daily and now the leading
newspaper in the nation, maintained the greatest degree of impartiality among the newspapers of Costa Rica. At the end of September, on the occasion of an attempt on the life of Manuel Mora,[51]
it summed up the issue of communism as being an electoral tactic
and reminded the Opposition that Mora was far more valuable to
them alive than dead since the agreements between Calderón
Guardia and Mora were of a personal nature. The pact, once

---

[48] *La Tribuna*, March 30, 1947, p. 1.

[49] *La Nación*, October 11, 1947, p. 1.

[50] *La Tribuna*, September 20, 1947, p. 4.

[51] Attempts were also made on the lives of Calderón Guardia and Manuel
Formoso, the editor of *La Tribuna*.

politically advantageous, had now become a great disadvantage because of international events. Moreover, as insiders of all political parties knew, communism was on the downtrend as evidenced by the mid-term elections and would continue to decline to a relative· ly insignificant and inoffensive position.[52]

At a crucial moment in the electoral campaign, Vanguardia Popular chose to issue an official declaration of adherence to the Comintern, coupled with a verbal attack on the United States. The declaration fell like a bomb in Costa Rica and throughout Central America.[53] The Picado administration and the candidacy of Calderón Guardia suffered the political effects of this abrupt about-face on the part of Mora in which he seemed to confirm the most telling attacks of the Opposition at a crucial period in the singularly intense and tumultuous political campaign.

The Opposition immediately seized the opportunity to discredit the National Republicans. Twenty-one members of Congress signed a petition asking the president to call a special session of Congress to outlaw Vanguardia Popular.[54] Such a procedure hardly would have been in keeping with either the nation's democratic traditions or its constitution.

One Opposition deputy, Fernando Vargas, later admitted that the petition, at least for him, was a political tactic designed for the limited purposes of the campaign. He considered the petition to be campaign propaganda that could be used to create a most embarrassing situation for the party in power. The Opposition in dwelling on the issue primarily wished to discredit the National Republicans.[55]

President Picado's reply to the petition, made in the same vein of moderation that characterized his conduct during the campaign, was to the effect that all political parties enjoyed equal legal protection and that he considered it inconvenient to call an extra-

[52] *La Nación,* September 28, 1947, p. 1.
[53] Ibid., October 22, 1947, p. 1.
[54] Ibid., October 28, 1947, p. 1.
[55] *La Gaceta,* November 4, 1949; a verbatim transcript of the debate of the Constituent Assembly of June 8, 1949.

ordinary session at a time when it would bring conflict to the country, already caught up in the emotionalism of the campaign.[56] Otto Cortés Fernández, a leading Opposition spokesman replied that Picado was morally unable to act against the Communist threat because he owed his present position to Vanguardia Popular.[57]

Ulate joined in the attack by using the top half of the front page of the *Diario de Costa Rica* to ask President Picado the oft-answered question as to whether or not the government was pro-Soviet. He asked for a direct answer, implying that the question had been repeatedly avoided. And despite the fact that the Opposition congressmen had petitioned the President to place Vanguardia Popular outside the law, Ulate stated that should he be elected the Communists would have complete freedom. They would not, however, be given special help and consideration such as they had had under the Picado administration.[58]

As the campaign entered its last phase in 1948, the issue of communism hurt the *calderonistas* internationally as well as domestically. Joshua Powers, a New York–based agency, withdrew advertising from *La Tribuna* because of its "Communist" sponsorship. The *Diario de Costa Rica* quoted *American Magazine* to the effect that Calderón Guardia had brought in six Communist deputies, and it showed on a map how almost all of Europe along with Costa Rica was strongly influenced by communism.[59] The same article was accompanied by a photograph of Calderón Guardia with Lombardo Toledano, the Mexican labor leader. Only two weeks before, the National Union party had described a chain of command, stretching from Moscow to Lombardo Toledano to Mora to Calderón Guardia, that threatened the whole continent.[60]

The receipt by the National Police of one-half of the small arms which had been ordered through commercial channels occasioned

[56] *La Nación*, October 29, 1947, p. 1.

[57] Ibid., October 30, 1947, p. 1.

[58] *Diario de Costa Rica*, November 1, 1947, p. 1.

[59] Ibid., February 1, 1948, p. 1.

[60] Ibid., January 11, 1948, p. 2.

an attack by Ulate. He even charged that the United States commercial attaché in Costa Rica, Frank P. Corrigan, was a Communist sympathizer because he had made the arrangements for obtaining weapons.[61]

The Opposition propagandists manipulated the issue of communism in order to tarnish Calderón Guardia with guilt by association. They emphasized the irrational elements of the issue, hardly touching on the question of the validity, or lack of such, of the Communist prognosis for the ills which beset Costa Rican society. Prior to 1945 there had been some rational debate on communism; however, in the electoral campaign of 1947–1948, the issue was used primarily to relate Calderón Guardia to an international conspiracy because of his political alliance with Mora.

The Cold War gave the distorted elements of the question precedence over the rational. The substance of communism in Costa Rica became ever more obscure. The small, poor, but somewhat influential party of Mora came to be viewed as an immediate threat to the nation rather than simply as a minor contender for power. Somehow, in some mysterious way, the Vanguardia Popular purportedly threatened the security of the whole hemisphere. In the irrational interpretation of the question, the junior members of a practical political alliance took on proportions which bore little relationship to their influence within that alliance.

Communism as a potential solution to national problems and Vanguardia Popular as a political capability were aspects of a vital question in Costa Rican society. However, within the framework of the 1948 electoral campaign and the Cold War, the real issue was obscured, supplanted by the distortions of a political issue fast leading the nation into a period of hysteria, fear, and violence.

[61] *La Tribuna*, January 15, 1948, p. 1.

CHAPTER 4

Fiscal Corruption and Mismanagement

Fiscal corruption and misman-
agement of government finances in Costa Rica between 1940 and
1948 were questions of sufficient importance to contribute to the
conditions which made revolution possible. They were not equal in
magnitude to the other major issues, but they did add significantly
to the widespread lack of confidence in the government and in the
National Republican party. As political questions, they had the
effect of contributing to the decline of Calderón Guardia's popularity.

One of the most important effects of the alleged misuse of power
by government officials was the alienation of many young men,
who either joined opposition groups in order to voice their dissatisfaction or, if already partisan, became more active in their resistance to the government. There probably were those in the ranks
of the Centro and Acción Demócrata who simply were looking to

attack Calderón Guardia and, regardless of reasons, would have found some issue on which they could focus their dissent. Since the Centro and, to a more limited extent, Acción Demócrata shared the *calderonistas'* concern for social justice and modernization, their claimed indignation over fiscal corruption could well have provided their only rationalization for failing to support a program which they should have embraced enthusiastically, the Centro in particular. The majority of their membership, however, accepted the purported offenses as fact, and their alienation was genuine.

Before the close of the first year of the Calderón Guardia administration, political rivals began to charge it with corrupt fiscal practices and mismanagement of government finances. Calderón Guardia himself later admitted that some members of his government had been dishonest.[1] Graft was portrayed as the fiscal equivalent to electoral chicanery. With considerable success, the enemies of the government created the image of the *calderonistas* as depraved self-seekers who sought public office mainly to enrich themselves at the expense of the nation. The alleged fiscal corruption of his successor, in part, motivated ex-President Cortés to organize the Democratic party. From 1940 to 1942. the Communists' attacks against dishonesty, graft, and mismanagement, formerly directed against Cortés, were shifted to Calderón Guardia.

The most telling examples of misuse of power were found in the conduct of the Development Ministry and the Ministry of Public Works during the period 1940 through 1943. Their malpractice consisted principally of letting out contracts without first asking for bids.[2]

[1] See *Diario de Costa Rica,* November 19, 1947, p. 2, for the salient paragraphs from Calderón Guardia's speech of November 17, 1947. He confessed that "Como gobernante en más de una ocasión cometí el error de confundir la lealtad personal con la lealtad del hombre de Estado, que son cosas diferentes. A la sombra de esos errores, muchos de mis amigos se beneficiaron y enriquecieron, gracias a que yo administré mal la hacienda pública." Also see *La Tribuna,* November 19, 1947, and *El Social Demócrata,* November 22, 1947.

[2] Note that the men directly concerned with its conduct, those who had served as secretaries during the period shadowed by charges of graft, the period of "contracts without bids," later became strong Oppositionists. When the "Special

Although all elements of the Opposition charged the National Republicans with misuse of government power, it was the Social Democrats who led the attack. They shrank from government corruption. Their idealism categorized it as another aspect of a decadent order and as one more item to be added to the multitude of sins which they charged to the "civil oligarchy."[3] These young men professed to believe that the self-seeking "civil oligarchy" ignored the needs of the nation. They believed that it was greatly lacking in rectitude and misused governmental power to create private wealth for itself; for instance, its members took bribes. They intended to perpetuate their power in order to enrich themselves, oblivious to the suffering of the poor and the perversion of the healthy customs of the nation. To the Social Democrats, it was not only the economically powerful and the professional politicians, in other words the "civil oligarchy," who failed to provide economic opportunity, but also the regime which they supported. Since the oligarchy controlled government and the economy, their overthrow was a precondition if the nation were to provide for the fuller realization of the economic aspirations and the talents of its citizens.

The charge of fiscal corruption was made particularly effective by the state of the nation's finances from 1940 to 1948. In order to implement its social legislation, the government inaugurated large-

---

Courts" were established under the Revolutionary Junta, those who had come over to the Opposition were not subject to "trials."

[3] The Centro had discovered a recognized phenomenon of democratic political organizations: that they tend to form within their number an elite or oligarchy of those most concerned with political affairs and those with financial power and concern for public affairs. Robert Michels first derived his theory of the "Iron Law of Oligarchies" from his experience in the German Social Democratic party shortly after the turn of the century. Subsequent research by such men as Vilfredo Pareto, Gaetano Mosca, and C. Wright Mills has tended to clarify the findings of Michels and to indicate that the "iron law" is not quite as strong as his terminology implied. I found no evidence that the *centristas* were aware of the large body of work on the phenomenon. They rather seem to have seen the existence of the "civil oligarchy" as a peculiarly Costa Rican phenomenon and one for which they could rightfully blame the *calderonistas*. See Robert Michels, *Political Parties*, pp. 15–39.

scale public expenditures and, by expanding its functions, appeared to create a large number of government positions with which it could reward friends and other "deserving individuals." The straitened circumstances of the public treasury in the postwar period and the reluctant passage of adequate revenue measures contributed to the impression that the regime incurred obligations beyond its ability to pay. In general, past Costa Rican governments had managed to balance their budgets. Costa Ricans prided themselves on their frugality.[4] It therefore seemed logical to many citizens to conclude that governments which spent in excess of even larger than "normal" budgets somehow had to be engaged in illicit activities.

Fiscal corruption defies measurement, for it is relative to what a given society tolerates at a given period in its development. In this respect, as in many others, Costa Rica evolved differently from those parts of Hispanic America where "the situation was . . . one of normal and expectable corruption."[5] Costa Rica expected much of her public officials and granted meager monetary rewards in return for dedicated service. The frugality and near austerity practiced by the tiller of the soil served also as the ideal for the public servant. His fellow citizens rewarded him with their esteem, not with their money.

This nineteenth-century tradition became progressively less suited to twentieth-century conditions. The steady increase of government functions required a growing number of public servants trained to specialized positions who could remain in public service. To the upper-class office holders of the previous century, compen-

---

[4] Charles M. Wilson, *Middle America*, p. 292. Also *La Nación*, December 6, 1947, p. 1, carries the following figures for three administrations: Cortés, a surplus of 8,211,564.48 colones; Calderón Guardia, a deficit of 79,149,061.88 colones; and Picado (for the first two years) a deficit of 27,636,759.66 colones.

Costa Rican budgets and deficits again rose precipitously in the period of the Junta and even greater budgets have become characteristic as the positive role of the state has continued to expand. The Junta and subsequent governments, however, enjoyed significantly greater revenues due to the income tax passed during the Picado administration.

[5] Charles Gibson, *Spain in America*, p. 108.

sation was almost beside the point; it was not to the twentieth-century public servants who were drawn heavily from the middle sectors of society. They found salary scales set for the old order inadequate for their requirements. To supplement these meager salaries, they found means of profiting in various ways—from the award of government contracts or by simultaneously holding more than one position. These practices, however, had been carried out on a modest level and the government operated on a small scale. Until 1940 the overall impression remained one of thrift. Costa Rican statesmen did not make fortunes through government service either directly or indirectly. The growth of business enterprises and of more elaborate governmental functions gave officials opportunity for graft and fiscal corruption on a larger scale.

Both *ambiance* and circumstances contributed to poor administration and fiscal difficulties during the Calderón Guardia administration. The very fact that the candidate achieved the presidency with overwhelming support at the polls encouraged his laxity in office; there seemed to be no truly significant threat to him or his party on the horizon. New departures, high adventure, sudden new opportunities, and crises charged the atmosphere of the Calderón Guardia administration and fostered a diminution of Costa Rican frugality. It was a wartime administration; it was an administration dedicated to rapid economic development and social change. The President faced great dislocations in the economy and attempted to compensate through public spending. The shortages of the wartime period and the allocation of scarce imports not only caused frictions but also provided a ready avenue for the misuse of government power.

Support of industrialization, coupled with sharp reductions in imports, afforded financial opportunity for enterprising men who held governmental positions or were close to the administration. These men seized the opportunities to produce formerly imported goods, to develop secondary and tertiary industries, and to provide products and services for an expanded internal market that was related to the prodigious road-building programs of the Cortés and Calderón Guardia administrations. The profit taking and the new affluence of a few middle-class men, who recognized the opportunities and exploited their connections with the government to secure them, upset many Costa Ricans. The increase in the magnitude of enterprises and graft suggested to some that all new wealth and its concomitants represented ill-gotten gains. Many considered the affluence of men close to the government as incontrovertible evidence of the deterioration of national values.

The Centro and Acción Demócrata made the most determined campaigns to expose dishonest practices in the government of Calderón Guardia. What they revealed, however, hardly seemed appropriate to the frequency and vehemence of their polemics. The construction of a modern suburban community, Barrio Escalante, on what was then the eastern outskirts of San José, elicited particularly irrational attacks. A political broadside distributed by them in 1946 illustrated their deep disapproval, tinged with a bit of envy:

We should take this nefarious tropical product [Calderón Guardia] to the defendant's bench to furnish there a reckoning of money received and paid by him and by his followers which would explain how it was that they entered [the government] without money and left with deposits in foreign banks, with large landholdings in Chomes, and with chalets and rich palaces in Barrio Escalante—Barrio a thousand times damned because it is a slap in the face to the honor of Costa Rica, that represents a derision and a national shame. The rich mansions of Barrio Escalante mean a mountain of corpses of undernourished children, great masses of sick people and hunger . . . the same hunger which Manuel Mora exploits.[6]

The condemnation of the *calderonistas* by the Centro and Acción Demócrata tended to be total but nonspecific. An Opposition leader, José Figueres, characterized the epoch as one when "all the vices of administrative dishonesty, opportunism, and favoritism came out of their lairs" but did not specify the dishonest acts.[7] There were constant references to "the nefarious Calderón Guardia" but

---

[6] "Hacia la reivindicación Nacional," *El Patriota No. 3.* "Meléndez Collection." It is interesting to note that similar neighborhoods have proliferated since the revolution.

[7] As quoted in Arturo Castro Esquivel, *José Figueres Ferrer*, p. 9.

the taking of accounts fell far short of what the revelations had seemed to promise.

Acción Demócrata began a series of articles in August, 1944, under the title "Official Gifts."[8] In the introduction to the series it asserted that these "gifts" totaled 800,000 colones (approximately $119,400) during the four years of Calderón Guardia's administration. The majority of the items subsequently listed proved to be official trips by Costa Rican government representatives to such gatherings as the inaugurations of heads of other Latin American states, or cultural, scientific, and educational meetings held outside the country to which Costa Rica sent a participant. The newspaper considered the various trips to have been superfluous and little more than pleasure jaunts. It did not, however, analyze them one by one so that its opinion could be closely scrutinized by the citizenry.

"Special services to the government" followed travel in the number of items noted and in the percentage of the total amount of the purported "official gifts" which they represented. *Acción Demócrata* claimed that the published lists were drawn up by employees of the Banco de Costa Rica and certified by the Centro del Control, a dependency of the national government.[9]

Acción Demócrata went to great extremes to try to illustrate Calderón Guardia's lack of thrift which it implied was indistinguishable from fiscal corruption. An example of this effort was the criticism it raised about the salary of 950 colones a month (approximately $159.00) paid to Santos León Herrera as Head Engineer of Public Works. It considered the salary excessive because it was only one hundred colones a month less than the salary of a cabinet member.[10]

The difficulty of proving alleged corruption or even of forming a strong community conscience against it was clearly revealed in the case of Alberto Martén. Martén, a professor of economics at the newly reestablished university and a close personal friend of the

[8] *Acción Demócrata*, August 5, 1944, p. 1.

[9] Ibid., August 10, 1944, p. 2.

[10] Ibid., August 12, 1944, p. 3.

exiled Figueres, received ten thousand colones from the government for special services in November, 1941. Since Martén helped edit *Acción Demócrata* and was in the first rank of the younger members of the Democratic party, the appearance of his name among those who had received payment for special services to the government proved most embarrassing. Martén reacted strongly but, in defending himself, he weakened the position of those who condemned the government for its lack of integrity. He asserted that there were perfectly valid reasons why his name appeared on the lists. He had received the ten thousand colones for his father, Ernesto Martén Carranza, who had had to leave Costa Rica for the United States for reasons of health.[11] If there were perfectly valid reasons why Alberto Martén received funds for his father for special services rendered to the government, could not there be perfectly valid reasons why others received similar funds?

Martén further weakened the campaign of *Acción Demócrata* to expose the alleged corruption of the Calderón Guardia administration by a blanket endorsement of the integrity of Carlos Manuel Escalante, who had served as secretary of finances under Calderón Guardia and who had approved the payment. Martén declared that Escalante had shown unquestionable honesty as a minister.[12]

Similar events throughout the period weakened the case for alleged fiscal malpractice. Almost all members of Calderón Guardia's cabinet had prominent defenders among the leadership of the Opposition. The courts functioned normally, but the charges of dishonesty in administration remained largely unproven assertions, published in the newspapers unsympathetic to the regime and solely for political purposes. Such coverage, of course, does not verify the absence of corruption in Calderón Guardia's administration; rather, it shows that the Opposition was unable fully to document a case for any significant instance. By linking corruption to poor administration, the Opposition implied that to prove the latter was also to prove the former.

Calderón Guardia excelled far more in the art of politics than in

[11] Ibid., p. 2.
[12] Ibid., p. 2.

administration. He was careless and gave his ministers too much of a free rein during his presidency. During the 1948 presidential campaign he himself admitted that inept administration of the finances of the nation while he was President had served to enrich some of his followers at the expense of Costa Rica.[13] The results of this lack of supervision contributed not only to disparage his own reputation but also, by association, to discredit his reform program.

The evidence that administrative shortcomings severely injured Calderón Guardia's prestige and political support is overwhelming. We have considered the predictably adverse opinion of the Opposition. A more damning statement, however, since it came from Ricardo Fernández, who was favorably disposed to Calderón Guardia, is that contained in the *Cartilla histórica de Costa Rica*: "After the two years had passed, Dr. Calderón Guardia had lost much of his prestige because of the liberality and the administrative disorder which was attributed principally to the Development Ministry."[14] He went on to assert that Calderón Guardia felt abandoned by his friends and turned to Vanguardia Popular rather than see his program undermined.[15]

The statements of the United States minister to Costa Rica, Robert M. Scotten, were another indication that fiscal mismanagement indeed had become a weighty issue. In April, 1942, he commented on the related questions of budgetary mismanagement, graft, and the loss of prestige which Calderón Guardia consequently had experienced:

While the financial difficulties of the government are of course partially due to the drop in bases of revenues caused by the war, government mismanagement appears to have produced a large part. . . . Calderón

---

[13] *El Social Demócrata*, November 22, 1947, p. 5.

[14] Ricardo Fernández Guardia. *Cartilla histórica de Costa Rica*, p. 146. Alfredo Volio, the key minister during the period in which so many contracts were granted without having been opened to bidding, later became a stalwart oppositionist. For a cutting appraisal of his contradictory actions, see *Trabajo*, January 18, 1947, p. 1.

[15] Calderón Guardia is reported to have spoken in a similar but less explicit vein as early as February 1947. See *La Tribuna*, February 16, 1947, p. 1.

is faced with a serious although perhaps not dangerous situation due to the somewhat precarious financial situation of the government but also to the widespread accusations of graft and mismanagement which are almost daily directed against him and especially against his brother, the Minister of the Interior.[16]

Scotten later recommended that the Department of State request that the Export Import Bank give favorable consideration to the negotiations then in progress with Carlos Manuel Escalante, the secretary of finances. He implied that he did not consider Calderón Guardia corrupt despite the "many accusations," since he had readily accepted the offer of American experts to help work out the serious and unprecedented fiscal problems of his wartime government.[17]

Dislocations within the Costa Rican economy made the charge of dishonesty seem more plausible. The lack of stability occasioned increased economic activity by the central government and gave the population the impression that the economy was faltering. The improvisations necessary to offset the effects of the war led to deficits in the national budget. Sudden shifts in marketing and manpower utilization patterns caused imbalances, both fiscal and economic, which the forces of opposition attributed to the corruption of the administration. Those sectors of the population which suffered the consequences of the dislocations were susceptible to anti–Calderón Guardia polemics.

Costa Rica was the nation of Central America with by far the greatest volume of external trade.[18] The disruption of trade occasioned by World War II hit Costa Rica as early as 1939, since much of her trade had been with Western Europe. In October, 1939, Costa

[16] U.S. Department of State, *Foreign Relations of the United States*, VI, *1942*, pp. 242–243. Note that no reference is made to the mounting opposition to the social reform program as a possibly deeper source of discontent.

[17] Ibid., p. 248, Scotten message is dated May 27, 1942.

[18] Sumner Wells clearly outlines Costa Rica's trading position: "For a small Latin American country, Costa Rica does a flourishing trade. In the 1929–1937 period, imports averaged $9,750,000 and exports $11,300,000—$33 per capita.

"Before World War II, 36 percent of Costa Rica's exports went to the United States . . . With World War II, however, imports rose sharply over exports" (*An Intelligent American's Guide to the Peace*, p. 195).

Rica received her first loan from the Export Import Bank to help her meet the exigencies of the new situation through the purchase of goods from the United States. By July, 1942, Costa Rica had received credits from the United States totaling more than sixteen million dollars; they had come in nearly equal parts from the Export Import Bank and the Public Works Administration.[19]

The normal receipts of the Costa Rican government came from customs duties, the liquor monopoly, railway earnings, and exportation, property, and conversion taxes. Of the three giving the highest income return, customs duties, the liquor monopoly, and exportation taxes, only the liquor monopoly was not adversely affected by the war.[20]

The Costa Rican government was called upon to make unprecedented outlays because of the demands of both the war and the reform program—a program initiated by Calderón Guardia at a time when normal sources of revenue were disrupted and in decline. The Calderón Guardia administration recorded sizable budgetary deficits during each of its four years. The situation was further complicated by monetary inflation.[21]

The cost of constructing the Pan American Highway contributed to the accumulative deficit of the regime more than any other single factor. This expenditure was attributable to Costa Rica's support of the United States in World War II.[22] Roads were needed, but highest priority in terms of purely national goals should have gone to the construction of penetration roads linking the frontiers of settlement to the populated areas of the nation. The Pan American Highway was essentially dictated by the military necessity of providing a link between the United States and the Panama Canal Zone. For this reason there were loan funds available for a crash

[19] Wilson, *Middle America*, p. 294. This is in addition to $550,000 in lend lease. See also Fernández Guardia, *Cartilla histórica*, p. 146.

[20] Wilson, *Middle America*, p. 292.

[21] *Surco*, no. 47 (May–June, 1944), pp. 46–47, charges the administration with ineptness in its program and enforcement of price controls. The rise in prices, however precipitous, closely paralleled that in the United States. See *La Nación*, January 23, 1948, p. 1.

[22] Wilson, *Middle America*, p. 292.

program of construction which did not represent the best allocation of Costa Rica's scant resources available for economic development.[23]

Although the charges of dishonesty raised against Calderón Guardia were related to fiscal affairs, his frequently cavalier attitude toward the spirit if not the letter of the law further antagonized those who opposed him. Perhaps the clearest example of this characteristic occurred in 1944 when the President decreed amnesty for some of his followers who had been found guilty of electoral offenses and of infractions related to fiscal affairs. The decrees were declared unconstitutional by the Supreme Court and principally served to demonstrate the President's inclination to misuse executive power.[24]

Teodoro Picado inherited the reputation of his predecessor when he assumed the presidency in May, 1944. He recognized that to still the political passions of the moment his government had to reestablish the image of fiscal integrity which the nation expected. Only a bold innovative program of tax reform and budgetary procedures could save Costa Rica from financial disaster.

The difficult economic situation which Picado faced became rapidly worse as coffee prices fell, reducing purchasing power both abroad and at home.[25] The declining volume of trade diminished revenues from taxes on imports and exports upon which Costa Rica depended heavily. In order to meet the government payroll, Picado had to resort to loans from private Costa Rican banks.[26]

Peace brought a new set of economic dislocations to the Costa Rican economy. The holders of the country's external debt, when an allied victory was assured, renewed pressure on Costa Rica to service her obligations.[27] The United States' interest in completing

[23] For a revealing account of the waste which accompanies a crash program such as the Pan American Highway in Costa Rica during the first years of World War II, see Alvaro Facio, "Forty-Million-Dollar Lesson," *The Inter-American* 3 (March, 1944): 10–12.

[24] *Surco*, no. 47 (May–June, 1944), p. 80.

[25] Fernández Guardia, *Cartilla histórica*, pp. 149–150.

[26] Ibid., p. 150.

[27] *The Inter-American* 4 (July, 1945): 43.

the Costa Rican segment of the Pan American Highway dwindled as the danger of attack on the Panama Canal Zone became more remote and as shipping became adequate in volume and generally safe in the Caribbean area. The crash program tapered off to a less costly pace. The net effect was that the regime still faced mounting deficits, in terms of 1936 colones, despite reduction in expenditures.

Picado approached the problem of impending financial disaster from three different angles. The first was administrative reform to foster more effective control and allocation of existing revenues. The second provided for long-range reform of bases for revenues, to make them less subject to the fluctuations of world trade and more compatible with the expanded services offered by the state. The third was a short-term attempt to prime the pump through a loan from the Export Import Bank for the creation of partially self-liquidating public works and to create other new revenues through minor changes.

Among the legacies he received from the previous administration, Picado had the benefit of the study of the Costa Rican fiscal organization carried out in 1943 under the supervision of Thomas Kekicht of the United States Treasury Department. The President appointed a committee composed of former secretaries of finance to develop a reorganization plan based on Kikicht's proposals. It recommended three laws which Picado's National Republicans pushed through Congress with the support of Vanguardia Popular. The first was the Ley Orgánica de la Controlaría General which, in effect, created a comptrollers' office to replace the inefficient Centro de Control. The Comptroller's Office would exercise general supervision over fiscal affairs. The second law was the Ley Orgánica de Presupuesto which gave "scientific" directives for drawing up and executing the budget. The third was the Ley Orgánica de la Tesorería Nacional whose purpose was the centralization of operations of all governmental offices receiving revenues.[28]

These laws provided a good base for ordering the nation's finances and for opening to scrutiny the financial affairs of the nation.

[28] *Acción Demócrata*, June 2, 1945, p. 1.

They laid the bases for the evolution of a modern and more efficient collection and allocation of revenues. However, much of public opinion which had originally called for fiscal order and reform now began to decry the new laws as simply devices for convincing the nation of the need for new taxes.[29]

The short-term efforts of the regime to create new revenue generally proved unsuccessful. The repeal of some customs exemptions brought new but not significant revenue, as did a 1 percent increase on the full delivered value of all imported merchandise.[30]

The great hope of the administration to relieve the fiscal and economic crisis was to obtain a loan for several million dollars from the Export Import Bank. The funds were needed for an economic development plan which included public works, stimulation of tourism, and agricultural development.[31] The program was not delineated in the national press. According to Fernández Guardia the project had been accepted in principle and had been submitted to detailed study when a small-scale revolt broke out.[32] Inexact and exaggerated coverage of the unsuccessful attempt at revolt resulted in the failure of the loan application; it presumably indicated that the stability necessary for the success of the plan did not exist.[33]

The establishment of direct progressive taxes represented the nation's hope for orderly progress and the opportunity to derive benefits from the new fiscal laws. To the National Republicans the most important, and politically dangerous of these, was the law concerning income tax. Without the passage of income tax legislation the National Republicans could not make their reform program viable nor could they counteract the charges of the Opposition that budgetary deficits demonstrated their corruption and lack of capacity to continue to govern the nation.

Previous regimes had considered the desirability of an income

[29] Fernández Guardia, *Cartilla histórica*, p. 150.

[30] *The Inter-American* 4 (November, 1945): 44, C.I.F. (cost, insurance, and freight).

[31] Fernández Guardia, *Cartilla histórica*, p. 151.

[32] An account of that uprising called the Almaticazo appears in chapter 5.

[33] Fernández Guardia, *Cartilla histórica*, p. 151.

tax but had never managed to institute one. President Alfredo González Flores (1914–1917) made the first and most serious attempt, and his effort contributed to his overthrow.[34]

In his second inaugural address in May, 1924, President Ricardo Jiménez, who had come to power with the help of the Reform party, proposed the establishment of an income tax. He recognized that the existing tax system in Costa Rica fell heavily on those least able to bear the burden. He also noted that the heavy dependence of the state on external-trade taxes made the development of governmental programs too susceptible to changes in the international situation.[35] Jiménez did not follow through on his proposal. León Cortés (1936–1940) went so far as to have a Chilean expert draw up a law which Cortés sent to Congress for its consideration, only to withdraw the proposal before any action had been taken.

The National Republican's. organized effort to put into law a meaningful tax reform provided the base for the final break with the majority of the nation's capitalists and the final coalescence of the Opposition. Picado's proposal of a new tax assured the Opposition a lavishly financed campaign designed to defeat his party, for the business and commercial sectors of the nation saw tax legislation as a threat to their interests. It was not the suggested rate which inspired the wrath of so many leading Costa Rican citizens, but the very idea of an income tax. The proposed rates were modest, ranging from 2 percent on incomes from 6,000 to 25,000 colones up to 20 percent on incomes in excess of 500,000 colones.[36]

When the draft of Picado's tax bill reached the floor of Congress, it immediately became the issue of the day. The Opposition legislators, who had been boycotting Congress in protest against alleged

[34] Carlos Monge Alfaro, *Historia de Costa Rica*, pp. 256–257. Carmen Lyra in a letter to *Trabajo*, January 17, 1947, p. 1, interprets the passage of the income tax as having been the main issue in González' overthrow. Hugo Navarro Bolandi (*La generación del 48*, p. 88) concurs in the opinion of Carmen Lyra. There are interesting parallels between the two periods. González also faced the dislocating effects of a great world war and like Picado did not have a strong personal following.

[35] Mario Sancho, *Memorias*, p. 176.

[36] *The Inter-American*, 4 (November, 1945): 44.

electoral fraud, returned to fight the proposal.[37] Although fiscal corruption and mismanagement continued to be political issues, there was little doubt that to the majority of the Opposition leaders graft was of far less consequence than the increasingly strong possibility of a progressive direct tax being placed on property and income.

Within the ranks of the Opposition, the Social Democrats found themselves in a most uncomfortable position. Many of their leaders, in accord with their socialist ideology, had previously spoken out in favor of direct and against indirect taxation.[38] They, however, found a variety of "reasons" for remaining Opposition members in good standing while still disputing the tax reform. They alleged that the bill was just a device employed by the government to obscure the real issues and to cover up its lack of sound fiscal practices. They objected to the specific law but not to the concept of direct taxation. Had the reform only been submitted to more study, Alberto Martén implied, the Social Democrats could have supported it:[39] "What we really are dealing with is an attempt once and for all to consolidate the social-Christian regime by means of financing its progressive activities which have constantly threatened them [the calderonistas] with bankruptcy."[40] Theoretically the reform was necessary but politically the Social Democrats had to stand and be counted as being in opposition to it.

Picado astutely linked the tax reform to a specific need for new revenue—the raising of schoolteachers' salaries. Education enjoys an almost sacred place in the minds and the hearts of Costa Ricans, and teachers' salaries had not kept pace with the steady rise in the cost of living during the wartime and postwar period. The Opposition could not deny the justice of the raise; it was reduced to the unconvincing argument that, if proper procedures had been used,

[37] See chapter 3 for the circumstances surrounding the boycott.

[38] A clear example is the denunciation by *Acción Demócrata* (June 2, 1945, p. 1) of Alvaro Bonilla's proposal for a paper tax to raise badly needed revenues: "El impuesto de papel sellado y timbre es la obra maestra de la incapacidad y la injusticia."

[39] Alberto Martén in *La Nación*, January 17, 1947, p. 4.

[40] *La Nación*, January 18, 1947, p. 4.

normal sources of revenue would have been sufficient to raise not only teachers' salaries but also those of other civil servants.

Interest groups, organizations, and individuals who had previously avoided involvement in public controversy felt compelled to speak out on the new tax question. *The Eco Católico*, the newspaper voice of the Costa Rican Catholic hierarchy, came out in favor of the reform: "The proportions established by the government are just and equitable."[41] The Chamber of Agriculture and the Coffee Growers Association (Sindicato Patronal del Café) opposed it even though they had hitherto remained silent on fiscal policy.[42] The nation's newspapers carried many declarations by groups and individuals, some in support, others in opposition to the new taxes.[43]

The National Republicans controlled Congress and successfully carried the measure to passage through heated debate. This enactment completed their basic legislative program. Once the law had been passed, debate on it quickly subsided, since the Opposition recognized that the law had wide support among the mass of the people.

Tax reform, however, continued to move the nation indirectly as the Opposition resumed its attack on the government for fiscal corruption and mismanagement. To many Opposition leaders, progressive income and land taxes represented serious departures from traditional thrift in government and were in themselves elements of fiscal mismanagement that provided the government with even more funds to squander.

Questions of graft and administration ineptness were important in the presidential campaign of 1947–1948, but Picado's administration came in for far less criticism than Calderón Guardia's. The Opposition recognized that public debate on the fiscal and tax re-

[41] *Eco Católico*, January 20, 1947. *La Tribuna*, January 12, 1947, p. 1, quotes a Catholic church dignitary to the effect that the tax reforms were inspired by the social teachings of the papal encyclicals.

[42] *La Tribuna*, January 10, 1947, p. 1.

[43] An example of individual advocacy was that of the wealthy painter Max Jiménez Huete.

forms which the President had successfully advocated would have worked to its disadvantage in appealing to uncommitted voters. The Social Democrats again came out with lists of "extravagances" and alleged graft. Some seemed justified although of minor importance, such as the charge that the Costa Rican consul in Brownsville, Texas spent more time in San José working for the party than in Texas.[44] Other charges seemed mere "nit-picking." They questioned the need for sending representatives to the inaugurations of the mayor of New Orleans and the presidents of Chile and of Cuba,[45] and they criticized the budget of the Costa Rican Embassy in Mexico.[46]

Some of the Social Democrats' minor criticisms seemed unnecessarily cruel, even for a heated political campaign, and rather far off the mark in exposing dishonest practices in government. An example was the proposal to discontinue Moisés Vicenzi's "botella," a position obtained through political influence. As director general of the National Library, he received a salary of less than one hundred dollars a month. The position, they alleged, had been an accepted "botella" for "old intellectuals" for several administrations. In time of fiscal duress the Social Democrats favored the abolition of such an unnecessary and "corrupt" practice.[47]

As a political issue the Opposition, however, preferred to emphasize the past transgressions of Calderón Guardia. He was the candidate and the Opposition could more readily document his errors. Calderón Guardia himself had admitted that there had been some dishonest officials in his government, and he joined in the general denunciation of graft, favoritism, and any use of government position or favor for private profit.

Much had been accomplished in the four years of the Picado administration to ensure to the Costa Rican citizen the high degree of fiscal integrity he expected of public servants. Measures had been passed to facilitate the exercise of a traditional rectitude in a

[44] *Acción Demócrata*, May 3, 1947, p. 1.
[45] Ibid., January 11, 1947, p. 1.
[46] Ibid., May 31, 1947, p. 1.
[47] Ibid., January 18, 1947, p. 1.

more modern setting and in a government with expanded and complex functions.

The polemics of the campaign obscured the real issue for the Costa Rican, the need for a more efficient administration. In the heat of the electoral contest most failed to realize how much had been accomplished. There had been corrupt practices but these were hardly the exclusive domain or invention of the *calderonistas*. The Opposition gave disproportionate emphasis to alleged fiscal corruption and tried to convince the public that all the fiscal difficulties of the administrations of Calderón Guardia and Picado resulted from their dishonest practices. The critics of the two regimes declined to recognize that those two administrations had been confronted by extraordinary circumstances, many of which were beyond the control of Costa Rica. The intense debate on fiscal affairs and corruption in government yielded some beneficial results for the long-range economic and political development of the nation, but at the time the controversy primarily aggravated political divisions among the Costa Rican people by further lessening their confidence in government.

CHAPTER 5

Conspiracy, Rebellion, and the Second Republic

IN COSTA RICA DURING THE 1940's, there were several groups or clusters of dissidents and more than one myth to justify revolution.[1] The theoretical framework upon which these myths were based included a formula for remedying the dsyfunctional conditions in Costa Rican society and presented to the believers a rationalization for rebellion. The dissenters assuaged their alienation from, or resentment toward, society by embracing a myth that justified insurrection in the name of national transformation and that could be achieved only when the nation conformed to the complete solution which the dissidents had either accepted or developed. In relation to the uprising of 1948, the Centro was the most significant of these groups. As early as 1940, it was organized and was formulating the theoretical frame of its revolution.

[1] Chapter 1, fn. 2.

However among the most significant of the views concerning the need for change were those of the Costa Rican governments between 1940 and 1948. They responded to the call for modernization. Their response elicited new resentment and new opposition groups, each with its own justification for an uprising, one looking back to a golden age of individualism, another patterning itself on contemporary European Social Democracy which looked forward to a new collective age.

The Communist party in 1940 had the most fully developed ideology of the protest groups. After 1942 it subordinated theory to the fulfillment of more practical measures designed to ameliorate the plight of the lower classes. Mora interpreted the period as leading toward the realization of the Communist social revolution without the need for an armed uprising.

The majority of the opposition forces resented the social reforms of Calderón Guardia. Basic human relationships were changed and many felt uncomfortable with the changes: a patrón could no longer deal arbitrarily with "his" worker. Among the members of polite society, there was near consensus that the nation simply could not function in the new manner. Those who thought in terms of insurrection cherished a myth of the golden age, of the age of Don Cleto and Don Ricardo—two outstanding exemplars of the Generation of 1889 who had dominated Costa Rican politics from 1906 to 1936. In that period, politics and statecraft were carried on among friends and acquaintances who readily understood one another. They thought in terms of nineteenth-century liberalism and of unrestrained small-unit capitalism. Their insurrection when it came was a nostalgic attempt at restoration. It was an effort to recover an idealized Costa Rica that they feared was disappearing, a nation without Communists, without social guarantees, and, preferably, without Calderón Guardia and his followers.

The Centro and Acción Demócrata formed part of the Opposition but shared few of its judgments, other than dislike or disapproval of the *calderonistas* and *vanguardistas*. They resented the state of affairs, but they moved beyond alienation with things as they were to the idea of a Second Republic which, as the name implied, would found a new republic and not just restore the old. The Second Republic was the particular myth used to justify their revolution. When other groups within the opposition collaborated with the Centro and Acción Demócrata, they did so without sharing their theoretical framework for the transformation and salvation of Costa Rica.

The Centro's study of national problems, and the solutions it proposed, provided the set of ideas and beliefs that the Social Democratic party, an outgrowth of the Centro, attempted to carry out. The *centristas* formulated their social vision and stated a new set of principles which they attempted to impose on the nation.

The Centro's political ambitions and its social origins led it to take a rather ambivalent position vis-à-vis social reform undertaken by Calderón Guardia:

> The President is engaged in defending the social guarantees as if they were instruments of social progress without political [in a derogatory sense—*politiquero*] content . . . In Costa Rica there do not exist conservatives or reactionary forces that see, in the advance which he proposes, an instrument against their class privileges or against their rights and powers . . . Our way of being . . . counsels us to accept an advance which seems simply correct, patriotic, and just. However, this acceptance is not convenient to the electoral interests of the governmental party. It had to invent an enemy: the reaction, the fifth column, the Opposition.[2]

The Centro set out with the long-range plan of developing a political party with an anti-Communist ideology, oriented to promoting the well-being of all. The plan called for a permanently organized, ideologically based political party, dedicated to the general welfare, political democracy, and a greater socialization of the economy. The program outlined by the Centro between 1940 and 1944 paralleled in many aspects that of the *calderonistas*. Both advocated rapid industrialization, greater productivity, and fuller participation of all citizens in national life and in the benefits of the increased productivity.[3]

[2] *Surco*, no. 47 (May–June, 1943), p. 84.
[3] Alberto Cañas, *Los ocho años*, p. 47.

Acción Demócrata fused with the Centro to form the Social Democratic party and contributed to the idea of the Second Republic. Ideologically, it stood somewhat to the Centro's right. Acción Demócrata emphasized political rather than social issues. It was reform minded and sought above all other objectives honest government and the improvement of electoral processes. In the economic sphere, it advocated a positive role for the state in regulating the economy but remained essentially capitalistic. The emblem of the party showed an edifice, Acción Demócrata, resting on three doric pillars "dignity," "responsibility," and "probity."[4] It stated that one of its major purposes would be to speak out on the question of public liberties and against "dogmatism, superstition, and fanaticism." "[Acción Demócrata] does not think that the truth takes refuge in any doctrine, in any political party, or any church. The truth is God and God is wherever there is light, justice and civilization." An indication that it adhered to the tenets of classical liberalism came in its avowal that "progress, like the movement of the heavenly bodies in the infinite, is irreversible."[5]

Acción Demócrata viewed itself as antithetical to the "unstable and amorphous" official party.[6] It condemned personalism and otherwise contrasted itself with the *calderonistas*. "The National Republican party is not really a political party, for it never consults the people. Our party will convert the citizen into the true support of national life: his ideals, yearnings, and necessities will be the substance and life of the fatherland."[7] It disclaimed international ideologies, but in its choice of feature articles for its newspaper it indicated its affinity for the United States, the Liberal party of Colombia, and Acción Democrática of Venezuela.[8]

Acción Demócrata defined its position on economic questions as favoring "honorable and progressive capitalism that works to create riches and social well-being; that pays taxes according to its eco-

[4] The emblem and motto appeared on all subsequent editions until the weekly changed its name to *El Social Demócrata* in May, 1947.

[5] *Acción Demócrata*, February 26, 1944, p. 1.

[6] Ibid., March 25, 1944, p. 1.

[7] Ibid., February 24, 1945, p. 2.

[8] Ibid., March 18, 1944, pp. 2–3.

nomic capacity; that treats its workers justly as human beings." As an example of what it preferred, Acción Demócrata cited José Figueres.[9]

Although it favored capitalism over communism or socialism, Acción Demócrata tried to identify its position more by analogy than by definition. It preferred the capitalism of Holland or Switzerland to the communism of Russia, or the socialism of Mexico, but the party hesitated to define its position.[10]

By September of 1944, perhaps as part of the effort to fuse with the Centro,[11] Acción Demócrata came out in support of the nationalization of electric power companies. It hastened to qualify its stand as not being dictated by ideological considerations but simply by the need to provide the means of developing a necessary service, since the present one had fallen into the hands of a "voracious trust which dominated nearly the whole American continent."[12] Its position by that time, although still limited to generalities, had moved much closer to that of the Centro and reflected the intransigence of the returned exile Figueres.

The major initial difference between the Centro and Acción Demócrata was the latter's active role in electoral politics in 1944.[13] There were, however, other differences, both in organization and orientation which pro–National Liberation authors, such as Alberto Cañas and Hugo Navarro Bolandi, have tended to minimize. In his discussion of the fusion of the two groups, for example, Navarro Bolandi almost passes over Acción Demócrata: ". . . a group of young men . . . limited to political things, followers of León Cortés."[14]

Acción Demócrata, however, brought many assets to the merger. It provided a more mature leadership, a functioning party, actual experience gained through participation in the 1944 election, and

[9] Ibid., p. 2.
[10] Ibid., p. 2.
[11] Although the fusion did not take place until March, 1945, *Acción Demócrata* announced it as "very proximate" (August 19, 1944, p. 1).
[12] *Acción Demócrata*, September 16, 1944, p. 1.
[13] Cañas, *Los ocho años*, p. 69.
[14] Hugo Navarro Bolandi, *La generación del 48*, p. 113.

a weekly newspaper, *Acción Demócrata*. The group did not enjoy the prestige or fame of the Centro; and it had fewer adherents. It too was composed largely of young men, but on the average they were twelve to fifteen years older than the *centristas*. Acción Demócrata counted among its assets José Figueres, who closely identified with the party during his last year of exile but did not confine his political role solely to it. To make it easy for the former members of the Centro to think of Figueres as one of their own is perhaps the reason that Acción Demócrata has been played down in National Liberation literature and the Centro's role made to seem dominant.[15]

In the first sentence of an editorial of August 12, 1944, *Acción Demócrata* touched on themes that were to be reiterated through the years by the Social Democrats: youth, the mystique of a generation, and a desperate, determined, and to-the-death fight against those who held back the integral transformation of Costa Rica.[16] All these factors indicated that Acción Demócrata was an active and a creative partner to the fusion.

Figueres more than any other Costa Rican of the period personified the rebel. Acción Demócrata seemed dedicated to advancing his cause, yet he stood outside the party's ranks. Essentially, his was an individual rebellion, but his presence brought together diverse elements who supported his justification for a revolt. Figueres was the prime mover of the revolution of 1948. The wellsprings of his alienation and his drive for power are of utmost importance to any understanding of the insurrectionary movement.

When did Figueres' rebellion begin? In political terms it certainly began with his audacious radio speech, severely critical of the Calderón Guardia administration, delivered at the studios of Station Latin America in San José on the evening of July 8, 1942. There seems to be no indication of prior political activity or concern by this solitary and ambitious man. The adulation of his supporters, the vituperation of his opponents, and the few introspective

---

15 Cañas, *Los ocho años*, p. 69. Also see *La Nación*, September 11, 1949, p. 10, concerning the organization of *Acción Demócrata*.

16 *Acción Demócrata*, August 12, 1944, p. 2.

remarks in his own works, however, give insights into the rebel in the making.

José María Figueres Ferrer was born on September 25, 1906, in San Ramón, Costa Rica, where his parents had arrived only months before from their native Barcelona.[17] He grew up in conflict with his devout Catholic parents, who insisted that he attend a religious secondary school. He submitted to their authority but passed through a period of "intense bitterness."[18] After graduation from secondary school, he struck out on his own for New York against his father's wishes. He remained in the United States for four years working at a variety of jobs to sustain himself while he learned English and privately studied other subjects.[19]

He returned to Costa Rica determined to make his mark. Again he set out on his own, this time to develop a plantation in the sparsely populated and rugged area to the southwest of Cartago. With his special talent for dramatizing, he named his property La Lucha sin Fin (The Endless Battle). His biographer–brother-in-law, Arturo Castro Esquivel, alleges that the name represented Figueres' philosophical conception of life "that obliges man to fight in bad times and to seek out battle in good times,"[20] a concept which he probably owed to his study of Herbert Spencer.[21]

The available sources on Figueres prior to his entry into public life in 1942 give the impression of a loner. Born of immigrant parents, he grew up in a home in which Catalán was spoken. He resented his small stature; he resented the restrictions imposed by his progenitors. He sustained himself by will, courage, and purpose in new and somewhat hostile environments and succeeded in the struggle.

In 1942, Figueres and two of his boyhood friends, Francisco Orlich and Alberto Martén, began a new struggle for much bigger stakes, national political power. The government faced a grave

[17] Arturo Castro Esquivel, *José Figueres Ferrer*, p. 15.

[18] Ibid., p. 17.

[19] Ibid., pp. 18–21.

[20] Ibid., p. 21.

[21] Ibid., pp. 17, 18, and 21. Castro Esquivel identifies Spencer, that propagator of Social Darwinism, as a major inspiration for Figueres' thought.

political crisis that was reflected by the success of independent candidates and Vanguardia Popular in the congressional elections of 1942. Orlich was one of the nonaffiliated aspirants elected to Congress.

Figueres entered public life with his radio attack on the government in July, 1942; Martén and Orlich accompanied him to Station Latin America.[22] In his speech, Figueres voiced profound disagreement with the policies and acts of the government. He criticized its conduct of the war, particularly its lack of initiative: "The only measures taken have come at the direct request of the American Legation." He charged the administration and the Communist party with mutual guilt for the riots in San José on July 4, 1942, following the march protesting the sinking of the ship *San Pablo* two days before. He then suggested that the government was in the hands of the Communists. He accused it of irresponsible management that was corrupting the people and leading the nation to fiscal ruin. He held the government culpable for the extent of damage caused by a plague of grasshoppers and in this context stated: "What have disappeared are the corn fields and what should have disappeared is the government." He sarcastically referred to the Social Security System as a "comedy."[23]

Before Figueres could finish his speech, police arrived to take him into custody. However, he managed to sum up his remarks before he was cut off: "What the government should do is go away."[24]

The Costa Rican government charged Figueres with having revealed military secrets in the course of his speech when he discussed gun emplacements along the coasts.[25] Allegations also circulated that he was accused of collaborating with Germans, helping them to avoid the confiscation of their Costa Rican property as

[22] Neither Figueres nor his followers shed much light on this aspect of his career. Since part of his political image as a "farmer-citizen-soldier" who spontaneously led a revolution in 1948 would be marred by admitting to prior political ambitions, Figueres has avoided clarification of his purpose in 1942.

[23] Castro Esquivel, *José Figueres Ferrer.* p. 29. See the text of Figueres' speech on pp. 27–35.

[24] Ibid., p. 35.

[25] *La Tribuna*, July 9, 1942, p. 1.

demanded by the law. It was also rumored that the government had exiled Figures at the request of the United States, its senior ally in the conflict.[26] The German most frequently mentioned in connection with Figueres was Federico Reimers, a prominent businessman.[27]

Calderón Guardia held Figueres incommunicado for three days and then exiled him.[28] Sympathizers and opponents give contradictory interpretations of the reasons for his expulsion. His opponents allege that it was for the same reasons for which he was imprisoned. His sympathizers view the event as a dictatorial act by Calderón Guardia who could tolerate no dissent.[29] Neither interpretation seems entirely plausible. Calderón Guardia certainly had harsher and more persistent critics, all of whom remained free to censure his every governmental act. There were no political prisoners and there was no other exile. It also seems most unlikely that the United States should have been that concerned about Figueres. The uniqueness of Figueres' case suggests that there was some underlying motive distinct from that of silencing an unknown political opponent, but it remains a matter of common conjecture as to what it might have been.

The government's decision to exile Figueres pushed him into open rebellion, and he became an immediate celebrity. Generalizing on his personal experience, he delineated the symptoms of tyranny in Costa Rica. His pamphlet, *Palabras gastadas*, written

[26] Manuel Mora Valverde, *Dos discursos*, p. 22 [Pamphlet]; José Albertazzi Avendaño, *La tragedia de Costa Rica*, p. 14. *La Tribuna* (July 9, 1942) expresses disagreement with the content of Figueres' speech and with the use of force by the government. On subsequent days it reported the allegations against Figueres, including his collaboration with local Germans to help them avoid confiscation of their properties and his divulgence of military secrets.

[27] Of interest in this regard is the fact, listed in the official record of Costa Rican government proceedings, that one of Figueres' first official acts following the revolution was to restore Reimers' property. *La Gaceta* (May 16, 1948, p. 713) recorded the act of April 30, 1948.

[28] *La Tribuna* (July 11, 1942, p. 1) reports that Figueres had departed for the United States. Castro Esquivel states that he went to Mexico by way of El Salvador and Guatemala (*José Figueres Ferrer*, pp. 38–43).

[29] Castro Esquivel, *José Figueres Ferrer*, pp. 35–38; and Robert Jackson Alexander, *Prophets of the Revolution: Profiles of Latin American Leaders*, p. 147.

in Mexico but published in Costa Rica, articulates the universal aspects of his own exile. The second paragraph of the first chapter, entitled "Democracia," begins: "Man lives in society and sustains a regulating state for his own benefit. From the moment in which that state prejudices him or disrespects his person, the contract is broken and the society ceases to exist."[30] This passage and his conduct after his expulsion suggest that Figueres gave transcendent value to his unique experience. His exile confirmed the resentment toward the administration he had expressed in his radio speech, and it universalized his rebellion. The "tyrant" had to fall, and with him the men and the system that sustained him. In their stead Figueres would erect the Second Republic.

From exile Figueres dedicated himself to the multifaceted task of engineering this downfall. He sought to ally himself with other rebels within Costa Rica and without, for his cause transcended national boundaries. He had to explain to his fellow citizens the depth of the crisis into which Costa Rica had been led. He had to develop the framework of his myth of revolution. Thus, at last, he began the real "battle." He conceived of himself as a rebel completely identified with a cause, the Second Republic.[31]

Calderón Guardia had broken the "contract" and, in so doing, had driven Figueres into an espousal of conflict on all levels. To save Costa Rica from the intolerable situation created by the *calderonistas*, he had to convince his fellow citizens that only a radical solution would suffice. As Alberto Cañas states it, "His occupation is now that of a conspirator."[32] He made a personal vow to "mercilessly wipe out the men of the established regime, to combat them

---

[30] José Figueres Ferrer, *Palabras gastadas*, p. 11. [Pamphlet.] "El hombre vive en sociedad y sostiene un Estado regulador, para beneficiarse. Desde el momento en que ese Estado le perjudica, o irrespecta su persona, se ha roto el contrato, y ha dejado de existir la sociedad."

[31] The first instance I found of Figueres' use of the term "Second Republic" was in the speech Figueres made on the occasion of his return from exile on May 23, 1944. See Castro Esquivel, *José Figueres Ferrer*, pp. 62–66.

[32] Cañas, *Los ocho años*, p. 58. Also see Bernaby (a pseudonym used by Alberto Cañas) in *La Nación*, May 7, 1948, p. 2. "Figueres había formulado claramente su ideal: Sólo por medio de la violencia será posible derrocar al régimen."

to the death if necessary, so that there would not remain one of their seeds and to make a new fatherland, a new Costa Rica."[33]

In Figueres' imagination, his enemy represented the synthesis of all the evils which had hindered Hispanic American development. His cause was not simply that of little Costa Rica but of America, as interpreted by one of his biographers: "Why fight only for Costa Rica rather than for [the] liberty and democracy of all the oppressed people of this continent? His conception of his destiny thus amplified enormously . . . and he made a vow of combatting them [the tyrants] with all his power."[34] Figueres exchanged views, counsel, and promises of help with exiles from other nations also residing in Mexico; the interchange led him to the larger battle for hemispheric freedom.[35]

The revolutionary ideology of Figueres was attractive mainly to the young. Through his contacts in Costa Rica, he recognized alienation among the youth and the consequent political potential of the Centro. The pamphlet *Palabras gastadas* made an overt appeal to Costa Rican youth to participate in the "reconstruction" of the nation.[36] And Martén further exhorted the young to: "read them [the pages of Figueres' pamphlet] with emotion-filled devotion," and entreated them as a distinct generation with a mission: "We receive the responsibility as well as the privilege of belonging to the generation of the twentieth century."[37]

In two publications, in 1943, Figueres began to sketch the framework for his new Costa Rica. In *Palabras gastadas* he combined rather exalted language with vague and unoriginal ideas: ". . . slow-

[33] Castro Esquivel, *José Figueres Ferrer*, p. 41.

[34] Ibid., p. 45.

[35] Ibid., p. 43. Also see Comisión Política de Vanguardia Popular, *Como y porqué cayó la democracia en Costa Rica*, p. 6. [Pamphlet.] For some insight into the ideas and activities of other exiles see Unión Democrática Centroamericana, *Por qué lucha Centro América*.

[36] Some of the references seemed mere flattery, for example, the following excerpt from Figueres' letter to Martén: "Por que yo conozco y veo, creciendo sobre los surcos que sus labores fecundaron una juventud de fuertes hombres y columna vertebral erecta, sobre los que puede descansar, segura, el arca de la República" (Figueres, *Palabras*, pp. 5–6).

[37] Figueres, *Palabras*, p. 7.

ly prepare man for the enjoyment of the heavenly kingdom, which technology [la técnica] must create here on earth."[38] His contribution, in March, 1943, to the book *Ideario Costarricense* contained the genesis of a plan for Costa Rica in the postwar period. He predicated the establishment of "tecnicismo profesional," of a career civil service. and of a national social conscience that would lead the state gradually to assume the direction of all economic activity within a democratic framework which would not only permit, but also encourage private investment.[39] He considered himself to be dedicated to the "liberation" of Costa Rica.[40]

From the day of his exile Figueres began to plan for revolution.[41] While still in Mexico he helped to establish and orient Acción Demócrata. He made important international contacts and, through his own writings and the efforts of Orlich and Martén, began to create a semilegendary figure with a mystique all his own: Figueres the self-made man; a leading capitalist; an important coffeegrower, yet a socialist; the philosopher-politician; and the ubiquitous revolutionary who was included in all opposition groups but exclusively allied to none.

Figueres returned from exile on May 23, 1944. By that time he was no longer an obscure farmer-businessman. As the only Costa Rican sent into political exile since the days of the Tinocos. he had become a symbol of resistance to the "tyranny" of Calderón Guardia. Figueres' close collaborators—Orlich. Martén, and Fernando Valverde—organized a rally to welcome him back to Costa Rica.

Figueres then made a speech from the balcony of Ulate's *Diario de Costa Rica* building in which he attacked Calderón Guardia and lamented the "state of dishonor and poverty" which he had encountered in Costa Rica.[42] Violence had to be met with violence, since the *calderonistas* would not respect the right of suffrage.[43] He

[38] Ibid., p. 36.

[39] Castro Esquivel, *José Figueres Ferrer*, pp. 52–55.

[40] Ibid., p. 42.

[41] Figueres made this assertion in his speech on the occasion of the opening of the National Assembly. *La Gaceta*, January 22, 1949.

[42] Castro Esquivel, *José Figueres Ferrer*, p. 64.

[43] Cañas, *Los ocho años*, p. 68.

called on Costa Ricans to remember the glories of 1856 and 1918.[44] He found the situation of Costa Rica similar to that of occupied France. He professed to see value in political discussions but maintained that political action could not bring about a transfer of power. He believed that the only verdict which the governmental forces would recognize would be a military one.[45] In closing he pledged himself to the founding of the Second Republic of Costa Rica.[46]

Acción Demócrata, under the editorship of Martén, was the voice of the newly founded party of the same name. It devoted much of its space to building up Figueres' image.[47] The lead editorial of its first number used as its theme a name given by Figueres to his first *finca*, La Lucha Sin Fin. *Acción Demócrata* asserted its devotion to "endless battle": "This is a weekly of battle, battle without end."[48] It gave over nearly the whole front page of its second issue to him, his picture, the speech which occasioned his exile, and his new work, "Canto a la libertad."[49] In an editorial of March 18, 1944, Figueres was the only example offered in an exposition on the qualities of the good capitalist.[50] The editions of May 13, 20, and 27, 1944, were largely given over to anticipating and recording his triumphant return.

Acción Demócrata devoted much of its space in the June, 1944, issues to Figueres' speaking tour to various sections of the nation—to the South, to Guanacaste, to Puntarenas, to Llano Grande, and to San Ramón. In these rallies, he reiterated the theme of a Second Republic to replace the first and preached his "gospel" of good

[44] Both were years of armed resistance.

[45] Cañas, *Los ocho años*, p. 68.

[46] Castro Esquivel, *José Figueres Ferrer*, p. 66; *Diario de Costa Rica*, May 23, 1944, p. 1.

[47] For example, it printed his pamphlet *Palabras Gastadas* in a series of articles beginning on June 17, 1944, p. 3.

[48] *Acción Demócrata*, February 26, 1944, p. 1. "Este semanario es de lucha, lucha sin fin."

[49] *Acción Demócrata*, March 4, 1944, p. 1. It also stated, "Acción Demócrata representa a la juventud costarricense limpia y honesta, de la cual el señor José Figueres es un brillante exponente . . ." (April 22, 1944, p. 1).

[50] Ibid., p. 2.

government and economic development through the application of hard work and technology.[51] In effect, he invited the nation to join his *lucha sin fin*. To start, of course, it would be necessary to overthrow the government and existing institutions.[52]

Under Figueres' guidance, *Acción Demócrata* began to use the amalgam of issues, ideals, ambitions, and analogies which were to serve the Social Democratic party, and by extension the Opposition, as justification for revolution. *Acción Demócrata* continued the appeal to youth which Figueres and Martén had employed in *Palabras gastadas*. The manner in which Figueres and his followers propagandized and manipulated the young is exemplified in the call to arms which appeared in bold letters in several editions of *Acción Demócrata*: "It is not behind a desk that the Allies fight for Democracy. It is with their hands on a rifle and in battle to the death with the enemy. It is also not in family conversations or in comfortable discussion groups that we have to save our Fatherland. Cooperate in this decisive battle."[53]

Acción Demócrata attempted by analogies to draw parallels between the situation in Costa Rica and those in other countries of Central America and the Caribbean in order to justify Figueres' planned insurrection. The analogies focused on the dictatorships of Ubico, Carías, and Trujillo and emphasized that those regimes were *de facto* governments as was that of Costa Rica.[54] *Acción Demócrata* praised the students of El Salvador and Nicaragua as belonging to a new generation that opposed dictatorship, and, in case anyone should miss the point, it drew the parallel between those valiant students of the new generation and the awakening spirit of resistance among the young in Costa Rica.[55]

The fusion of Acción Demócrata with the Centro to form the Social Democratic party on March 10, 1945, was a key event in the

---

[51] See Figueres, *Palabras*, p. 7, for the use of the term "Evangelic."

[52] See *Acción Demócrata*, June 3, 10, 17, and 24, 1944.

[53] Ibid., December 16, 1944, p. 2.

[54] July 1, 1944, p. 2 is an example when in its lead editorial it called for the overthrow of the dictatorships of Ubico, Carías, Samoza, and any other Caribbean government which had not been elected by free elections.

[55] Ibid., July 8, 1944, p. 1.

preparation of the revolution.[56] This is not meant to imply that the new party was exclusively a device by means of which Figueres hoped to advance his plan for revolution. It was a legitimate political party which took stands on national issues and participated in political contests. Its organization, however, provided Figueres with a much stronger political base, and it gave him the number of potential soldiers he needed to convince his co-conspirators in other nations that he did indeed have the men, as well as the money and the ideas, necessary to carry out a successful revolt against the Costa Rican government.

In Figueres' plan the Social Democratic party was just one element. He was a member of its executive committee, but he was first and foremost a conspirator and, as such, worked on many levels. His basic aims were simple: he was to become the arbiter of the nation's destiny, and Calderón Guardia and *calderonismo* were to be eliminated as factors in national life. To realize his goals he was simultaneously a member of various organizations oriented to electoral and conspiratorial ends. He was part of an international conspiracy to eliminate dictatorship in the Caribbean area and to reestablish the Union of Central America. He was a member of the Democratic party and of a dissident group within that party which called itself "Authentic Cortesism." Figueres organized and financed, or arranged to have financed, a small terrorist group which was identified with the newly formed Social Democratic party, but which owed its primary allegiance to him and his revolution.

The ideas of the Centro prevailed in the name selected for the new party and in the manifesto it issued. In consequence, its economic program was considerably to the left of that advocated by Acción Demócrata and Figueres.[57] Two points in the Social Democratic manifesto seemed particularly ominous for the peace of Costa Rica: first, it condemned the "coup d'état of 1944," the Opposition's name for the fraudulent election of 1944, not because it was a coup

---

[56] Cañas, *Los ocho años*, p. 69; *La Nación*, September 11, 1949, p. 10; *Acción Demócrata*, March 17, 1945; and Castro Esquivel, *José Figueres Ferrer*, p. 70.

[57] The manifesto of the party was carried in *Acción Demócrata*, March 17, 1945, p. 3.

but because it did not establish a better system; second, the manifesto stated that the purpose of the Social Democrats was to reorganize the nation. Equally ominous was the declaration that "the ideological party [Social Democratic] organizes and arms itself not for a battle but for a war. In the ultimate combat we will triumph and we will renew the Fatherland to its very seeds."[58]

The objective of the Social Democratic party was determined by Figueres. At the close of the convention at which the party was founded, he stated: "The motto which directs us—'We are going to establish the Second Republic.' "[59] By October, 1946, *Acción Demócrata* suggested a new motto: "Elections No; Rebellion Yes."[60] Carlos Monge Alfaro, vice-president of the Executive Committee in 1947, wrote immediately after the revolution: "The role represented by the Social Democratic party and José Figueres in the political process . . . consisted precisely in determining the manner of organizing an uprising against the government."[61]

The Social Democratic party from its formation played down its ideological position and channeled its efforts into preparations for the uprising, the details of which remained largely in Figueres' hands. As a minority party within the Opposition, it endeavored to keep the larger political groups from reaching an entente with the progovernment parties and to exact an ever-harder line from the Opposition candidates.[62] The Social Democrats cherished slight hope of coming to power by means of an election. Their position within the Opposition was analogous to that of the Vanguardia Popular in the Bloque de la Victoria. They could exact concessions from the larger parties in exchange for the militant support, ideas, and propaganda efforts. Their only hope of achieving power was by means of an armed uprising.

The first attempt at insurrection came on the night of June 24,

---

[58] Ibid., February 3, 1945, p. 2.

[59] Castro Esquivel, *José Figueres Ferrer*, p. 70. The new party published its statutes in March, 1945, which included a list of the executive committee.

[60] *Acción Demócrata*, October 16, 1946, p. 1.

[61] *El Social Demócrata*, May 6, 1948, p. 6.

[62] See chapter 6.

1946. Even though Figueres was planning an armed insurrection, he was not involved in this initial venture. Fernando Castro Cervantes, Fernando Valverde, and Arturo Quiros organized this abortive effort known in Costa Rica as "the Almaticazo" (for the radio station Alma Tica, which was to have been the congregation point for the rebels).[63] The plan called for the seizure of San José by armed bands made up of young Costa Ricans, mostly Social Democrats, and Nicaraguan mercenaries with military experience. Success of the enterprise depended heavily on the latter, who did not fulfill their bargain.[64] Fernando Castro Cervantes provided most of the capital, 200,000 colones, for the ill-fated venture.[65] The government took some 200 prisoners, and decommissioned great quantities of arms, ammunition, dynamite, and bombs.[66] Picado went to the police station to see that the frustrated rebels were freed.[67] He continued to think that time and traditional Costa Rican concord would resolve the crisis.

The debacle strengthened Figueres' position. He had opposed the movement as amateurish and misconceived. After the failure, he met with the organizers of the aborted revolution to explain his conspiracy and to invite their participation.

Figueres' plan involved action on several levels. First, political activity had to be maintained, since most of the Opposition still thought in terms of an electoral contest. On every feasible occasion the Opposition had to be indoctrinated as to the futility of elections and oriented to associate the idea of revolution with him.[68] Second,

[63] A chronicle of the events, purportedly by an unidentified participant, appears in Cañas, *Los ocho años*, pp. 79–82. Both Cañas and Rafael Obregón Loría, *Conflictos militares y políticos de Costa Rica*, p. 115, have partial lists of the participants as did the news story in *La Tribuna*, June 26, 1946.

[64] Obregón Loría, *Conflictos militares*, p. 115.

[65] *Diario de Costa Rica*, February 11, 1949, p. 1. Also see *La Nación*, February 19, 1949, p. 1.

[66] *La Tribuna*, June 26, 1946, p. 1.

[67] Obregón Loría, *Conflictos militares*, p. 115.

[68] This aspect of his plan proved successful on two important counts: (1) the Opposition diverted a portion of their campaign funds to Figueres to prepare the revolution, and (2) when he finally brought off his revolution he did so under the cover of the chaotic electoral situation in March, 1948.

a select group within the Opposition, under Figueres' direction, should dedicate itself to terroristic and propagandistic activities to help create circumstances propitious to revolution. This group had to keep the regime under the maximum possible pressure and simultaneously discredit its efforts to combat such subversion by accusing it of using dictatorial and militaristic practices. Third, the Costa Rican insurrectionists should make contact through Figueres with Caribbean exiles intent on the overthrow of dictators in that general area. This collaboration would add to the ranks of trained, dedicated, professional military men, obviating the need for simple mercenaries, such as those employed in the Almaticazo. The Caribbean exiles had contacts for acquiring arms and would help to finance their acquisition. A propaganda campaign linking Calderón Guardia and Picado to Somoza would be launched to condition public opinion and the mass of young sympathizers within the Social Democratic party to accept foreign support.

Figueres already had made some progress on his plan through the efforts of his Nicaraguan allies in Mexico—Rosendo Argüello, Edelberto Torres, and others.[69] The process of acquiring arms on a large scale, however, proved a slow one. Figueres and his close Costa Rican associates were impatient to put "Plan Sunday" into operation, preoccupied as they were with the fear that the major political groups would reach an entente, the possible "infamous" political transaction continually denounced by the Social Democrats.[70] "Plan Sunday" called for arms to be introduced through the

---

[69] For a detailed chronicle of this aspect of Figueres' plan, see Rosendo Argüello, hijo, *Quienes y como nos traicionaron.* This account was written by his closest collaborator, who believed that Figueres had betrayed the Nicaraguans by not aiding them in an attempt to overthrow Somoza. The author is understandably bitter against his former ally. The chronicle is plausible if one ignores the attacks on Figueres for alleged acts of cowardice and other personal shortcomings. See also, Castro Esquivel, *José Figueres Ferrer*, p. 110; and Movimiento Liberación Nacional, *Los pagos de la guerra de Liberación Nacional*, pp. 31–33.

[70] The "ingroup" of Figueres' conspiracy included Francisco and Cornelio Orlich, Gonzalo Facio, Alberto Martén, Fernando Valverde, Daniel Oduber, Fernando Figuls, and others. The evidence is not clear to what degree the more extensive group, which called itself proudly "the terrorist group," was privy to

small port of Dominical on the Pacific coast of Costa Rica[71] and to be transported from there to a feeder road leading to San Isidro del General and the Pan American Highway, giving relatively easy access to Figueres' farms. Figueres built up a small store of arms but never in quantities sufficient to carry out the revolt.[72] On one occasion, Argüello and Torres accumulated what was thought to be a sufficient stock to launch the revolution, but Mexican authorities captured the arms as the Nicaraguans were about to ship them to Costa Rica in August, 1947.[73]

Terrorism began in 1945 but did not become serious until late in 1946 when Mora's home was partially destroyed by dynamite.[74] The timing of the intensification of activity by Figueres' terrorist group coincided with the acquisition of the cache of arms in Mexico, thought sufficient to begin the uprising. The majority of the terrorist acts were directed against public services, waterlines, electrical installations, and railroads, all of which would serve to disrupt the normal activities of the populace, thus reminding them that resistance to the regime continued. Terrorism also harassed the government.[75]

Organized cells within the Social Democratic party in Cartago, however, carried on a more systematic campaign of subversion in an attempt to bring about a general strike. The situation there became particularly tense in early May of 1947 when workers, returning by train from a May Day celebration in San José, were set upon and stoned by awaiting youths. A street brawl followed between *vanguardistas* and youths favoring the Opposition. An as-

---

the details of the larger conspiracy. The "ingroup" expanded with new developments between 1945 and 1948.

[71] Argüello, *Quienes y como*, p. 25.

[72] Ibid., pp. 19–27.

[73] *La Nación*, February 16, 1947, p. 5; *Trabajo*, February 15, 1947, p. 1; and Argüello, *Quienes y como*, p. 26.

[74] *La Tribuna*, January 22, 1948, p. 5.

[75] Ibid., January 22, 1948, p. 5, carries a résumé of the terrorist acts until that date and *Trabajo* (May 24, 1947, p. 1) carries an extensive article on the terrorist activities. *Trabajo* (January 11, 1947, p. 1) reports that the Political Bureau of Vanguardia Popular had called on President Picado to take decisive action against terrorism in a resolution sent to him in January, 1947.

sault on the Vanguardia Popular club, which occasioned an exchange of shots, culminated the evening's activities.[76]

Prior to the Cartago incident, there had been street clashes among
partisans of the various political parties which the police were unable to control. The Opposition employed groups of young men,
organized in neighborhood brigades, who met in the halls of the
Social Democratic party. They called themselves "the resistance,"
perhaps in response to Figueres' oft-repeated comparison of Costa
Rica with wartime France. The "resistance" carried blackjacks and,
in groups of ten, went out into the streets to "bait" the police, to
torment a drunken *calderonista*, or to assault *vanguardistas* as on
the occasion of the May Day celebration.

The Social Democrats in organizing street gangs emulated the
tactics that had been employed by the governmental partisans as
early as 1943. The harassment of Opposition rallies and leaders
had reached alarming proportions during Picado's campaign for
the presidency. Pro–Calderón Guardia workers manufactured
blackjacks in the workshops of the Ministry of Public Works and
used them to intimidate those who opposed the government. All too
frequently policemen loyal to the government became involved as
participants in street disorders. The net result was an ever-escalating
level of violence that perturbed moderate leaders both within and
outside government circles.

One group of young men under the direction of Joaquín Garro
called itself "Brigada Canta Rana." Garro, with his hat pulled
down and his collar turned up, went through the streets accompanied by his "brigade"; their cry was "we want Communist
blood."[77]

The commander of the army in Cartago (Comandante de Plaza)
openly favored the youths and therefore restrained the police from
taking strong action against them. His assistant, however, forced his
superior's resignation and the "resistance" began to lose control of
the streets, despite valiant help from Opposition leaders, such as

[76] *La Nación*, May 3, 1947, p. 1, and *La Tribuna*, May 3, 1947, p. 1.
[77] *La Prensa Libre*, July 30, 1948, p. 3.

Fernando Volio Sancho, Alfredo Volio Mata, and Bruce Masís.[78]
The new commander, Víctor M. Vaglio, to the "great indignation"
of the "resistance," brought police from San José to help put down
the violence in the streets. That step began the chain of events
leading to a *huelga de brazos caidos* (sit-down strike).

The importation of police gave the Opposition in Cartago opportunity to play on wounded local pride. *La Prensa Libre* carried a
report by José R. Cordero Croceri, a participant in the events, who
wrote: "We could not have permitted such a humiliation." The
brigades were determined to "fight for liberty." Groups of students
with blackjacks attacked and beat individual policemen. When
other police arrived to rescue their colleagues, they were restrained
from doing so by armed, mature members of the Opposition who
were always nearby to assist the youths.[79] The police, who, up to
that time, had used nightsticks as weapons, now began to use or
threatened to use firearms.

On July 2, 1947, the Opposition leaders canvassed the hinterland
around Cartago in order to swell their ranks for an anticipated
showdown. Trucks were also "coming and going from the barracks." "That night each [member of the resistance] armed himself
as best he could. Those who had revolvers put them under their
shirts." The first encounter of the evening, "by a group under the
leadership of Alfredo Volio," was an assault on a Communist, who
offered no resistance. At nine o'clock a great number of young men
confronted the police at Almacén Masís e Hijos and there beat another Communist for having shouted "Viva Calderón Guardia."
With that a pitched battle began between the police and the "resistance" who were reinforced by other members of the Opposition.[80] The police used tear gas, which Otilio Ulate, the Opposition
presidential candidate, considered an abomination.[81] They did not
use their firearms, but one man was injured when a policeman

[78] Ibid., August 6, 1948, p. 3.
[79] Ibid., August 11, 1948, p. 3.
[80] Ibid., August 16, 1948, p. 9.
[81] See letter from Ulate to Picado in Roberto Fernández Durán, *La huelga de brazos caidos*, p. 10.

struck him with the edge rather than the flat side of his sword. The police pursued the armed youths, including Joaquín Garro, into a movie theatre, and, when the youths opened fire while inside the cinema, the officers again used tear gas but were unable to capture them.

The fighting continued on a reduced scale the following day. Cartago, on July 21, was in a state of rebellion. The casualties for all sides were two dead and approximately fifteen wounded. The Opposition brought in arms from outside, started a strike, and fired on any policeman who tried to leave his barracks.[82] The campaign culminated in the so-called *Huelga de brazos caídos*, which, in fact, more closely approximated a lockout. The only significant group to strike were the bank employees, and the real thrust of the movement lay in the voluntary closing of business establishments.[83]

The Opposition leaders in San José called for a national sit-down strike to protest the "arbitrariness and cruelty" of the government forces in Cartago. Figueres wired Argüello to send arms from Mexico, but the Nicaraguan managed to send only a few small arms and one machine gun; it is likely that the *figueristas* hoped to bring down the government at that time, as Argüello claimed.[84] Certainly, they had fresh in mind the efficacy of the general strike technique which had been used to bring about the resignation in 1944 of Jorge Ubico in Guatemala and of Maximiliano Hernández Martínez in El Salvador.[85]

The banks and most commercial establishments in San José observed the lockout. When the government forced the banks to open, despite the absence of most of their regular employees, a deliberate run was made on the banks by Opposition depositors in order to force their closure. The generally pacific strike entered a more

[82] Cordero Croceri, *La Prensa Libre*, September 8, 1948, p. 2.

[83] The best treatment of the movement leading up to the strike appeared as a series in *La Prensa Libre* (July, August, and September, 1948, José R. Cordero Croceri, "Historia del civismo estudiantil").

[84] Argüello, *Quienes y como*, pp. 22–23.

[85] *Acción Demócrata* (April 29, 1944, pp. 1–2, and May 13, 1944, p. 1) comments extensively and glowingly on the success of the general strike in El Salvador.

violent stage on July 26 when workers from the coasts arrived in the capital to stage progovernment and pro-Vanguardia demonstrations as they sacked some business establishments which had participated in the lockout.[86]

The government overreacted to the threat of widespread civil disobedience. Unable to declare a state of siege because of the numerical strength of the Opposition in Congress, Picado tried to confront organized dissent with force. Merchants and professionals were intimidated; bank employees were threatened with dismissal and military service. The police and military forces patrolled the streets, reinforced by workers' militia. The governmental forces interpreted the strike as a prelude to an armed uprising. San José appeared to be a city beseiged by its own security forces.

The majority of the closed businesses reopened on July 28 to avoid further damage by progovernment demonstrations. The active protest by the Opposition continued, however. The government threatened even more drastic action and based it on a twofold justification: the strike violated the Labor Code and closed shops worked a real hardship on the poor of the city. To counter the latter, the Opposition established a system of food distribution which relieved the plight of the urban poor, dependent on daily purchases for their sustenance.

On August 2, the Opposition repeated a tactic used successfully in 1943. A body of women marched on the presidential palace to petition for guarantees that a free election would be held. President Picado did not receive them and they were dispersed by force. The government was discredited because shots were fired into the air, apparently to frighten the congregated women, although it is not certain who perpetrated the action.

The following day the government, the official party, and the Opposition reached an agreement, "El Pacto del honor." It guaran-

---

[86] The workers from the coast were called *mariachis* by the citizens of San José because of their use of blankets for protection from the cool nights. The blankets were associated with Mexican sarapes and then with Mexican entertainers, the *mariachis*. The Opposition seized on the term as clever and degrading and from that time forward applied it to those who favored the government.

teed free elections and provided that during the last week of the campaign the Electoral Tribunal would be in charge of the complete electoral process. It further stated that during the last eight days of the campaign there would be no public political activity by either side.[87]

The "terrorist group" intensified its efforts beginning in August, 1947. It continued the sabotage of public facilities and it also added more daring and potentially disruptive undertakings. Twice the group attempted to assassinate Calderón Guardia; both attempts failed.[88] It succeeded in blowing up Mora's automobile and the home of Manuel Formoso, the editor of *La Tribuna*, but did not injure either of the principals. In November, it bombed *La Tribuna*, killing one person and injuring twelve. Serious rioting followed in the capital as progovernment forces tried to retaliate.[89] Although the government identified most of the leaders of the group, it did not proceed against them.[90] But unless Figueres could manage to devise and execute a new plan for obtaining the necessary arms and trained officers essential for the projected insurrection, the efforts of the terrorists would be of little use.

Figueres by August, 1947, had failed to achieve his bold plans of 1943–1945. Despite the activities of his "terrorist group," he had not been able to bring off a general strike let alone bring down the government. His last great hope remained with his international connections. The failure of Dominican exiles to launch an attack on their homeland from Cuba had resulted in the transfer of their arsenal to Guatemala, where there it came under the control of President Juan José Arévalo and Colonel Francisco Arana. Figueres and his Nicaraguan allies formed one of several groups vying for use of the arsenal, which nominally still belonged to General Juan Rodríguez of the Dominican Republic.[91]

[87] Castro Esquivel, *Los ocho años*, p. 90. Similar accounts appear in the progovernment and antigovernment press.

[88] *La Tribuna*, August 12, 1947, p. 1, and October 23, 1947, p. 1.

[89] *La Nación*, November 4, 1947, p. 1.

[90] *La Tribuna* (November 6, 1947, p. 5) named many of the leaders along with their photographs.

[91] Argüello, *Quienes y como*, p. 28.

Arévalo planned to see the arms employed to achieve a Central American Union under a democratic government and to overthrow dictatorships in the Caribbean. Figueres and his agents in Guatemala, Argüello and later Argüello's Costa Rican brother-in-law, Fernando Figuls, convinced Arévalo of their Unionism and of their willingness to fight in the larger battle of the Caribbean. In the context of the fight against tyranny, Figueres convinced Arévalo that the battle should begin in Costa Rica: (1) Costa Rica was militarily the weakest nation in the Caribbean area; (2) an attack could be launched against Somoza's Nicaragua over a long land frontier, difficult to control; (3) the conditions for revolution had been prepared in Costa Rica where Figueres had five hundred trained men, but few arms.[92] On December 16, 1947, Figueres and Argüello signed the Pact of the Caribbean along with other exile leaders, pledging themselves to battle to free the area of dictatorships.[93]

Figueres, in effect, pledged the resources of his nation, which had traditionally pursued a policy of isolationism, to a protracted, costly, and rather dubious international venture. This step, in late 1947, however, seemed essential if Figueres were to found the Second Republic. Arévalo's subsequent vacillation as to whether or not he should send arms and men to Figueres caused Figueres many tense moments, but at the precise moment when he had to act, both men and arms were made available.

[92] See Ibid., pp. 30–38, and fol. 1, item 92, "Murray Collection."

[93] See Argüello, *Quienes y como*, pp. 118–122, for the text of the pact; or see Otilio Ulate, *¿Hacia dónde lleva a Costa Rica el Señor Presidente Figueres?*, pp. 20–21. [Pamphlet.] A copy of the document itself is in the "Murray Collection."

CHAPTER **6**

The Electoral Question

Eᴸᴇᴄᴛɪᴏɴꜱ ᴘᴇʀᴇɴɴɪᴀʟʟʏ ᴍᴏᴠᴇᴅ
Cᴏꜱᴛᴀ Rɪᴄᴀɴꜱ to great activity and to mutual recrimination. It had
long since been resolved that the only legitimate means to power
was by election based on universal manhood suffrage.[1] The mechanism of the electoral process, however, was deficient, and a variety
of devices had evolved which corrupted the right of suffrage.
Throughout the period from 1940 to 1948 Costa Rica was particularly torn by the electoral choices it had to make. Increasing social
tension and great international insecurity posed questions which
provoked unusual controversy over the individuals and party best

[1] Charles W. Anderson, *Politics and Economic Change in Latin America*, pp.
108–109, discusses the question of governmental legitimacy in Latin America in
general. Costa Rica is one of the few exceptions in that only an electoral victory
gives one an accepted claim to office.

qualified to lead the nation. At the same time, the nation faced related problems concerning methods of making the vote effective; for instance, ensuring that each eligible voter cast only one vote and that only these votes would be counted.

The electoral question precipitated the crisis that led to the revolution. Each of the two major groups, united behind its presidential candidate, charged the other with serious offenses against the letter and the spirit of the law. In effect, each accused the other of attempting to obstruct the expression of the will of the people. The major thrust of the issue was directed against the *calderonistas*, the party in power.

In broad outline the question seemed patently simple as interpreted by the Opposition—the National Republicans had resorted to fraud to win the elections of 1942, 1944, and 1946.[2] On the other hand, the parties supporting the government accused the Opposition of simply wanting to divert popular attention from the real issue, the social question, by confusing popular opinion with their unsubstantiated charges of fraud. The government tried to assuage the discontent of the Opposition with a variety of measures short of turning over the executive branch of government to it.

There are three distinct chronological phases to the electoral issue. The first covers the period from 1940 to the presidential elections of February 13, 1944; it was during these years that Calderón Guardia emerged as a new *caudillo civil* with a great popular following.[3] The second marks the period between February 13, 1944, and February 8, 1948, which, in effect, was just one long campaign for the 1948 presidential election. The third phase extends through the months of February and March of 1948, during

[2] The Opposition generally ignored the elections of 1938 and 1940, for their inclusion would have served to discredit the memory of León Cortés Castro, whom it portrayed as a martyr for the right of suffrage.

[3] The *caudillo civil* in Costa Rica is a political leader who through a combination of charisma and anticharisma develops a large and loyal personal following. It is a concept analogous to the *caudillo* or man on horseback with the significant difference that he is not a military figure. As the term is used in Costa Rica, the *caudillo civil* attracts his following in the countryside and the small towns more than in the cities.

which the followers of the two candidates sought a détente until they realized that the verdict was no longer theirs to deliver.

Citizens of Costa Rica, from the late nineteenth century onward, had an exalted idea of the inviolability of the vote and of the electoral process, holding them to be the political foundation of the republic. Notwithstanding, various techniques of manipulation and outright chicanery were widely enough practiced to form, in effect, a part of the electoral process.[4] Almost every election prompted charges and countercharges of fraud, but the prestige of the Grand Electoral Council, selected to scrutinize the votes cast, was usually sufficient to curtail flagrant abuses.

The conduct of President Cortés during the 1940 election had seriously disparaged the right of suffrage. Calderón Guardia in his inaugural address therefore tried to reassure the nation by promising a new and more effective electoral law. His one attempt at electoral reform, however, was condemned by his opponents. Since the measure would have centralized more control in the hands of the chief executive, they considered it a device to thwart the popular will. In the face of partisan protest, Calderón Guardia withdrew the bill from further consideration by Congress.

The intense political activity that took place between Calderón Guardia's inauguration and the 1944 election centered on the various facets of his reform program rather than on corruption of the right of suffrage. A major voice clamoring for electoral reform silenced itself in 1942 when the Communists changed from opposing the government to supporting it.

Politically, the defection of ex-President León Cortés from the National Republican party in 1941 to form the Democratic party constituted a grave threat to the new administration. The Costa Rican voter was still wedded to personalism and Cortés was a widely known and respected *caudillo civil*. This new party attracted

---

[4] Carlos Luis Fallas, *Mamita Yunai*, pp. 59–68. In this autobiographical novel, Fallas gives an example of what was probably the most flagrant form of fraud: a whole community of Talamanca Indians went through what to them was a meaningless sham under the direction of voting inspectors, who returned to the capital with predetermined results of the voting.

much of the elite, which was intransigently opposed to even moderate social change. Despite the obvious widely accepted need for social reform, Cortés' platform proposed no significant innovation; it simply stated the intent not to abrogate social legislation already in effect.[5]

Cortés' program was reactionary, not conservative. He appealed to the peasantry to protect its "way of life" and to follow the wisdom of its fathers. He did not propose a return to the nation of small farmers, but rather championed the maintenance of the status quo in which the small farmer, once the economic mainstay of the nation, had been reduced to a most inferior position. He advocated a "return" to domination by the coffee interests whose leadership had resulted in a reduced level of entrepreneurship and a gradual impoverishment of the countryside.

During the first two years of Calderón Guardia's administration, his reform program was hampered by a number of extraordinary developments related to World War II. As an ally of the United States, Costa Rica undertook to build a somewhat more professional army despite a tradition of distinct opposition to a standing military force. It also accepted a military training mission and an air detachment from the United States, since its proximity to the Panama Canal gave it great strategic importance.[6]

Perhaps the most disruptive step Costa Rica was called upon to take in consequence of its role as a belligerent in the war was the suppression of resident German nationals. British intelligence officers with the support of the United States, even prior to that country's entrance into the war, compiled lists of German firms and nationals in Latin America. These rosters, generally referred to as "black lists" were presented to the various governments in Central America and their cooperation was sought, at the very least, to make it impossible for Germans to engage in international trade. In Central America the procedure generally went beyond

[5] León Cortés Castro, *Programa de gobierno y orientaciones generales del Partido Demócrata,* p. 122. [Pamphlet.]

[6] Juan Rojas Suárez, *Costa Rica en la Segunda Guerra Mundial,* pp. 74–75.

mere trade restriction. German nationals were put in concentration camps either in the United States or in Central America.

Costa Rica deported more than two hundred Germans, placed German-owned businesses under Costa Rican administrators, installed a concentration camp utilizing the German Club and part of La Sabana airport, and expropriated German-owned farms.[7] Surprisingly little of the criticism provoked by these actions was directed against the United States; most of it was voiced against Calderón Guardia.

All these pressures, combined with the domestic issues of social reform and purported corruption in the administration, resulted in a marked decline in the popularity of Calderón Guardia. This loss of confidence was manifested in the congressional election of 1942 in which, despite the control of the electoral machinery by the government, competing parties made great gains. The Communist party received 16,198 votes of the 100,296 votes cast, an increase of almost 6,000 over its showing in 1940. Independents and members of smaller parties polled another 20,642 votes.[8]

The struggle for the political allegiance and support of the working classes became three-sided during the Calderón Guardia administration. The Communist party to a large extent had dominated the nascent labor movement until Calderón Guardia made his direct appeal to the masses. The Communists continued to provide much of the leadership for the labor movement although the personalistic figure of Calderón Guardia captured the imagination

[7] Ibid., pp. 42–50, and Edward N. Barnhart, "Citizenship and Political Tests in Latin American Republics in World War II," *Hispanic American Historical Review* 42 (1962): 297–332. The Germans in general were highly respected in Costa Rica, and enjoyed a position of some influence in the Cortés administration. There followed a public outcry against expropriation by the government. The German-language school maintained by the German community also catered to the local elite and had helped establish close relationships between the two groups. The Germans had not isolated themselves from the Costa Ricans; they were well integrated as members of the business and large-unit agricultural community. Examples of this integration are Federico Reimers and the Niehaus family who later benefited directly from the victory of National Liberation.

[8] *La Tribuna*, February 19, 1942, p. 1.

of much of organized labor after 1943, when the Labor Code was enacted, giving labor legal status and the express right to organize for the first time in Costa Rican history. The third contender for labor's support was Father Benjamín Núñez, who organized a new labor organization popularly referred to as Rerum Novarum.

The election of 1944 marked the beginning of a new phase in the electoral issue. In preparation for the contest, the National Republicans and Vanguardia Popular formed their political alliance, christened the Bloque de la Victoria. The alliance chose Teodoro Picado as their candidate, and both groups mutually pledged to work for an honest administration and for the passage of a specified program of social reform. The National Republicans believed the alliance was necessary to forestall a second presidency for León Cortés. Many individuals of liberal orientation feared that a second Cortés presidency would have disastrous results for the program of reform which had been initiated.

Cortés carried out a vigorous campaign that was actually begun just as his first administration terminated. He concentrated his efforts on the countryside, where the majority of Costa Rican voters lived and where personalism was most pronounced. He appealed to these folk to protect their way of life. their religion, and their honor from the "red hordes."[9] Relentlessly he linked the National Republicans with Vanguardia Popular and identified both simply as Communists.[10]

Both the Centro and Otilio Ulate, the publisher of the *Diario de Costa Rica* and a leading opposition figure, remained on the sidelines during the contest in 1944. They discredited Cortés as a candidate because of his authoritarian reputation and his silence on the issue of social reform.

[9] See *La Prensa Libre* or *Diario de Costa Rica* for the period of November, 1943, through January, 1944. There an almost daily repetition of this theme may be found. A second theme that Cortés employed extensively was *volver*, "to return" [to days past].

[10] His tactics were almost identical to but more vociferous than those he had employed in the election of 1936 against Octavio Beeche. The names had simply been changed; rather than "Beeche-Comunismo" he attacked "Picado-Comunismo" or "Calderon-Comunismo."

The government employed every means at its command to assure Picado's victory. It used official vehicles to transport Picado's followers, allowed police to intimidate participants in Cortés' rallies, and acquiesced in the employment of gangs of toughs to harass opponents. The violence reached a climax in San José on the Sunday before the election. Cortés' forces organized a demonstration in the capital to which they brought nearly as many people from the countryside as there were residents of San José. Street clashes that day resulted in one dead, and forty-eight injured. Consequently, during the last week of the campaign, Calderón Guardia prohibited the two parties that supported Picado from holding further political rallies.

Election day, February 13, proved as violent as had the campaign. Four deaths were registered. The official verdict gave Picado a majority of nearly 30,000 of the 136,806 votes cast. The evidence of fraud and intimidation on the part of the government was most convincing; the only question seemed to be whether their tactics had been sufficiently widespread to deprive Cortés of a majority. Those who had opposed the government, however, acted on the assumption that Cortés had been defrauded of victory, as he most probably was.

The dust had hardly settled from the election when the various opposition groups turned their attention to the next presidential election, which would take place in February of 1948. Acción Demócrata, originally an activist group with the Democratic party, almost immediately established itself as an independent political party. All the opposition groups recognized that only through resolute action over the next four years could they hope to deny Calderón Guardia a second term as president.

Calderón Guardia had largely replaced the Communists in the popular mind as the proponent of reform and transformation. His great following enabled him to threaten the privileges of the oligarchy far more ominously than did the minuscule and vulnerable Vanguardia Popular. His rise in popularity also threatened those segments of his opposition whose hopes of political power rested on their own programs for reform and transformation. Acción

Demócrata and the Centro therefore sought to discredit him not by criticizing his reform program, but by charging him with fraud. It was not credible to them that an oligarch should stake out for himself the fertile political terrain of non-Communist social and economic reform. And by the elite he was deemed a traitor for having carried out any program of social reform. Both oligarchs and reformers agreed that a second term for Calderón Guardia had to be avoided at all costs.

The prominent leaders of the major parties recognized that Costa Rica faced a grave political crisis. All attempted to pacify the nation. Calderón Guardia left the country to practice medicine in New York shortly after his term ended.[11] Cortés counseled his followers against insurrection and, at least momentarily, removed himself from active controversy. Picado, first as President-elect and then as President. attempted to quiet the nation and to meet his opponents' challenge by promising fiscal integrity and new legislation to prevent dishonesty in government.

The most far-reaching consequence of the fraudulent election of 1944 was to bring the several opposition groups together in a political pact. The question of fraud was the principal issue upon which they could and did unite. The "imposition" of Picado created a problem which for many citizens eclipsed all other aspects of national life. Electoral purification became the primary question which had to be solved to assure meaningful political activity in Costa Rica.[12]

The question of the inviolability of the suffrage brought Acción Demócrata and the Centro into conversations which led to the formation of the Social Democratic party. The purported fraud provided the basis for the effective cooperation of the revolutionary-minded, largely middle-class young men of the Centro with the more "traditional" political groups. The suffrage question transformed the various groups opposing the government into *the Opposition*. "The Opposition maintains itself united and thus will main-

---

[11] Calderón Guardia returned in September, 1946.
[12] *Acción Demócrata*, November 5, 1944, p. 1.

tain itself until its objective is realized, to reestablish the right of suffrage and to behead the civil oligarchy."[13]

A statement by Otilio Ulate shows clearly the primacy he assigned to the suffrage issue: "We all know that the fundamental problem of Costa Rica is that of liberty of suffrage. Liberty of suffrage does not exist in our nation. Liberty of suffrage will not exist until the governing regime—that is, the established system in power—has disappeared from the political scene."[14]

The Opposition, particularly the Social Democrats, tried to establish a popular conception of the Calderón-Picado period as one of cruel dictatorship approaching the notorious regimes maintained by Anastasio Somoza in Nicaragua and Rafael Trujillo in the Dominican Republic. Other than the suffrage question, the Opposition really had little on which to fault the executive in democratic procedures. Press freedom existed to the point of license; newspapers were permitted to print even outrageous personal attacks against the President. The rights of organization and assembly were scrupulously respected. The courts maintained their independence as evidenced by their ruling that two of Calderón Guardia's decrees of amnesty were unconstitutional. There were no secret police, no arbitrary arrests, and no political prisoners. There was only one political exile, José Figueres, and he returned to the country within two years. He freely attended political rallies and spoke openly, advocating insurrection.[15] The military establishment was small, composed entirely of volunteers and led by nonprofessional officers. Such a force could not support an oppressive government.

The attacks by the Social Democrats were not always consistent. At times they characterized the government as dictatorial, at other times as militaristic or comparable to the most regressive regimes of Latin America. On occasion, as though recognizing the incredibility of their charges, they moderated their accusations, charging that

[13] Ibid., June 15, 1946, p. 1.
[14] Ibid., January 23, 1946, p. 1.
[15] See chapter 5.

the regime was sinister not so much because of its actions as because of what it might become. In this milder vein of criticism, they found the government "pseudodemocratic":

We are not going to say that in Costa Rica we live a tyranny of blood and fire; we are not going to repeat the same nonsense from which the adulators of the government defend it every day. No, in Costa Rica no one is jailed, at least not now, . . . we do believe that this blessed government . . . can fall on the list of hypocritical governments to which a distinguished North American official [Spruille Braden, Assistant Secretary of State] made reference.

Mr. Braden began his definition of the pseudodemocratic governments of this continent by saying that they are those which deny democratic rights to the people that they pretend to represent; and what has been the phenomenon which Costa Ricans have observed? That of a government that says it represents the people when it only represents a clique and an extremist minority party [Vanguardia Popular] and that denies the democratic right of the citizens to elect [their representatives].[16]

Picado soon learned that "restoration of the right of suffrage" would be judged accomplished only when the Opposition attained an electoral victory. The Social Democrats stated the dictum, "the government must permit free elections and be defeated or the people will drive it from power."[17]

The irregularities of the campaign of 1943–1944 led not only to vehement protest from the Opposition but also to deep concern within the forces which supported the government. Most politically aware Costa Ricans recognized that the voting mechanism was defective and the process confused.[18] Vanguardia Popular immediately renewed its call for a just and comprehensive electoral code. It had an enlightened self-interest in reform, for it recognized that its cooperation with the National Republicans was transitory.

Picado and his close personal followers put top priority on the writing and passage of an advanced electoral code by the new ad-

[16] *Acción Demócrata*, January 26, 1946, p. 2.
[17] Ibid., January 12, 1946, p. 3.
[18] José Figueres Ferrer, *Estos diez años*, p. 21. [Pamphlet.]

ministration. In 1945 he presented an enlightened and comprehensive draft that received merited general acclaim. The code was approved in the last months of 1945, too late for its rather complex provisions to be put into effect for the 1946 congressional election.

President Picado used the new code, even though it was not yet in effect, as a guide for conducting the 1946 election. The polling proceeded smoothly with few disputes; those which occurred the President arbitrated. In at least one instance, at the request of the Opposition, he decreed a rerun of the voting in a certain district.

Picado's conciliatory efforts received favorable comment from the press.[19] Even the Social Democrats' newspaper, *Acción Demócrata*, gave him credit for his just supervision of the electoral process in 1946.[20]

The election confirmed a trend away from the National Republicans.[21] Their margin of victory had grown smaller in each successive election after 1940. In 1946, 44 percent of the popular vote went to the Opposition compared to 50 percent for the *calderonistas*. The Opposition elected ten of their candidates to Congress compared to eleven for the National Republicans and two for Vanguardia Popular.[22]

The Communists also suffered a decline in strength. It became essential to them to maintain their alliance with the government if they were to continue to influence its policy. The possibility of their becoming an independent political force had been undoubtedly lessened when they entered the coalition with Calderón Guardia.

The results of the election encouraged the *calderonistas*' foes, but the National Republicans, even without the popular figure of Calderón Guardia at the head of the ticket, had obtained an electoral advantage. It then became obvious that the Opposition's cam-

[19] *La Nación*, February 20, 1946, p. 1.

[20] *Acción Demócrata*, February 16, 1946, p. 1.

[21] During the third term of Ricardo Jiménez, from 1932 to 1936, the National Republicans became a party of national consensus which was only weakly challenged electorally in the elections of 1938, and 1940.

[22] Alberto Cañas, *Los ocho años*, p. 71.

paign had to be greatly intensified if Calderón Guardia were to be defeated in the coming presidential race of 1948. The Opposition at this point began its boycott of Congress in a canny maneuver to link Communism and electoral fraud in the popular mind.[23]

The spirit of compromise that had long characterized Costa Rican political life expressed itself in the period of crisis between 1946 and 1948 in the many attempts to reach a transaction which would avert possible bitterness and bloodshed. Picado did not believe that a revolution could take place even though there was talk of one, nor did he think that anyone else believed it possible.[24] This conviction conditioned his response to the Opposition and to his critics within governmental circles. He sought compromise and he presumed that the leadership of the Opposition did so as well.

The first attempt to reach an agreement came almost immediately after Picado assumed office in May, 1944. Ricardo Fernández related that the President was approached by *cortesista* leaders but that he found their conditions unacceptable. They asked him to break completely with Vanguardia Popular, which had supported him in the past election.[25]

Following the 1946 off-year election, Cortés himself approached Picado to ask him to reconsider his alliance with Vanguardia Popular. He assured him of ample support from the business community and of his personal cooperation in order to save the nation from even graver ills due to political excesses. Picado was still considering Cortés' proposal at the time of the ex-President's death, March 3, 1946.[26]

After the death of Cortés, representatives of Cortés' Democratic party conferred with Picado and Calderón Guardia. Since Calderón Guardia remained in New York, Fernando Castro Cervantes, president of the executive committee of the party, discussed the possibility of a political transaction with Calderón Guardia's brother,

[23] See chapter 3.
[24] Teodoro Picado, *El Pacto de la Embajada de Mexico*, p. 7. [Pamphlet.]
[25] Ricardo Fernández Guardia, *Cartilla histórica de Costa Rica*, p. 149.
[26] Ibid., p. 151.

Francisco.[27] Castro Cervantes thus followed the initiative of the deceased leader of his party, ex-President Cortés.

Otilio Ulate also conducted talks with Picado almost simultaneously with those Castro Cervantes was holding with Francisco Calderón Guardia. Ulate was interested mainly in obtaining from the President a personal guarantee to uphold the new electoral code in the forthcoming campaign, but the *cortesistas* accused him of having sought a political compromise.[28]

The hope of an agreement to avoid the predictable excesses of the 1947–1948 campaign ended in mutual recriminations within Opposition circles. The Social Democrats and Figueres made "transaction" a pejorative in the Opposition's vocabulary. Their determination to prevent compromise resulted in the discrediting of that time-honored method of controlling political tensions used previously to avoid reaching a position of no-return or a showdown.[29]

For Figueres and the Social Democrats, compromise with the government was neither convenient nor admissible. In a speech he made in August, 1946, Figueres clarified his position: "A transition candidate, which would again protect them from attack [*que les guarde otra vez las espaldas*], is the ideal 'out' for the official politicians. . . . Let us abandon once and for all the idea of a simple political battle."[30]

The Social Democrats' position within the inner councils of the Opposition made a transaction a near impossibility. To the young men of the Social Democratic party a fight to the finish represented heroism and purity. If all was "bad" then all must be changed. Compromise was a tactic of the old-style politicians; they viewed it with disdain.

The Opposition overcame the greatest threat to its continued unity in 1947 with the selection of a single candidate for the presi-

[27] Cañas, *Los ocho años*, p. 78.

[28] Ibid., pp. 78–79.

[29] For Figueres' categorical denial of the possible efficacy of any transaction see *Acción Demócrata*, August 31, 1946, p. 1.

[30] Arturo Castro Esquivel, *José Figueres Ferrer*, pp. 84–86.

dency to oppose Calderón Guardia who it was correctly assumed would be the official candidate in 1948. On February 13, 1947, the third anniversary of the defeat of León Cortés Castro, the Opposition held a convention in the National Stadium to nominate a single candidate for the approaching election. The heterogeneous nature of the forces represented was evident in the selection of delegates. Among the participants there were members of the executive committees of three parties; deputies to National Congress; municipal councilmen; former judges, secretaries of state, and deputies of Opposition sympathy; and professionals, priests, and university professors sympathetic to the cause. Also present were the directors of the Chambers of Agriculture and Commerce, and the Coffee Growers Association, as well as the executive members of all private banks. The convention also included members of social and sport clubs, and worker and student organizations whose assistance had been especially requested by the Social Democrats.[31] Fourteen individuals received votes for the nomination, but three candidates obtained preponderant support from the delegates. They were Otilio Ulate, Fernando Castro Cervantes, and José Figueres.[32]

The conventioneers envisioned each of the candidates as representing a particular sector within the Opposition: "The big businessmen and conservative mentalities lean toward Castro; the mature intellectuals and young businessmen are with Ulate; and the students, young intellectuals, and 'hot heads' have voted for Figueres."[33] On the third ballot the young men who had previously voted for Figueres threw their support to Ulate who thus became the Opposition candidate.

For the moment the differences among the Opposition parties were minimized. They were able to present a united front against Communism and the arbitrary practices of the *calderonistas*.[34] In

[31] Cañas, *Los ocho años*, p. 84.

[32] Ulate was the candidate of Unión Nacional; Cervantes of Partido Demócrata; and Figueres of Partido Cortesista formed by a dissident group of Partido Demócrata (ibid., p. 83).

[33] Ibid., p. 85.

[34] Hugo Navarro Bolandi, *La generación del 48*, pp. 113–115.

this spirit of unity, Ulate appointed Figueres his campaign manager, although in practice Dr. Carlos Luis Valverde served as such.

The National Republicans countered the Opposition convention with one of their own. On March 23, 1947, they pointedly invited the participation of all Costa Ricans, thereby emphasizing to the populace the almost complete absence of a similar representation of the lower classes at the Opposition convention. The invitation was not to aid in choosing the candidate, but rather to acclaim the already selected standard-bearer, Calderón Guardia.[35].

The die was cast for a fight to the finish as both sides resolved to seek the banner of legitimacy by an electoral victory. A hard contest seemed a certainty. In late March, however, the *calderonistas* made a last attempt to reach a political transaction, hoping to avoid the ominous campaign which lay ahead. The *Diario de Costa Rica* claimed that Ulate knew nothing of the maneuver, but that the compromise candidate would be a member of the Opposition "who enjoys the confidence of Dr. Calderón."[36] Calderón Guardia would withdraw from the race if agreement could be reached.

Once more the Social Democrats led the effort to avert a transaction. They revealed that the compromise solution involved the candidacy of Castro Cervantes and the exclusion of Communists from the new Directory of Congress to be chosen in May. Oppositionists along with *calderonistas* were to form the new Directory, which would include Fernando Lara of the Democratic party as vice president.[37] Not all of the members of the Opposition approved of the Social Democrats' intransigence on the question of political transaction.[38] The opinion of these young men, however, prevailed; referring to themselves they claimed that the ideological parties "have developed a social conscience among the people" and therefore compromises could not take place.[39]

[35] *New York Times*, March 24, 1947, p. 10. *La Nación*, March 24, 1947, p. 1.
[36] *Diario de Costa Rica*, March 29, 1947.
[37] Ibid., April 30, 1947, p. 1.
[38] The most outspoken of those who disapproved of the tactics of the Social Democrats was Lic. Víctor Guardia Quirós.
[39] *Acción Demócrata*, May 3, 1947.

The key to the nation's hope for a fair election was the Electoral Tribunal formed under the new Electoral Code. The tribunal consisted of three leading citizens chosen by the three branches of government, and a substitute chosen by Congress. Congress had originally appointed Octavio Beeche, but he departed for the United States in late 1947 for medical treatment, and Maximiliano Koberg Bolandi was chosen as his substitute. The Supreme Court named José María Vargas, and Picado named Gerardo Guzmán. The various political parties agreed that these men inspired confidence and they were thought to be above political controversy. They gave renewed hope for a fair electoral race.[40]

The Opposition, particularly the Social Democrats, almost daily questioned the possibility of a verifiably fair election. Ulate publicly expressed his lack of confidence in the Electoral Code. He stated that it had been emitted only to calm internal public opinion and to serve as propaganda outside the country.[41]

The Electoral Tribunal had demanded full guarantees from the government that it would establish the necessary conditions to assure free elections. In early February the Tribunal's members threatened to resign en masse if such conditions were not established within thirty days.[42] In March, the tribunal recognized that Picado intended to exert the weight of his office toward the task of providing free elections.[43] His government accepted the decisions of the tribunal members, modified the electoral legislation at their request, and provided the necessary financial support which exceeded that granted by any previous government.[44]

Picado, however, found himself in a weak position to influence the course of events. Since he could not stand for reelection, his power of persuasion diminished as the presidential election approached. He was further handicapped because his personal following was scant in comparison with that of Calderón Guardia

[40] *La Nación*, March 13, 1947, p. 1.
[41] Ibid., March 14, 1947, p. 1.
[42] *Diario de Costa Rica*, February 7, 1947, p. 1.
[43] *La Nación*, March 15, 1947, p. 1.
[44] *Diario de Costa Rica*, July 19, 1960, p. 2.

or even of Mora. Since much of the military establishment and the police force gave first political allegiance to Calderón Guardia, Picado's task was all the more difficult.

On a visit to the Civil Registry (not to be confused with the Electoral Registry) in September, 1947, Guzmán, secretary of the Tribunal Electoral, discovered that the National Republicans' applications were being processed far more rapidly than those of the Opposition, and he found obvious signs of conflict between some supervisors and employees.[45] In addition, he uncovered clear evidence of fraud which included false declarations of age by minors, invented names, and duplicate registration, all of which he charged to the responsibility of the National Republican Party.[46]

Not all the *calderonistas* shared Picado's hope for a free election nor perhaps his interest that there should be one. From early 1947 they focused their discontent on the office of the Electoral Registry which, under the direction of Lic. Benjamín Odio, they denounced as an Opposition stronghold. Vanguardia Popular joined in this denunciation and, during working hours in the closing months of the campaign, they maintained an almost constant demonstration in front of the Electoral Registry protesting the alleged partiality of its operation.

The Electoral Registry faced a tremendous task in preparing to implement the electoral laws. Odio found the records in poor condition, an atmosphere of neglect reigning in the office, and the employees divided according to their political inclinations. Odio's own sympathies most likely proved a major obstacle to the proper execution of his duties, for he was a follower of Figueres. In the closing days of the campaign, members of the Social Democratic party guarded the Electoral Registry because they feared that the progovernment demonstrators would attack Odio and his subordinates.

The voting took place on Sunday, February 8, 1948, in an atmosphere of great calm that belied the tension which gripped the nation. The early returns were inconclusive but indicated a trend for Ulate. René Picado, public safety secretary, and brother of the

45 *La Nación*, September 23, 1947, p. 1.
46 *El Social Demócrata*, September 27, 1947, p. 1.

President, told reporters that he believed that the election had been "fair and free." At the close of the day the unofficial returns showed Ulate to be the victor by a substantial margin, approximately ten thousand votes.

On election day the Electoral Tribunal had realized that incorrectly prepared voting sheets were preventing many citizens from exercising their right to vote. According to the new Electoral Code, the number, name, place of residence, and voting table shown on the voter identification cards had to agree with the corresponding data entered on the electoral materials at the polling place, or the voter would be disqualified. Such discrepancies were sufficiently numerous that in the afternoon of election day the tribunal sent telegrams instructing all polling places to relax the close legal scrutiny and to permit those with identification cards to vote. However, the volume of business handled by the telegraph offices on election day had slowed delivery to the extent that many outlying communities received this directive only after the polls closed.

For a number of reasons other than relaxation of the scrutiny of identification cards, the polls were seriously congested during the afternoon. Many citizens found that the voting lists called for them to vote in a district other than their own. The tribunal had previously ruled that individuals expecting to vote outside their home districts would be allowed to exercise the suffrage exclusively between the hours of two and four in the afternoon. The Opposition instructed its followers to vote in the morning, but to return to the polls in the afternoon ostensibly to prevent government partisans from voting illegally at more than one polling place. Their delaying tactics during these hours insured that those waiting in line would have time to vote only once and, also, that some might be denied the vote.[47] The net effect was to reduce the number of ballots cast.

With the closing of the polls on the evening of February 8, the Electoral Tribunal became the center of interest and attention for the hopes and anxieties of the nation. The Electoral Code provided that the tribunal should scrutinize the whole voting process. Its

[47] Cañas. *Los ocho años,* pp. 111–112.

members were to go over the voting rolls, not merely recount the totals sent in by the various regions. It was to make a provisional declaration on February 25 which was to be sent to the Congress for the final declaration of the results. In order to preclude any intervention on the part of the executive, Congress was to convene in an extraordinary session on March 1 for the express purpose of considering the vote of the past election. The tribunal, however, recognized that despite the clear provisions of the code, it faced a serious crisis in which the future of the republic seemed to hang in balance.[48]

The calm of voting day gave way to agitation as the National Republicans took stock of the result and discerned the pattern of what they considered to have been a particularly galling "fraud." While, in principal, all sides condemned electoral fraud, in practice, it was recognized as being largely within the province of the party in power to carry it out. Many National Republicans reacted vehemently against what they considered to be not only fraud, but also a tremendous affront to their prerogatives. To them the President's good intention of preventing a repetition of the fraud committed in 1944 had led to a most ironic reversal for their own party. They concluded that they had been beaten at their own game.

On February 9, René Picado reversed his opinion that the election had been fair and free. Calderón Guardia on the advice of his brother, Francisco, had already prepared a statement to acknowledge his defeat.[49] However, convinced by some of his followers that a massive fraud had been committed against the National Republicans and specifically against his candidacy, or perhaps simply convinced that the party could exact concessions from Ulate, he did not acknowledge the defeat.

There appeared to be cause for suspicion. Despite a rapidly growing population and the vast interest generated by the campaign, the number of votes cast was smaller than in any previous presidential campaign since 1936. The decrease was most drastically evident in

[48] The provisions are clearly defined in *Código Electoral.*
[49] Cañas, *Los ocho años,* p. 113.

those areas outside San José where the strength of the National Republicans and Vanguardia Popular was most pronounced.[50] Tales circulated throughout the republic of well-known and obscure supporters of the two parties being denied the right of suffrage for technical reasons. The National Republicans took their charges of fraud to the Electoral Tribunal, but it declined to consider them.

The tribunal recognized the dangerous political situation in which the country found itself, but its work failed to progress with sufficient rapidity to meet the deadline of February 25.[51] The tribunal seemed to be avoiding the final verdict, perhaps with the hope that the candidates would come to some extra-official agreement which would tranquilize public opinion. In the tribunal's view, the charges of fraud were a matter for Congress to settle, yet the nation awaited its verdict and thought of its decision as final.[52] Constant turmoil and agitation around the tribunal's offices added to its inquietude, the members even fearing for their personal safety.[53]

Benjamín Odio, the director of the Electoral Registry, left the capital before the electoral process was complete to join the Figueres forces in the south, where he became an officer of the insurrectionary Army of National Liberation.[54] His demonstrated connection with the *figueristas*, and the post of foreign minister with which he was rewarded by the Junta would seem at the very least to cloud his claim to impartiality. If the problems he faced as director of the registry had been, indeed, impossible to solve in the interval between his appointment and the election, it would have seemed incumbent on him to so inform the nation. Under such

[50] Puntarenas and Puerto Limón were strongholds (the 1966 election indicates that they still are) of the progovernment parties, and voting there was proportionately lower than in the other provinces.

[51] Maximiliano Koberg Bolandi, "Koberg Memoranda," "Memorandum Number Seven," p. 1. Koberg became a member of the Electoral Tribunal in December, 1947, to substitute for Octavio Beeche who departed for New Orleans for urgent medical reasons and did not return until after the revolution. At the insistence of the other two members, Koberg Bolandi served as president. Koberg prepared a series of ten memoranda in the early 1950's on the electoral question.

[52] *La Nación*, February 11, 1948, p. 1.

[53] Cañas, *Los ochos años*, p. 114.

[54] Rafael Obregón Loría, *Conflictos militares y políticos de Costa Rica*, p. 117.

circumstances, a political transaction arranged to preserve constitutional government while the means of guaranteeing free elections were established would have been appropriate.

It could be argued that Odio recognized the futility of expecting the *calderonistas* to accept the verdict of a free election and, therefore, fled to the south to Figueres' *finca* to protect himself.[55] Subsequent events and revelations concerning the activities of Figueres in preparing the revolt, however, indicate that Odio's fortunes were linked closely with the revolutionary movement.

By February 11, street demonstrations by *calderonistas* and *vanguardistas*, who had begun their protest on the day following the elections, had reached near riot proportions. They streamed through the streets of the capital and congregated in front of the Gran Hotel Costa Rica, where scrutiny of the ballots was taking place, shouting: "We want to vote."[56]

Probably not even Calderón Guardia himself had a clear idea of what redress he sought in the period immediately following the election. At the very least, he expected to reach a compromise solution in which neither he nor Ulate would serve as president. To all appearances, he had several advantages over Ulate. His party, with the support of Vanguardia Popular, would still enjoy a slight majority when the new Congress was seated and the majority of the army officers were pro–Calderón Guardia.

That the tribunal was in fact pro-Opposition was concluded by the National Republicans, and the refusal by the tribunal to consider the charges of fraud gave more credibility to the National Republicans' allegation that the electoral rolls had been tampered with. The very inertia of the tribunal in making its count indicated to the *calderonistas* an uncertainty on the part of the Opposition.

Calderón Guardia believed that he, in fact, still retained control of the situation and that Ulate would have to deal with him. Since Congress had to pass on the election, Calderón Guardia's supporters could override the verdict of the tribunal should that become necessary. His bargaining position seemed strong, and Ulate at first

[55] Cañas, *Los ocho años*, p. 113.
[56] *Newsweek*, February 2, 1948, p. 40, and Cañas, *Los ocho años*, p. 113.

indicated his willingness to enter into discussions. Demonstrations by Calderón Guardia's followers, protesting the allegedly vast numbers denied the vote, gave new determination to the ex-President and to his party. Calderón Guardia assumed each day that passed without a decision from the Electoral Tribunal would add to the debility of the Opposition, indicating that it was unsure of its triumph. This presumption led him to ignore counsels of restraint within his party reminding him that the *calderonistas* had too little to gain and perhaps much to lose in questioning the results of the contest.

The members of the Electoral Tribunal held the key to the political crisis that Costa Rica faced. Their position became ever more uncomfortable. The nation awaited their verdict but as mutually antagonistic camps ready to contest it rather than abide by it. To add to the tribunal's discomfort, unidentified persons succeeded in burning some of the voting materials.[57]

Despite the expectancy of the nation, the tribunal was unable to complete the scrutiny by the deadline provided by the law. On February 25, they had counted only one-third of the votes. In order to abide by the letter of the Electoral Code, the tribunal officially closed the scrutiny and went into secret session under tremendous pressures.[58]

On February 28, a provisional declaration was made, based largely on the count of the vote submitted by telegrams from the many polling places; a count carried out by the *fiscales* of Unión Nacional.[59] However, one of the three members, Koberg, withheld his vote because he considered the count incomplete. The announced official returns showed Ulate elected with 54,931 votes to Calderón Guardia's 44,438. The final act was to be confirmation by Congress.

By issuing its verdict at the last moment, the tribunal added to

[57] Koberg, "Koberg Memoranda," "Memorandum Number Eight," p. 23, and Cañas, *Los ocho años*, p. 113.

[58] Koberg, "Koberg Memoranda," "Memorandum Number Nine," p. 2. Cañas (*Los ocho años*, p. 116) treats the subject of the verdict but clearly implies that February 28 was the day stipulated by the Electoral Code rather than February 25.

[59] Koberg, "Koberg Memoranda," "Memorandum Number Nine," p. 2.

the tension and anxiety of a crucial moment for the nation. Its last-minute decision and the extraordinary session of Congress for March 1 gave the various factions little time to appraise the political situation and come up with an alternate to a war of nerves or arms. The *calderonistas* regarded the verdict and particularly the manner in which the tribunal counted the votes as partisan acts of the Opposition, not as acts rendered by an impartial judge.

The *calderonistas* believed that the Opposition had become adamant. Ulate had announced in the *Diario de Costa Rica*, on February 18, that he would no longer even discuss a compromise. This new attitude of Ulate and the manner in which the tribunal rendered its decision appeared as a direct challenge to Calderón Guardia. In a colossal political blunder, the *calderonistas* and *vanguardistas* accepted the challenge. Calderón Guardia put his personal ambition above the national good and the fortunes of the great majority of his followers.

On March 1, Congress, in an undisciplined and vehement session, annulled the election by a vote of twenty-six to nineteen.[60] According to José Albertazzi Avendaño, the National Republican leader in Congress, the progovernment congressmen intended to elect Calderón Guardia first designate to the presidency when the new Congress convened on May 1, and in the absence of an elected President he would serve as such for the next four years.[61] Mora concurred in Albertazzi's appraisal of the intentions of Calderón Guardia's supporters.[62] The *calderonistas* claimed that a new election was an impossibility because of the disarray of the voting apparatus and somehow concluded that this justified their imposing their candidate by electing him first designate.

The actions of March 1 closed the way to any alternative other

[60] *Newsweek*, March 15, 1948, p. 42. *Newsweek* (February 9, 1948, p. 32) reports the composition of the Congress to be as follows: National Republicans, 16; Vanguardia Popular, 8; Opposition, 21.

[61] José Albertazzi Avendaño, *La tragedia de Costa Rica*, p. 83.

[62] Comisión Política de Vanguardia Popular, *Como y porqué cayó la democracia en Costa Rica*, p. 10. [Pamphlet.]

than insurrection. The moderates on both sides found themselves pushed into the background. The progovernment men presumed that they had the power to prevail and, for the moment, their estimate was accurate. On the same day that Congress annulled the election, Juan José Tavío, the Cuban-born chief of police, went with a contingent of policemen, in a coordinated show of force, to inspect the home of Dr. Carlos Luis Valverde, acting campaign manager for Unión Nacional.[63] Tavío did so without authorization from the secretary of public security and, it would seem, against his expressed wishes—a clear indication that the Picados were not in full control of their subordinates. The police surrounded Valverde's home where Opposition leaders, including Ulate and Figueres, had gathered. Figueres had departed shortly before the police arrived. As two policemen climbed the wall of the garden, shots rang out from within the house killing them both. The police answered with superior fire and Valverde fell mortally wounded at his front door. His position and the angle at which the bullet entered his body indicated that he had attempted to signal for a cessation of the firing.[64] The police then entered the house, ransacked it, and seized their arms. Ulate had escaped to a neighboring house, but he was captured on the following day and imprisoned.

Archbishop Sanabria, working with the diplomatic corps, managed to convince *ulatistas* and *calderonistas* of the desirability of a truce.[65] Ulate was then released from custody and immediately went into hiding. The truce lasted until March 8 and then was extended to March 10. By that time, it was obvious that a compromise

[63] According to Cañas (*Los ochos años*, p. 107), Tavío arose as leader during the attempt at a general strike in July, 1947. He kept his business open every day during the strike and on its eighth day appeared in uniform. One difficulty faced by the government had been the reluctance of its officials to use force against other Costa Ricans. Tavío had no such qualms; he played a prominent role until he went into exile at the close of the revolution.

[64] The best account of the events surrounding the death of Valverde appears in the *Diario de Costa Rica* on December, 7–8, 11–13, 1952. A more partisan account is found in Cañas, *Los ocho años*, pp. 117–118.

[65] Castro Esquivel, *José Figueres Ferrer*, p. 105.

solution was unattainable, since neither side would consent to any solution that did not include immediate recognition of its candidate as President.

Ulate had a clear claim to the presidency. He had received the majority of the votes cast, and his victory had been affirmed by the Electoral Tribunal. His claim was clouded by Congress' annulment of the election as fraudulent and by the manner in which the tribunal had scrutinized the ballots and delayed announcing the results.

Calderón Guardia had no claim to the presidency. Legally the annulment should have been followed by a rerun, but the *calderonistas* with the support of the Vanguardia Popular congressmen intended to gain by parliamentary maneuver what they had not gained at the polls. Perhaps their position could have been defended had Congress called for a new election in April as provided by the Electoral Code. But Calderón Guardia and his supporters intended to stay in power, thus seeming to confirm what Figueres had maintained since his return in 1944, that the *calderonistas* would only accept a verdict rendered by superior force.

The electoral process had broken down completely. Despite the efforts of many in both political camps to resolve the resulting impasse, there seemed to be no solution. The *calderonistas*, with the events of March 1, 1948, had taken a position which allowed them little room for maneuvering. Their position had hardened and they were determined to elect Calderón Guardia as first designate to the presidency when the new Congress met on May 1. The Opposition, on the other hand, had resolved that Ulate's victory of February 8 would not be denied him.

CHAPTER 7

Revolution and Negotiated Peace

THE CONSPIRACY TO OVERTHROW the Costa Rican government and establish the Second Republic assumed its definitive character when Figueres signed the Pact of the Caribbean on December 16, 1947. From that date onward his organization in Costa Rica was complete. It included armed elements dedicated to terrorism, men in training for anticipated military action, an efficient propaganda and subversion apparatus, and the necessary financial backing. Figueres needed only an opportunity to put his mechanism in motion under conditions giving some promise of success. The idea of an armed uprising had been generally accepted. However, he could hope to bring off the planned revolt only with the tacit approval of the *ulatistas*. He could not expect that support while the majority, even some within the Social Democratic party, still hoped for a victory at the polls. The aftermath of the election of 1948 removed that deterrent.

Figueres stood alone in more than one sense. He had dedicated years of his life to the conspiracy and had overextended the credit of his commercial enterprises in order to help finance the effort. Only Fernando Castro Cervantes had contributed comparable sums, but he had done so with great circumspection and without jeopardizing his fortune.[1] Figueres served as the only Costa Rican link with the coalition of Caribbean forces dedicated to overthrowing the various dictatorships that afflicted the region. Figueres' commitment to a war against Caribbean tyrannies was personal;[2] it may have been shared by some of his followers, but certainly it was not representative of the consensus of even the Social Democratic party. As the insurrectionary movement evolved, it became even more distinctly Figueres'. He stood to lose most if revolution failed. If it succeeded, he was assured of a prominent position in Costa Rican politics and was likely to become the arbiter of the nation's destinies, as well as an international figure of some stature. Previous efforts to organize and bring off an insurrection having failed, Figueres could only continue to plan, keep up with events, mend fences when necessary, and hope that somehow the results of the election would not be accepted by all sides. That they were not, had, of course, not been left to chance.[3]

Figueres' most important lieutenant in Costa Rica during the last months preceding the revolution was Alexander Murray, a Canadian citizen reared in Costa Rica.[4] Murray had been trained by the British intelligence in Canada and had served in Great Britain

[1] Castro Cervantes, according to *La Nación* (February 19, 1949, p. 1), wanted to avoid another administration by Calderón Guardia, for he thought it would lead the nation to civil war. He believed that the prolonged political crisis was leading the nation toward war and therefore sought a pacific solution from 1945 forward. However, at the same time, he contributed to the revolutionary coffers.

[2] See chapter 5.

[3] See chapter 6.

[4] Dr. Rosendo Argüello, hijo, identifies Murray as a most amiable gentleman, a Canadian citizen, who had worked with British intelligence in France during World War II (*Quienes y como nos traicionaron*, p. 60 [Pamphlet]. In a three-page cable message to Mr. Luce, publisher of *Time* magazine, Murray identified himself as a British subject, born in Costa Rica ("Murray Collection," fol. III, item 15).

during World War II; his capabilities included "unarmed combat, surveillance, the arts of sabotage, the fabrication of explosive and incendiary devices using materials easily purchased. He could make and write with secret inks, use different kinds of codes and ciphers for communicating with other agents."[5] This expertise and experience Murray put at the disposal of the conspirators. His contribution to the cause of the Second Republic probably was exceeded only by that of Figueres himself.

Throughout January, 1948, Figueres and Argüello struggled with the problem of how to transport the arms, obtained under the terms of the Pact of the Caribbean, from Guatemala to Costa Rica. They considered shipping them overland by bus, by launch to Dominical, by unregistered flight, or by a flight registered for David, Panama, which enroute would land in Costa Rica.[6] In addition to the indecision of the conspirators on the best manner of getting the arms into the country, the shipment was also delayed because of Arévalo's reluctance to release the arms, and the appeals from other exile groups who desired them for their own insurrections.

As the election drew near, Figueres seemed optimistic about his military prospects. In January, 1948, he wrote Argüello in Guatemala that since signing the pact he had revived the organization which had been partially disbanded since August, 1947: "Even though it seems a lie, there are 450 boys duly distributed in groups, ready for action. They have enough training, speaking in Costa Rican terms. They are all persons of some culture. Here the *peón* does not lend himself to these affairs."[7]

When Calderón Guardia decided to charge fraud, following Ulate's apparent electoral victory, the justification for an insurrection seemed at hand. If the *calderonistas* remained adamant, Figueres could count on support from the mass of the Opposition to protect the electoral victory of Ulate. However, the possible occurrence of two events might remove the ostensible cause of the revolution:

[5] H. Montgomery Hyde, *Room 3603*, p. 227. Murray's activities during the war are mentioned in Bruce Marshall, *The White Rabbit*, p. 45.

[6] "Murray Collection," fol. I, item 61.

[7] Ibid., fol. I, item 53.

Calderón Guardia might accept Ulate's victory either before or
after the verdict of the Electoral Tribunal; or the *ulatistas* and
calderonistas might reach a mutually acceptable compromise. The
specter of an "infamous" political transaction, narrowly averted in
the period 1944 through 1946, returned to haunt Figueres' plans for
the establishment of the Second Republic.

The impasse following the election was unprecedented in Costa
Rican experience. Not even the most astute politicians could calcu-
late a basis for an accord. The *ulatistas* affirmed their determination
to accept only the verdict that had been "popularly reached at the
polls." In the chaos and uncertainty of those days, the Electoral
Tribunal failed to assert its full authority. Its belated verdict left
virtually no time for the followers of Ulate and Calderón Guardia
to seek an *entente*.[8]

The *calderonistas* interpreted the tribunal's vacillation as an indication that it was an Opposition redoubt. The various factors supporting this thesis were the tribunal's refusal to consider the charge
of fraud, its incomplete scrutiny of the votes cast, its use of members of the Opposition as guards, and its final recourse to the count
of the *ulatistas*. Seen in this context the tribunal's final verdict was
construed as being merely another move in a long war of nerves.

The *calderonistas*, in general, thought that Picado had reacted
far too circumspectly to the threat of their adversaries. They resolved to frustrate Ulate's election by making use of the advantage
given them by their majority in Congress and their control of the
nation's military forces and the police. The alternative, in their
opinion, was to accept the ignominious defeat that the Opposition
had been able to "fraudulently" engineer because of Picado's mis-
judgment of the tenor of the struggle.

On March 1, 1948, the *calderonistas* accepted the challenge of the
Opposition that they interpreted as being implicit in the verdict of
the tribunal, and, using their majority in the Congress, they an-

---

[8] The verdict was expected on February 25, but the tribunal tried to follow
the letter of the law by formally closing its scrutiny of the election while, in
fact, continuing it in closed session. The verdict was finally rendered on February 28.

nulled Ulate's election. Tavío's attack on the Opposition leaders assembled at Carlos Luis Valverde's home and the death of Valverde himself, further lessened the possibility for a peaceful settlement.

There were renewed efforts at compromise but with slight hope of success, each side having first to appreciate the strength of its adversary before agreement would be broached. The *calderonistas*, convinced that they had predominant power and had been pushed to the extreme by the insurgency of the Opposition, were determined, after the events of March 1, to exact harsh terms from the *ulatistas*.[9] Their terms became far less rigid after the initial skirmishes of the armed conflict,[10] but by then the initiative belonged to Figueres and he had spelled out his terms on repeated occasions. His firm purpose was to establish the Second Republic and this could be accomplished only after the fall of the first.

With the events of March 1, the long political conflict was converted into a contest of arms. The *calderonistas* and *vanguardistas* miscalculated the force at the disposition of the Opposition. They had never quite taken seriously the threat posed by Figueres or the Social Democratic party, nor were they fully aware of Figueres' international activities and connections.

On March 10, 1948, Figueres' forces, having made themselves fast on his farm La Lucha, began what they called "The War of National Liberation." After informing his supporters in San José

[9] Comisión Política de Vanguardia Popular writes concerning Calderón Guardia's position: "Dr. Calderón Guardia meanwhile opposed, with all his power, possible transactions; he expected that Congress which was to convene on May 1 would be inclined in his favor, since he had been defeated by fraud and it would elect him First Designate to the Presidency of the Republic, from which position he would assume command" (*Como y porqué cayó la democracia en Costa Rica*, p. 9).

[10] Ulate and Calderón Guardia arrived at a compromise solution at the end of March that was acceptable to Manuel Mora. The key to the agreement called for Congress to elect Dr. Julio César Ovares, a member of Unión Nacional, as the first designate to the presidency. He then would serve as the chief executive for a period of two years to conciliate the nation and prepare it for new elections (Teodoro Picado, *El Pacto de la Embajada de Mexico*, p. 7 [Pamphlet]). *La Nación* on the occasion of the death of Dr. Ovares carried a two-column biographical sketch (June 14, 1964, p. 16).

of his decision to begin hostilities, Figueres sent out two groups, one to block the Pan American Highway and the other to capture San Isidro del General.[11] On the morning of March 12, they captured the town and, with assistance from TACA (Transportes Aéreos Centro Americanos) employees in San José, took three DC-3 airplanes which belonged to the airline. They immediately dispatched the planes to Guatemala to pick up the officers and the arms provided by General Juan Rodríguez with the approval of President Arévalo and Colonels Arbenz and Arana.[12] The DC-3's made nineteen trips for arms, ammunition, and men during the forty days of conflict which followed.[13]

On March 12, the Costa Rican government sent an exploratory group, under Colonel Rigoberto Pacheco Tinoco, south on the Pan American Highway to investigate rumors that Figueres was preparing a revolt. A National Liberation force ambushed them from the heights on either side of the highway not far from La Lucha. Three officers died in the encounter. Among them was the commander of the force.[14]

On the afternoon of March 12, the revolutionaries assumed easily defended positions in an area along the highway called La Sierra. There, later in the day, they withstood the initial government offensive and from their superior placement inflicted heavy casualties on their adversaries, forcing them to withdraw in general

[11] San Isidro is the principal populated area in the valley of El General; it is located about ninety-five miles south of San José on the Pan American Highway. La Lucha is between Cartago and San Isidro.

[12] The influence of Arana was of crucial and revealing importance, for as head of the armed forces he had ultimate control of the arms. The Guatemalan constitution, at that time, made the military virtually a fourth power along with the executive, the legislative, and the judicial.

[13] *Time*, March 29, 1948, p. 42. Rafael Obregón Loría, *Conflictos militares y políticos de Costa Rica*, p. 117; and Arturo Castro Esquivel, *José Figueres Ferrer*, p. 42.

[14] Obregón Loría, *Conflictos militares*, p. 117. Picado (*El Pacto*, p. 7) describes the military establishment as being composed of less than three hundred men, who with very few exceptions lacked formal training and battle experience. Pacheco was an exception, for he had served as a noncommissioned officer in the Spanish Army of Africa.

panic.[15] Had the government troops pressed their attack at this time, it is possible that they could have changed the course of the revolution and perhaps even have forced its leaders to flee the country, since the arms and men from Guatemala had yet to reach the insurgents.

On the following day, two rebel groups returned to La Lucha from San Isidro del General. They were under the command of Miguel Angel Ramírez, a native of the Dominican Republic who had been appointed chief of staff of the Army of National Liberation upon his arrival from Guatemala.[16] He reached La Lucha in time to direct the defense against an intense government attack on the morning of March 14. The government forces had withdrawn toward nightfall because they were unfamiliar with the region. When they renewed their attack the following morning they were routed.[17] During the night the long-awaited military equipment had arrived from San Isidro.

For greater security Figueres moved his general headquarters to the town of Santa María de Dota. The troops evacuated his farms which were subsequently burned by government forces. Figueres' army was augmented each day with fresh contingents of men, generally of the middle class and between the ages of seventeen and thirty who arrived at Santa María de Dota for training and assignment to one of the areas of operation.[18] There the Costa Ricans received intensive military training from the experienced men who had come from Guatemala.

The role of this group, later called the Caribbean Legion, has been one of the most debated of the revolution. Figueres' opponents, by exaggerating its importance, tried to demean the efforts of the Army of National Liberation. On the other hand, Figueres and his

[15] Teodoro Picado, "Comentario sobre el folleto *Como y porqué cayó la democracia en Costa Rica*," p. 5.

[16] Obregón Loría, *Conflictos militares*, p. 118.

[17] Argüello, *Quienes y como*, pp. 39–40.

[18] Obregón Loría, *Conflictos militares*, p. 118. Carlos María Jiménez, *La legión Caribe*, pp. 11–34, gives a good description of how the youths reached the area of operations. His comments throughout the work are suggestive as to their social position and motivation.

followers, once in power, tried to minimize the contribution of the Legion's non–Costa Rican forces to their victory. They pointed out that throughout the conflict the vast majority of the troops were Costa Rican and that political control had remained firmly in Figueres' hands. In addition, the whole network of intelligence and subversion operated under Murray, who, although not Costa Rican, was completely identified with Figueres and apparently had no connections with the Caribbean Legion.

The contributions of the Caribbean Legion to the struggle were crucial. Without the almost unlimited supply of arms, ammunition, and fuel that Figueres, because of his association with the Legion, had been able to obtain from Guatemala, a successful revolt could hardly have been staged. If Figueres had chosen to revolt with an ill-equipped force, the government troops easily could have defeated the Army of National Liberation. The legion also supplied critical military skills that the traditionally pacific Costa Ricans lacked. The general staff of the revolutionary army was composed of exiles from Caribbean nations who had accompanied the arms from Guatemala. The exile group gave the insurrectionaries a technical military advantage over the regular forces of the Costa Rican army. The enthusiasm, youth, dedication, and generally high level of vitality of the Costa Rican revolutionaries combined well with the skilled leadership of the legion.[19]

The *legionarios* took part in the Costa Rican conflict in order to establish a base for their subsequent activities. Their numbers increased throughout the forty-day campaign. Their role was far more important than that of simple custodians of "hardware." Once Figueres was in power, the mere presence of hundreds of loyal, armed, and militarily organized foreigners discouraged efforts at a counterrevolution.

At the beginning of the campaign, the revolutionaries fought defensive battles in San Isidro del General and along the Pan Ameri-

---

[19] The best single source on the role of the Caribbean Legion is found in Argüello, *Quienes y como.* Almost all contemporary accounts of the fighting recognize that the legion made a significant contribution. Several of these are by members of the legion.

can Highway. They needed the former for logistical reasons and the latter because its familiar terrain worked to their advantage. The general headquarters were defended on all sides with detachments of only small units of thirty to forty men, leaving the bulk of the men in Santa María de Dota to prepare for the offensive.

A second group of revolutionaries fought skirmishes to the north of the city of Alajuela in the cantons of San Ramón and San Carlos. The group led by Francisco Orlich managed to capture and hold San Ramón for two hours, on the first day of the revolution, and then carried out a strategy of distracting the government forces from the southern front.[20]

The government responded weakly to the uprising. Picado wanted to avoid bloodshed, and he seemed to proceed on the premise that the presumably greater force at the disposition of the government would easily permit it to contain the rebellion. He almost immediately accepted the idea of workers' militias[21] to supplement the meager army of some three hundred men.[22] The volunteers supplemented the regular troops and also formed independent units. These units proved the most effective forces under Picado's command, particularly when contrasted with certain shortcomings of the regular forces. Several of the government's messages intercept-

---

[20] Obregón Loría, *Conflictos militares*, p. 120; Maurilio Arias, "En Tilarán y Cañas si existió segundo frente," *Diario de Costa Rica*, June 11, 1948, p. 2; Alvaro Chacón Jinesta, "Operaciones en el frente norte," *Diario de Costa Rica*, May 1, 1948, p. 3.

[21] Comisión Política de Vanguardia Popular, *Como y porqué cayó la democracia en Costa Rica*, p. 9. Picado saw the irony of his having accepted support of the workers: "The backing which the working classes gave me, with admirable resolution and abnegation, served as a pretext so that it was said that my government was in the hands of the reds, and that a regime of the center . . . which on international questions always loyally seconded the democratic policy of the United States, was 'Communist.'

"I could not refuse the support which the workers valiantly gave me, but I understood that their help served as a source of scandal and seemed to prove malevolent international propaganda, which I had no means to counter, and which presented Costa Rica as a second Czechoslovakia, as Haya de la Torre has called it" (*El Pacto*, pp. 9–10).

[22] Picado, *El Pacto*, p. 7: "The army was ridiculously small, it did not surpass three hundred men."

ed by Alex Murray's intelligence net revealed the ineptness and lack of dedication of many of the untrained officers of the Costa Rican military establishment as well as their difficulty in establishing the necessary rapport with their heterogeneous troops.[23]

Irregular government troops controlled the banana zone around Golfito, on the Pacific coast. One of their assignments was to recapture San Isidro del General. Under the command of Carlos Luis Fallas, the labor leader, and General Toribio Tijerino they set out from Dominical for their objective.[24] Tijerino had earned his rank in the Nicaraguan army, Guardia Nacional, before being exiled and becoming a resident of Costa Rica. The rival forces skirmished all along the route until the government contingent finally reached San Isidro. There the battle lasted thirty-six hours, during the course of which control of the town briefly passed to Fallas' men. After suffering heavy losses and exhausting their supplies, the government forces withdrew to return to the coast. As they retreated General Tijerino was killed.

In the wake of a bitter battle at El Empalme, March 14 and 15, Picado decided on a policy of containing the insurgents within the limited area they controlled along the Pan American Highway. The only exception to this general rule was that the militia, under the command of Fallas, was to carry out an offensive in the south. The government established a defense perimeter which ran from Casamata, a populated area on the Pan American Highway between Cartago and El Empalme, and Frailes, to a western locality in the canton of Desamparados.[25]

The inadequately trained government forces carelessly expended

---

[23] An example of the first-mentioned phenomenon appears in "Murray Collection," fol. IX, item 21. The commander in chief writes to inquire about the absence of his field commander. The acting commander answers that he had been in charge for four days and that the commander comes and goes.

A good example of the lack of rapport appears in fol. IX, item 9: "Tell him that these people are unbearable; even I am fed up with them . . . send our people."

[24] Fallas had some military fame as the organizer of armed resistance in the labor strife of 1934 in the banana plantations of the Atlantic coast. See Obregón Loría, *Conflictos militares*, p. 114.

[25] Obregón Loría, Ibid., p. 119.

their arms and ammunition during the first days of the revolution and then experienced difficulty in obtaining new supplies. The United States publicly refused to grant the export permit necessary for the purchase of small arms.[26] General Anastasio Somoza, whose friendship had been carefully cultivated by the National Republican administrations, offered armed men, but no arms. Mexico consistently manifested interest in the *calderonistas'* cause but found itself unable to help the government when it was in dire need.[27]

The Costa Rican officers themselves seemed to have been reluctant to arm the swelling numbers of irregulars who volunteered to defend the government even as well as circumstances permitted.[28] The volunteers were mostly workers from the coasts, *mariachis* who were ready to fight to protect their social gains of the past eight years. They received virtually no training and were sent to the front in an atmosphere of disorganization and growing indifference on the part of politically appointed officers.

In the capital of San José, Manuel Mora continually strengthened his position. He held in reserve a disciplined force of 1,500 *vanguardista* workers, for he realized that his alliance with the government was seriously strained and that San José remained the key to victory. By the third week of the revolution, it was obvious that neither Picado nor Calderón Guardia controlled Mora or the general situation in San José. The Vanguardia Popular leader was quoted as saying: "The people must seal their social gains with blood," and "I will not compromise or throw away anything for which I have fought for twenty-five years."[29]

More than any other group allied with the government Van-

[26] Picado, "Comentario sobre . . . *Como y porqué*," p. 1.

[27] "Murray Collection," fol. II, item 21, contains the official permission granted by President Miguel Alemán of Mexico to Captain Enrique Wallberg to serve with the Costa Rican forces. In fol. VII, item 18, Murray somewhat cryptically told Figueres: "Government desperately trying to get more arms. Sent 24,000 dollars to Mexico. Plane sent to get them will not come back."

[28] Comisión Política de Vanguardia Popular. *Como y porqué*, p. 9. Carlos Luis Fallas, *Reseña de la intervención y penetración yanqui en Centro América*, p. 12. [Pamphlet.]

[29] *Time*, April 19, 1948, p. 42. Mora had brought the *mariachis* to San José again, on March 8, as he had done in the general strike of 1947.

guardia Popular had reasons for strong prosecution of the conflict and a last-ditch defense, since the Opposition had promised to dissolve the group if they came to power. Ironically, Vanguardia Popular, a part of an international movement, found itself isolated with only somewhat indifferent support from the very government it was defending. The Social Democrats, on the other hand, a purely indigenous party, received crucial assistance from other democratic elements in the Caribbean area and significant, if not open, assistance from the United States.[30]

The Army of National Liberation continued to fight defensively until April 10 when the long and well-planned offensive began. A specially trained group under the command of Mayor Horacio Ornes departed from Santa María de Dota for San Isidro del General.[31] It flew to Altamira in the north, only thirty-one miles from the Nicaraguan border, as a diversionary tactic.[32] While waiting in Altamira to resume the flight to Puerto Limón, its real objective, the group sustained several unsuccessful bombing raids carried out by the converted DC-3's which the government used to drop the homemade bombs manufactured by Julio López Masegosa.[33]

[30] Picado lists the assistance from the United States in his "Comentario sobre *Como y porqué*": "It is true that the State Department encouraged the Costa Rican Opposition. We cite a few cases: (a) It was prohibited that the manufacturer of submachine guns, Thompson, sell us 50 pieces and the State Department made the prohibition public; (b) the American government reduced an order for 50 Reising submachine guns to 25; (c) Don Otilio Ulate, the visible adversary of the government over which I presided, was treated with great affection in various ways by the American government; (d) the military attaché of the American Embassy frequented with assiduity oppositionist circles" (p. 1). Later Picado acknowledges that "it is true that the Public Roads Administration helped the rebels and that Figueres obtained a plane in the Canal Zone" (p. 5).

Comisión Política de Vanguardia Popular, *Como y porqué* (pp. 3–6), discusses the assistance but with much less plausibility. Several items in the "Murray Collection" indicate that Col. J. R. Hughes did in fact assist the insurrectionists. See also, José Albertazzi Avendaño, *La tragedia de Costa Rica*, and Picado, *El Pacto*, p. 10. *La Nación*, May 8, 1948, reported Hughes among those honored by Figueres for having contributed to the insurrection.

[31] Obregón Loría, *Conflictos militares*, p. 119.

[32] This movement, perhaps, convinced Somoza of the desirability of sending his troops into Costa Rica, for shortly thereafter they occupied Ciudad Quesada.

[33] López Masegosa fought in the Spanish Civil War as a Republican, then es-

On April 11, Ornes took Puerto Limón by surprise. Within a few hours, his men were in control of the city except for some resistance from Vanguardia Popular snipers. The revolutionaries suffered only two fatalities in the operation. The following day, they repulsed the government force sent to retake Puerto Limón, at the nearby town of Moín.

The next objective of the revolutionary offensive was Costa Rica's second largest city, Cartago, approximately twelve miles from the capital. Figueres departed from Santa María de Dota on April 10 with nearly six hundred men. He intended to take the city by surprise by avoiding the roads and passing through the forest to infiltrate across the patrolled enemy lines between Casamata and Frailes. The plan called for the force to enter Cartago on the morning of April 11. This effort would coordinate with the capture of Puerto Limón by interdicting the railroad between San José and the coast and thus prevent government reinforcements from reaching the port.[34] The march through rugged terrain was more arduous than anticipated, however, and the party had to stop for the day in order to avoid discovery by loyalist troops. On April 12, the revolutionaries quickly occupied Cartago and fortified the heights of Ochomogo, which overlooked the road from San José. Within a matter of hours the only remaining resistance was the Cartago barracks. With the fall of Cartago, the minister of foreign relations convoked a special meeting of the diplomatic corps accredited in San José.

Picado had been dispirited since mid-March when, after the first government offenses, he recognized that the revolutionaries had the will and the capacity for strong resistance which, along with the international implications, meant a long and bloody struggle. He had little heart for the contest; many of the revolutionaries were sons or relatives of personal friends and some were even his former students.

The President was greatly distressed by the intrusion of the in-

---

tablished himself in Costa Rica where he owned a brewery. For his role in defending the Picado government, see Argüello, *Quienes y como*, p. 40.

[34] Then as now, no highway ran between Puerto Limón and the interior.

ternational situation on the affairs of the nation and feared for the more than five hundred political prisoners arrested during the revolution. He stated that it had been very difficult to put friends in prison[35] and realized that many of them would have been sacrificed had he decided to defend San José.

Throughout the campaign, the revolutionaries made extensive use of propaganda and subversion in San José. The intelligence network coordinated by Murray kept Figueres and his men fully advised as to the state of government forces. They even succeeded in intercepting messages from the government to its field commanders. A series of broadsides containing a number of deliberately misleading items, signed with the pseudonym "B. Marstad, Correspondent on the Southern Front," served to confuse the enemy as well as the foreign press.[36] Through his contact with Edward "Ted" Scott of the *Panama American*, Murray was able to extend adroit rumormongering beyond Costa Rica.[37]

In two radio messages to the nation, Figueres explained the significance of the revolution and exhorted those not fighting at the front to carry on a campaign of civil disobedience. He also forcefully disputed the allegation that National Liberation was a rightist movement, as the foreign press at first represented it and as the government continued to do throughout the struggle. He pledged to honor the election of Ulate, but he also stressed that his movement was not going to reestablish a nineteenth-century liberal democracy and would, instead, found the Second Republic. He made it clear that the new regime would be socialist and that welfare leg-

---

[35] Picado, *El Pacto*, p. 12.

[36] "Murray Collection," fol. II, item 23.

[37] The role of Edward "Ted" Scott of the *Panama American* remains perplexing. It would seem that he was actively collaborating with the Figueres forces, particularly with Alex Murray, Figueres' principal contact in San José during the insurrection. One item in the "Murray Collection" clearly indicates that Scott collaborated or, at least, took more than a normal journalistic interest in the uprising. In a letter to Scott dated April 14, 1948, Murray explained, "I am writing this letter to you in order to see if you will help lick these bastard Communists here in Costa Rica." He went on to ask him to contact a Mr. Aguilar who had $20,000 with which to buy arms (Fol. II, item 26).

islation would be extended, not abrogated.[38] His emphasis on the social orientation of his revolution was such that Murray warned him to be more cautious until after victory, since some of his supporters in San José were apprehensive about his leftist pronouncements.[39] The largely rightist Opposition accepted his statements only because they considered them necessary to neutralize elements sympathetic to the government.

On April 13, a cease fire was arranged and the diplomatic corps began conversations with the revolutionary forces.[40] The Papal Nuncio, Luigi Centoz, and the United States ambassador, Nathaniel P. Davis, acted in the name of the diplomatic corps. Negotiations began for the transfer of authority in San José and the arrival of the Army of National Liberation.

On April 14, Picado privately decided to turn over the presidency to Santos León Herrera, the third designate to the presidency, and to that effect sent him a note asking him to return from his farm to San José.[41] This was Picado's method of preserving the constitutional transfer of power, providing that it prove acceptable to all parties to the negotiations.

Seven times in five days "a black Cadillac, flying a small American flag and with a yellow and white papal banner draped across its hood, carried United States Ambassador Nathaniel P. Davis and the Papal Nuncio Luigi Centoz" to Figueres' headquarters in Cartago. It also carried Figueres' special emissary, Father Benjamín Núñez, to negotiate with government representatives in San José.[42]

---

[38] Arturo Castro Esquivel, *José Figueres Ferrer*, pp. 116–119, quotes the text of the two official pronouncements of National Liberation authorized by Figueres during the conflict. On pp. 124–127, Castro Esquivel cites Figueres' statement from Cartago on what had been the purposes of the revolution and his plan for the future of Costa Rica.

[39] "Murray Collection," fol. VII, item 17.

[40] Picado, *El Pacto*, p. 12.

[41] Ibid., pp. 16–17.

[42] Ibid., pp. 16–18. Picado refused to consider the first proposal, which Davis and Centoz brought back from Cartago. In it, Figueres proposed that he, Fernando Valverde, and Alberto Martén be elected by Congress as first, second, and third designates to the presidency respectively. That is to say, a new government was to be formed by the revolutionaries under the existing constitution and Fi-

The National Republican leaders prepared to abandon San José. Picado's wife was already in Managua. *Vanguardia Popular*, however, virtually controlled San José and impeded any general exodus. It was ready to accept the unhappy alternative of plunging the nation into a full-scale civil war should the terms of the surrender be unacceptable.[43] Understandably, Mora saw *Vanguardia Popular*'s existence in jeopardy and refused to accept Picado's orders to give up his barracks.

Vanguardistas had seized the airport and blocked both railroads leading out from the capital. They began positioning political prisoners on the top floors of prominent buildings to discourage air attacks should the situation reach a showdown.[44] Mora's defiance reached the point of forbidding Calderón Guardia and Picado to leave the country and announcing that he would continue to fight as long as necessary.

Somoza was disposed to send his troops from Nicaragua to pacify Costa Rica on his own terms but offered no further assistance to the Costa Rican government.[45] His major concern was to defeat Fi-

---

gueres as first designate would assume the presidency. This proposal which would have led to immediate difficulties with the *ulatistas* is reproduced in Picado, *El Pacto*, opposite p. 12.

Núñez early joined the struggle against Calderón Guardia. In 1943, he organized the Confederación Costarricense de Trabajadores Rerum Novarum which identified itself closely with other elements in opposition to the National Republicans. Rerum Novarum competed directly with the CTCR (Confederación de Trabajadores de Costa Rica) for the adherence of the organized labor unions and in the organization of new unions. Núñez' involvement with social reform and the labor movement reflected the interest of his mentor and patron, Archbishop Víctor Manuel Sanabria.

[43] *Time*, April 5, 1948, p. 38.

[44] In Murray's letter to Scott (See fn. 37 of this chapter), his opinion on April 14, 1948, was that "these arms must come forward because it is certain that the Communists will keep on fighting. . . ." ("Murray Collection," fol. II, item 26). In another instance, Murray told Figueres that political prisoners in San José were being put on the top floors of buildings to discourage bombing. and that locomotives had been placed across the railroad tracks to stop anyone from entering or leaving the city by train. He advised him against insisting on unconditional surrender, since he thought the Communists were ready to fight to the last ("Murray Collection," fol. VII, item 10).

[45] Picado had gone secretly to Managua at the request of Somoza. There the

gueres' forces because he presumed that the Caribbean Legion considered his overthrow a prime goal. He feared that, once in power, Figueres would allow his allies the use of Costa Rican territory as a base for their activities.

Vanguardia Popular viewed Nicaraguan attempts at pacification with a wary eye, since it looked upon Somoza as a "puppet" of the United States. Mora appealed to all forces in the nation to be prepared to repel the proposed Nicaraguan intervention. He announced that Vanguardia Popular was willing to close ranks with National Liberation to oppose the troops should Somoza send them into Costa Rica.[46]

President Picado realized that a Nicaraguan invasion would unite his people, but he was also aware that tremendous suffering and destruction would accompany a "pacification" effort against a united Costa Rica. He did not doubt the valor of this people; however, he realized that they were ill-equipped to encounter the vastly superior military establishment of the Somoza dictatorship.

The events that took place from the occupation of Cartago by the Army of National Liberation, on April 12, until the signing of the pact that ended the conflict were most varied and complex. Distinct interests were at play, and decisions that could affect life in Costa Rica for the next decades hung in the balance, although the nation was hardly aware of the transcendent nature of the period. The military posture of the revolutionaries had improved immensely. After the insurgents captured the nation's major port on the Atlantic, their allies could ship men and arms in quantities limited only by the size of the ocean-going vessels.

---

terms and nature of assistance to be offered by Nicaragua to Costa Rica were made clear. Picado was presented with a letter in which he was to ask for assistance "against Figueres and communism." He was then to leave San José and establish a temporary capital in Liberia in the province of Guanacaste. The Guardia Nacional of Nicaragua would then "pacify" Costa Rica. The most complete account of the affair appears in Comisión Política de Vanguardia Popular, *Como y porqué*, p. 10. Picado, in his "Comments," "Comentario sobre . . . *Como y porqué*," asserts that the account was accurate with the exception that no representative of the United States participated in the affair as asserted by Vanguardia Popular (p. 5).

[46] Comisión Política de Vanguardia Popular, *Como y porqué*, pp. 13–14.

At the very moment when Figueres began his negotiations with the diplomatic corps on April 13, the bloodiest battle of the conflict was raging at El Tejar, a small town a few miles south of Cartago. The bulk of the government forces, which had maintained the front at Casamata, had come into contact with a platoon of the Army of National Liberation, engaged in mopping-up exercises in the vicinity of El Tejar. Although it might have seemed reasonable to assume that the government forces were moving on toward Cartago, that was not the case. The forces were in disarray and, it would seem, their movements lacked coordination from the high command in San José. There was as yet no movement of troops from the capital, even though General Roberto Tinoco and his men still defended the Cartago barracks.[47] The most reasonable explanation for the presence of troops from Casamata is that they did not realize that Cartago had fallen and were returning to San José for provisions and instructions. On route they encountered a small contingent of insurgents outside El Tejar, which immediately broke for cover. The remnants of the patrol alerted their comrades in Cartago to the approach of the government troops that they had encountered.

When the government troops reached the plaza of El Tejar, the revolutionaries had made themselves fast. They cut down the government troops in what must be described as a slaughter. The estimates of the government casualties ran as high as 400 with at least 190 dead. The revolutionaries lost only 14 men.[48]

The President became even more convinced that the nation desperately needed an end to the conflict. A negotiated peace with Figueres, to which Vanguardia Popular would accede, recommended itself to him rather than unconditional surrender, for the government still commanded most of the nation, had the capacity to hold San José, and could possibly retake Cartago. In addition, the fact that revolutionaries had reached the *meseta central*, seemed to indi-

[47] Argüello, *Quienes y como*, pp. 48–51.
[48] Argüello attributes the high casualties of the government to atrocities on the part of a few of the Costa Rican revolutionary leaders. There is no corroboration for his assertion in other accounts (ibid., pp. 50–53).

cate that within a matter of days the situation would degenerate into civil war. On April 15, therefore, the President, having first explained to Roberto Tinoco the futility of further defense, surrendered the Cartago barracks. The peace negotiations prospered even though the *vanguardistas* continued preparing for combat in San José, and the revolutionaries accepted increasing numbers of recruits in Cartago.

On April 16, the secretary of foreign relations replied to a note from the Nicaraguan government in which Nicaragua requested Costa Rica to secure its northern frontier against any revolutionary activities that could result in an invasion of Nicaragua. The Costa Rican government stated its inability to give such guarantees and granted permission to Nicaragua to fortify the frontier for its own protection.[49]

On April 17, three seemingly disparate events took place that had significant effects on the tactical and strategic posture of the government and further endangered both Picado's position and the future of the nation. The first was a warning by Figueres that, if the Communists continued to resist, the Army of National Liberation would have to march on the capital. He further stated that no concessions would be made to conflict with anti-Communist policies of the United States.[50] American concern over the extent of Communist influence in the Americas had increased dramatically following the Bogotazo of April 9. 1948.[51] Figueres, recognizing the interest and influence of the United States in Central America, wanted to leave no possible doubt as to the position of his movement vis-à-vis the Cold War.

The second event of April 17 was the occupation of Villa Quesada in northern Costa Rica by a Nicaraguan airborne expeditionary force. Somoza intended to meet any threatened invasion of his

---

[49] Enrique Guier, *Defensa de los Señores Licenciados Don Teodoro Picado y Don Vicente Urcuyo*, pp. 14–21. [Pamphlet.]

[50] *Newsweek*, April 26, 1948, p. 42, quotes Figueres.

[51] Vernon L. Fluharty, *The Dance of the Millions: Military Rule and the Social Revolution in Colombia* (pp. 100–107), contains a good account of the events in Bogotá on April 9, 1948.

country outside Nicaraguan borders. He was also prepared to move against the Army of National Liberation and Vanguardia Popular, if necessary. These Nicaraguan troops remained on Costa Rican soil until after the peace was signed and Vanguardia Popular disarmed. They evacuated Costa Rican territory on April 21.[52]

The third event of that fated day concerned information received by Picado that a United States force had been organized in the Canal Zone. It was on standby status ready to be transported to Costa Rica and, in the character of a police force, would end the hostilities now that the combatants had been clearly identified as Communists and seemed to be in control of San José.[53]

Thus by the evening of April 17, the situation in Costa Rica had become an extremely grave one. The country confronted the strong possibility of an unprecedented holocaust; Figueres' forces were poised in Cartago, Mora's followers were preparing to resist in San José, hundreds of political prisoners were gathered on the top floors of buildings in the capital, the Nicaraguan National Guard occupied Villa Quesada, and Picado faced the possibility of intervention by United States forces. Under such pressing circumstances, a swiftly achieved negotiated peace became an absolute necessity.

In a letter dated April 18 and addressed to Calderón Guardia and Mora, Picado expressed his conviction that the attempt to hold San José would be futile and catastrophic. He guaranteed a general amnesty, and he assured them that the labor movement would not suffer reprisals for the support it had given to the government.[54]

In response to the grave situation which Costa Rica faced, the diplomatic corps met in the Mexican Embassy on April 18 to consider means of terminating the negotiations quickly. On the following day, in the presence of the members of the diplomatic corps, Picado and Núñez signed a pact ending the conflict. This pact pro-

---

52 Guier, *Defensa*, pp. 22–24; and Comisión Política de Vanguardia Popular, *Como y porqué*, p. 11.

53 Ricardo Fernández Guardia, *Cartilla histórica de Costa Rica*, p. 155. Albertazzi (*La tragedia*, p. 76) reports that Figueres received planes from the Canal Zone. Also see Comisión Política de Vanguardia Popular, *Como y porqué*, p. 1.

54 Picado, *El Pacto*, pp. 5–6.

vided for the interim presidency of Santos León Herrera, the third designate. It gave the critical position of secretary of public security to Miguel Brenes Gutiérrez, who commanded the respect of both sides.[55]

The Pact of the Mexican Embassy was not based on a victor's demand for unconditional terms but rather provided generous terms for the departure of the National Republican and Vanguardia Popular leaders. The pact guaranteed the lives and property of the vanquished and provided for indemnification to all victims of the conflict, regardless of the side on which they had fought. It prohibited reprisals and stipulated that a general amnesty would be decreed. Finally, it stated that "the social rights and guarantees of all employees and workers would be respected and extended."[56] Mora's influence was particularly important for the inclusion of this final point, point seven, of the pact.[57]

The negotiated peace was consistent with Picado's character and his stance during his presidency. Throughout the conflict, the President had tried to hold together a nation riven by insurrection and the consequent serious dislocations. His many talents were characterized by an innate civility, and he had tried to maintain a standard of rational behavior throughout the conflict. When Aureo Morales, a man who had been in public service since the Cortés administration, went berserk and sought vengeance against his adversaries, Picado impartially ordered his capture during the last desperate weeks of the struggle, despite the fact that Morales was a colonel in the government forces.[58] On the previous day, April 5, the President ordered the release of a judge who had been taken prisoner in Guanacaste.[59] That this affair came to his attention through the Supreme Court indicates that the judicial system re-

[55] Ibid., p. 18, and Guier, *Defensa*, pp. 28–29.

[56] Ibid., pp. 19–20. *La Prensa Libre*, April 20, 1948, p. 2. On the same date in *La Prensa Libre* the Mexican Embassy published a communique of the diplomatic corps which summarized the negotiations.

[57] Obregón Loría, *Conflictos militares*, pp. 123–124.

[58] "Murray Collection," fol. IX, item 9.

[59] "Murray Collection," fol. IX, item 7.

mained operative despite the conflict. Perhaps the most convincing evidence of Picado's restrained and civil conduct was published unintentionally by his opponents in 1949. In a pamphlet dedicated "to the heroic dead" of the "War of Liberation," only two victims are listed as being from the city of San José. Although the loss of two lives is to be regretted, it seems almost a tribute to the government in power that only two insurrectionists lost their lives in the capital despite the hundreds of political prisoners, the presence of irregular troops, the existence of an active center of insurrectionary propaganda, and an inflamed atmosphere.[60]

On April 24, Figueres entered San José at the head of the Army of National Liberation, thus ending the bloodiest revolution in Costa Rican history. An estimated two thousand men were killed of which fewer than one hundred were from among the revolutionaries.[61] The National Liberation Movement had successfully carried out the military aspect of its program and now faced the task of founding the often-promised Second Republic.

On the occasion of the victory parade, on April 28, Figueres spoke of the causes of the revolution which went back to the election of 1940 and even before that. He referred to the *mariachis* as victims of the war. Suffrage and justice were the lost "jewels" of the "First Republic" and they would now be restored. He emphasized that the careful planning which distinguished the revolutionary movement would also characterize the Second Republic.[62]

The skillful execution of the movement had indeed contrasted sharply with the conduct of the National Republican government. The leaders of the Vanguardia Popular and the National Republican parties apparently had never considered seriously the possibility of a revolution when they called for the annulment of the election.[63] With its army, undisciplined and unready, the government

[60] See *La Guerra de la Liberación*, pp. 3–7. [Pamphlet.] The *figueristas* listed sixty-seven of their number as having been killed in the conflict which included two killed in San José in underground activities.

[61] Ibid., p. 7.

[62] Castro Esquivel, *José Figueres Ferrer*, pp. 146–150.

[63] "The general tendency of Costa Ricans was to resolve their political conflicts by means of conversations and transactions, conciliatory agreements. The

had weakly replied to the rebel challenge. The initially inadequate response simplified the revolutionaries' task of obtaining outside aid and of securing their position in the broken terrain of the south. The government's heavy reliance on Vanguardia Popular during the conflict proved an even greater miscalculation than its lack of preparation. Largely because of this association, the revolutionaries were able to utilize the new international situation to their advantage. The government thus found itself unable to obtain arms, and particularly ammunition, which limited the use of some of its best weapons. The control that Mora, through Vanguardia Popular, exerted over San José in the last days of the conflict helped convince Picado that the national good would be served by negotiations.

A political struggle, which had been transpiring at a secondary level in Costa Rica throughout the eight years prior to the revolution, was resolved in the last days of the military conflict. Both the National Liberation movement and the Vanguardia Popular had formed permanent ideologically based political parties. The latter represented the most dedicated group within the government, and the former, the one within the Opposition. Each had a program for Costa Rica which emphasized a planned economy and social guarantees. Both repudiated the oligarchy and dismissed nineteenth-century liberal thought as an adequate basis for a changing society. The National Liberation movement favored state ownership of only a few basic industries, whereas Vanguardia Popular postulated it for all means of production. When the revolution broke out, the confrontation was every day more apparent and direct.

As the conflict between the government and the revolutionaries deepened, these two minority elements, the Vanguardia Popular and the National Liberation movement, were counterpoised and

---

proof of this is that even in the midst of civil war Dr. Calderón Guardia, Otilio Ulate, and Manuel Mora, leader of the Vanguardia Popular, agreed that Dr. Julio César Ovares should become President; the formula failed as I have been told, because of the opposition of the Figueres group . . ." (Picado, *El Pacto*, p. 7).

reserved their choicest invective for each other. In late April, 1948, when the interim government was being formed, and with the inauguration of the Founding Junta of the Second Republic on May 8, 1948, there was little doubt as to the victor.[64]

[64] In the interim government, José Figueres, Fernando Valverde Vega, and Alberto Martén headed all the ministries (Castro Esquivel, *José Figueres Ferrer*, p. 134).

CHAPTER 8

Epilogue

Fᴵᴳᵁᴱᴿᴱˢ ˢᵁᶜᶜᴱᴱᴰᴱᴰ in making his
revolution. He persevered through partisan politics, ever-changing
patterns of international conspiracy, financial difficulties, arms
seizures, and finally a forty-day test of arms. On the path from
solitary rebel to the role of *caudillo* of the new order, he assumed
many often-contradictory obligations, both within and without
Costa Rica. These various commitments limited him and his followers in the realization of their revolutionary program. The great
mass of the Opposition expected Figueres' government to emphasize stability and pacification, for them the task of the victorious
revolution was one of restoration. The Social Democrats saw victory as only the beginning: the moment had arrived for the Generation of 1948 to transform Costa Rica. However, Figueres had yet
another moral debt, that to the Caribbean Legion. His agreement
to aid in the overthrow of dictatorships in the Caribbean conflicted

with the expectations of most of the Costa Ricans who had supported the revolution with their attention focused on domestic
rather than international questions.

Figueres' most pressing and immediate political problem was
how to reconcile his plans for the transformation of Costa Rica with
Ulate's clear claim to the presidency. The revolution ostensibly
sought to defend his election. However, Ulate definitely was a man
for the "first republic," given to pacific solutions and a strong
advocate of civil liberties. Had the uprising served merely to confirm Ulate's election, as so many thought it had, there would have
been no attempt to found the Second Republic.

On May 1, 1948, Figueres signed a pact with Ulate that removed
the last great obstacle to the founding of the Second Republic.
Figueres now had the opportunity to try to fit Costa Rica to his
ideas.[1] The Figueres-Ulate Pact, the first political transaction of
the new order, provided that a revolutionary junta should govern
for a period of eighteen months, during which time a constituent
assembly would be elected to enact a new constitution.[2] The constituent assembly would ratify the election of Ulate as the first
President of the Second Republic.[3]

With these agreements, Figueres, at the head of the National
Liberation movement, established a de facto government which
he controlled as President of the Founding Junta of the Second
Republic.[4] So empowered, the men of National Liberation en-

[1] Arturo Castro Esquivel, *José Figueres Ferrer*, pp. 152–153; and Marco Tulio
Zeledón, *Historia constitucional de Costa Rica en el bienio 1948–1949*, pp. 35–36.

[2] Zeledón (*Historia constitucional*, pp. 7–8 and 37) discusses the abrogation of
the Constitution of 1871 on May 8, 1948, by Decree Law No. 2. In the 1948 election for delegates to the Constituent Assembly the Social Democrats polled only
6,411 votes out of 82,000 (*La Nación*, December 10, 1948, p. 1).

[3] See *La Nación*, May 2, 1948, p. 11, and Zeledón, *Historia constitucional*,
p. 36, for the provisions of the agreement.

[4] Castro Esquivel, *José Figueres Ferrer*, pp. 159–160. Figueres organized the
junta along the lines of a president and his cabinet. The men chosen were drawn
from the inner circle of the revolutionary movement. For himself, he took the
title of President and commander in chief of the Regular Army of the Republic.
The Cabinet was made up as follows: minister of government, Fernando Valverde Vega; minister of public security, Edgar Cardona Quirós; minister of
public education, Professor Uladislao Gámez Solano; minister of labor, Father

deavored to fit the nation to the theoretical framework which they had developed for it.

The Pact of the Mexican Embassy had saved the people of Costa Rica from what would have been an extremely costly and bloody civil war between the Army of National Liberation and the Vanguardia Popular.[5] It saved the nation from further humiliation at the hands of foreign citizens and governments. It was a wise conclusion to the struggle which had rent the Costa Rican people. It promised concord, reconstruction, and the salvage of the rich Costa . Rican heritage of constitutional government.

. If one discounted the alien forces present in Costa Rica at the time the agreement was reached, the Pact of the Mexican Embassy reflected the power relationship then existing. The government had not been prostrated; it controlled most of the republic. Had Picado been willing to accept full-scale Nicaraguan intervention, the Army of National Liberation could have been dealt with in short order. The National Republicans remained the largest single political party in the nation. Vanguardia Popular had evidenced great vitality and determination during the struggle, despite the vacillations of the executive whom it supported. The agreement had provided for a negotiated peace, without limiting the basic rights of the vanquished. It established just bases for continuity and pacification.[6]

The Pact of the Mexican Embassy, however, was an obstacle to the Junta's program, for it contradicted one of the major premises of the Second Republic—that the old regime represented a de-

---

Benjamín Núñez; minister of justice, Gonzalo Facio Segreda; minister of economy, Alberto Martén; minister of public health, Dr. Raúl Blanco Cervantes; and minister of agriculture and industry, Dr. Bruce Masís Dibiassi.

[5] For a text of the pact see Teodoro Picado, *El Pacto de la Embajada de México*, pp. 18–20 [Pamphlet]; Rafael Obregón Loría, *Conflictos militares y políticos de Costa Rica*. pp. 122 and 124; or Comisión Política de Vanguardia Popular, *Como y porqué cayó la democracia en Costa Rica*, p. 12–13 [Pamphlet].

[6] For discussions of the provisions of the pact which brought the armed conflict to a close, see Picado, *El Pacto*, pp. 12–20; Zeledón. *Historia constitucional*, pp. 30–32; Enrique Guier, *Defensa de los Señores Licenciados Don Teodoro Picado y Don Vicente Urcuyo*, pp. 28–29 [Pamphlet], and Castro Esquivel, *José Figueres Ferrer*, p. 123.

pravity that could not be tolerated. Figueres had asserted on August 25, 1946, in a radio address to the nation: "Here the only thing that goes badly is everything, a whole political-social system in decadence that cannot be maintained. Here we should seek only a total transformation."[7]

Vanguardia Popular and the National Republican party were obstacles to "total transformation," as was the pact. Many of the members of both groups were forced into exile or imprisoned, and their goods were confiscated by "special courts."[8] They were dismissed from public and private employment, contrary to the law and the Pact of the Mexican Embassy. Vanguardia Popular as an organization was proscribed. On June 22, 1948, by Decree Law 77, the Revolutionary Junta, with Figueres at its head, declared the pact dissolved.[9]

Even before the junta had begun implementing its program, it had used up much of its political capital. The supporters of the Second Republic constituted only a small minority within the ranks of the Opposition, and the Junta further alienated potential support for any program of reform by its violation of the Pact of the Mexican Embassy. Although the adherents of National Liberation considered themselves to be socialists and therefore to the political left of the National Republicans, the insurrection weakened the left and fortified the right by virtually eliminating the *calderonistas* and *vanguardistas* from the political spectrum. Only the members of the Social Democratic party remained on the left. When the extent of their international obligations became known, the junta lost

[7] Castro Esquivel, *José Figueres Ferrer*, p. 86.

[8] The "special courts," the Court of Immediate Sanctions, and the Tribunal of Probity, were established outside the judicial system. These courts operated on the basis of lists of the accused published by the junta. The accused then had to appear before the court within a matter of months to defend themselves or be found guilty automatically. There was no appeal. The lists were purely partisan; anyone who had come over to the Opposition during the political struggle was not subjected to revolutionary "justice." See Zeledón, *Historia constitucional*, pp. 40–42 and pp. 44–53.

[9] Ibid., pp. 57–59.

further support. The very presence of hundreds of uniformed Caribbean exiles rankled many Costa Ricans.

The meagerness of the junta's political base became manifest as it began the creative aspects of its program. It met much the same resistance that had been brought to bear against the reform program of the previous governments. The ire expressed by the junta's opposition, however, was even more intense, for many of those dissenting had made great sacrifices for Figueres' revolution. They had fought alongside his men; they had contributed money, supplies, time, shelter, and countless other services. Their privileges were being threatened even more perniciously by the junta than they had been by *caldero-comunismo*. The euphoria from a victory over the "bad Costa Ricans" came to an abrupt end with Decree Laws 70 and 71 of June 21, 1948, which provided, respectively, for a 10 percent forced contribution from private capital and for the nationalization of the banking system.[10]

Although the reaction to earlier decrees had been mild, despite certain encroachments on cherished elements of the national tradition, the present reaction represented the true nature of the Opposition. Previously it had opposed Calderón Guardia, Picado, and Vanguardia Popular because their programs of government had conflicted with personal interests. Efforts to solve the social question and provide a more ample and dignified way of life for the mass of Costa Ricans had elicited from this group a strong dissidence which coalesced in the "great civic movement, the Opposition," and in the Army of National Liberation. It was the junta that now threatened established interests, and former allies within the Opposition became vehemently antijunta and remained so to its end.

The junta realized only a small part of the work that it had planned. The Second Republic was founded in name only, since the Constituent Assembly, when it met, would not accept, even as a base for discussion, the draft of a new constitution drawn up by a committee appointed by the junta. The draft was discarded and the

---

[10] Castro Esquivel, *José Figueres Ferrer*, pp. 163–168; Zeledón (*Historia constitucional*) reproduced the texts of the decrees on pp. 54–57.

Constitution of 1871 was simply modified to serve the Second Republic as it had served the first. The name, Second Republic, fell rapidly into disuse.

Figueres and the junta passed eighteen stormy months in power, then reestablished constitutional government and transferred authority to Ulate. They had not succeeded in transforming the nation according to their theoretical framework. Even with the powers of a de facto regime, their concrete realizations in social and economic reform did not equal those of the National Republican governments of Picado and Calderón Guardia. The great achievements of the junta were the nationalization of the banking system, which remains a burning issue in Costa Rica, the dissolution of the army, and the establishment of National Liberation as a viable political movement.

The revolution and the junta consolidated the reform program of the previous eight years by moving the center of controversy farther to the left. The full meaning of the goals of the Second Republic, as revealed in the decree laws and the draft constitution, so alarmed most of Figueres' former allies that the reform measures passed by the previous two regimes no longer seemed radical. Within a few years Calderón Guardia's program became part of the accepted heritage of the past, although he himself remained a controversial figure.

During the next decades, as the young men of the Social Democratic party, catapulted by the revolution into areas of national decision making, advocated and pursued ever more profound and audacious programs of modernization, the social reforms which had precipitated the revolution ceased to be at issue. The accelerated trend toward the establishment of state-owned autonomous institutions seemed so ominous to the guardians of the status quo that they readily incorporated the positive role of the state as espoused by the *calderonistas* into their concept of the proper role of the nation. The time span of nostalgic looks backward into the past shortened. The conservatives no longer looked back to the golden days of Don Cleto and Don Ricardo but simply to the days before National Liberation, for the present plans for economic development and modernization were far more comprehensive than had been those of the National Republicans.

An important effect of the revolution, along with the political crisis which preceded it and the program of the junta, was the rededication of Costa Ricans to the maintenance of civil government, the peaceful transfer of power from one popularly elected candidate to another, and a perfecting of the electoral process. Figueres, the junta, and the Constituent Assembly all contributed to strengthen these convictions. The bitterness engendered by the whole process of the revolution proved anew to the Costa Rican people that, even though representative government can be slow and at times unresponsive, it is an effective safeguard against governmental excesses. All subsequent governments have worked to make elections as nearly perfect as possible. The Electoral Tribunal has become a permanent and adequately financed body, one not likely to invite improvisation or to fall into the abuse which handicapped its efforts in 1948.

National Liberation, under the perennial leadership of José Figueres, has been in power, or near to it, since the Army of National Liberation first marched into San José. As a political party, National Liberation has been able to achieve many aspects of its program that it was unable to do through the Founding Junta of the Second Republic. The junta, however, clearly indicated the direction that Costa Rican development would follow for the next two decades. The young men of the Centro, the Generation of 1948, have had ample opportunity to apply their solutions to national problems and with results worthy of Costa Rica's rich democratic traditions. With the passage of time they have found that their plans for improving economic, social, and political conditions in Costa Rica were generally complementary rather than antagonistic to those of the National Republicans.

SELECTED BIBLIOGRAPHY

MATERIAL IN PRIVATE COLLECTIONS

Koberg Bolandi, Maximiliano. "Koberg Memoranda."
A collection of ten memoranda prepared by Maximiliano Koberg Bolandi, a member of the Costa Rica Electoral Tribunal in 1947–1948 (in the files of Maximiliano Koberg Bolandi in San José).

Meléndez Ch., Carlos. "Meléndez Collection."
Photographs, pamphlets, broadsides, newsclippings, letters, and other miscellaneous items dealing with the period 1942–1949, collected by Professor Carlos Meléndez Ch. (in the files of Carlos Meléndez Ch. in Heredia, Costa Rica).

Murray, Alexander. "Murray Collection."
A collection of primary source material concerning the revolution, conserved by Alexander Murray, one of the principal revolutionaries. It contains letters, messages in plain language and in code, broadsides, intercepted government messages, and other miscellaneous items from the years 1947 and 1948 (in the files of Alexander Murray in San José).

Picado, Teodoro. "Comentario sobre el folleto *Como y porqué cayó la democracia en Costa Rica*."
Written by ex-President Picado as to the veracity of the many assertions contained in that pamphlet which included events in which he was a principal (copy in the files of the author).

PAMPHLETS

Acción Demócrata. *Declaración de principios y reglamento interno.* San José: Imprenta Borrasé, 1944.

Alexander, Robert. *Labor Parties of Latin America.* New York: League for Industrial Democracy, 1942.

———. *Labour Movements in Latin America.* [London: Fabian Publications, 1947.]

Argüello, Dr. Rosendo, hijo. *El impostor que siendo un pigmeo quiere pasar a la historia como un gigante.* [Managua, 1958.]

Brenes Mesén, Roberto. *El político.* San José, 1942.

Busey, James L. *Latin American Political Guide.* [Boulder, Col.: Printed Page, 1963.]

———. *Notes on Costa Rican Democracy.* [Boulder, Col.: University of Colorado Press, 1962.]

Caja Costarricense de Seguro Social. *¿Qué es el Seguro Social?* San José: Imprenta Nacional, 1942.

Calderón Guardia, Dr. Rafael Angel. *Discurso del señor Presidente de la República Dr. Don Rafael Angel Calderón Guardia leído ante el Congreso el 8 de Mayo de 1944.* San José: Imprenta Nacional, 1944.

———. *El gobernante y el hombre frente al problema social costarricense.* San José, 1944.

Centro para el estudio de problemas nacionales. *El Partido Comunista de Costa Rica enjuiciado por sus hechos.* San Jose: Imprenta Borrasé, 1943.

Comisión Política de Vanguardia Popular. *Como y porqué cayó la democracia en Costa Rica.* [Guatemala City, 1949.]

———. *Por qué lucha Vanguardia Popular.* San José: Ediciones Vanguardia, 1945.

———. *Los sucesos de Costa Rica.* [Guatemala City, 1948.]

———. *Trabajo en su trece aniversario.* San José, 1944.

Comité Costa Rica–Unión Soviética. *¿Será posible una tercera guerra mundial?* San José: Trejos Hermanos, 1946.

Cortés Castro, León. *Programa de gobierno y orientaciones generales del Partido Demócrata.* San José: Imprenta Borrasé, 1941.

Diario de Costa Rica. *El opio de las garantías sociales.* San José: Imprenta Trejos Hermanos, 1942.

Dillon, Dorothy. *International Communism and Latin America: Perspectives and Prospects.* [Gainesville, Fla.: University of Florida Press, 1962.]

Documentos relativos a la situación creada entre Costa Rica y Nicaragua. [Washington, D.C.: Unión Panamericana, 1961.]

Facio, Rodrigo. *El Centro ante las garantías sociales.* San José: Imprenta Borrasé, 1943.

Fallas, Carlos Luis. *El canal de Nicaragua y nuestra soberanía.* San José: Publicaciones de la Unión de Mujeres Carmen Lyra, 1950.

———. *Don Bárbaro.* San José: Imprenta Elena, 1960.

————. *La gran huelga bananera del Atlántico de 1934*. San José: Publicaciones de la CGTC, 1955.

————. *Reseña de la intervención y penetración yanqui en Centro América*. [Mexico City: Fondo de Cultura Popular, 1954.]

————; Mora, Eduardo; and Ferreto, Arnoldo. *Calderón Guardia, José Figueres y Otilio Ulate*. San José, 1955.

Fernández Durán, Roberto. *La huelga de brazos caídos*. San José: Editorial Liberación Nacional, 1953.

Ferreto, Arnoldo. *Los principios de organización del Partido Vanguardia Popular*. San José: Ediciones Vanguardia, 1946.

Figueres Ferrer, José. *Las causas de la bonanza*. San José: Imprenta La Republica, 1954.

————. *Los deberes de mi destino*. San José: Imprenta Vargas, 1957.

————. *Dos revoluciones*. San José: Imprenta Tormo, 1962.

————. *Las elecciones de 1958 y el futuro de un gran movimiento popular*. San José: Imprenta Nacional, 1958.

————. *Estos diez años*. San José: Imprenta Nacional, 1958.

————. *La imparcialidad del presidente*. San José: Imprenta Nacional, 1957.

————. *Mensaje de José Figueres a la conferencia interamericana prodemocracia y libertad celebrada en la Habana el 12 de Mayo de 1950*. San José: Imprenta Española, 1950.

————. *Mensaje presidencial presentado a la Asamblea Nacional Constituyente de la Segunda República de Costa Rica*. San José: Imprenta Atenea, 1949.

————. *Palabras gastadas*. San José: Imprenta Española, 1943.

————. *Los tres grandes cambios de la humanidad*. San José: Imprenta Nacional, 1948.

Formoso, Manuel. *Recurso de inconstitucionalidad de Manuel Formoso Peña sobre los decretos leyes de intervención y de probidad*. San José: Imprenta La Nacion, 1950.

Garro, Joaquín. *La derrota del partido Liberación Nacional*. San José: Imprenta Vargas, 1958.

Gil Pacheco, Rufino. *La nacionalización bancaria*. San José: Imprenta Tormo, 1962.

La guerra de la liberación 1948. San José: Librería e Imprenta Atenea, 1949.

Guier, Enrique. *Defensa de los Señores Licenciados Don Teodoro Picado y Don Vicente Urcuyo*. San José: Imprenta La Nacion, 1950.

Ibarra Mayorga, Francisco. *La tragedia del nicaragüense en Costa Rica*. San José: Imprenta Borrasé, 1948.

Kantor, Harry. *The Costa Rican Election of 1953: A Case Study.* [Gainesville, Fla.: University of Florida Press, 1958.]

Lacayo L., Chester. *Los osados: Noguera Gómez y sus hombres.* San José, 1944.

Martén, Alberto. *El comunismo vencido.* San José: Imprenta Borrasé, 1952.

Monge, Luis Alberto. *No hay revolución sin libertad.* San Jose: Imprenta Tormo, 1961.

Mora Valverde, Manuel. *Defiende la Revolución Cubana y aborda la crisis del café en Costa Rica.* San José: Imprenta Tormo, 1959.

———. *Dos discursos.* San José, 1959.

———. *Dos discursos de actualidad.* San José: Imprenta Tormo, 1958.

———. *Dos discursos en defensa de Vanguardia Popular.* San José, 1959.

———. *Dos discursos en respuesta a los falsos defensores de la democracia y de la independencia de las pequeñas naciones.* San José, 1940.

———. *Nuestra soberanía frente al Departamento de Estado.* San Jose, 1940.

———. *Por la afirmación de nuestra democracia: Por el progreso y bienestar de nuestra nación.* San José, 1959.

———. *Porqué Vanguardia Popular sigue apoyando al gobierno.* San José: Imprenta La Tribuna, 1945.

Moviemiento Liberación Nacional. *Los pagos de la guerra de Liberación Nacional.* San José: Editorial Liberación Nacional, 1953.

Núñez, Francisco María. *Seguro Social.* San José: Imprenta Borrasé, 1941.

Núñez Quesada, Fernando. *Recurso de inconstitucionalidad de Víctor Wolf: Refutación a la contestación de la Procuraduría General de la República.* San José: Imprenta La Nación, 1950.

La obra social de Presidente Calderón Guardia. San José: Imprenta Nacional, 1944.

Ortiz, Santiago. *Primera aplicación del Tratado Interamericano de Asistencia Recíproca.* [Washington, D.C.: Unión Panamericana, 1949.]

Partido Liberación Nacional. *José Figueres: Su gesta libertaria.* San José: Editorial Eloy Morua Carrillo, 1952.

———. *Política campesina y ley de reforma agraria.* San José: Editorial Eloy Morua Carrillo, 1962.

Partido Social Demócrata. *Estatuto Constitucional del Partido Social Demócrata—fundado el 11 de Marzo de 1945.* San José: Tipográfica Nacional, 1945.

————. *Resumen del programa de gobierno.* San José: Imprenta Borrasé, 1949.

————. *Aspiraciones campesinas.* San José: Imprenta Tormo, 1948.

Picado, Teodoro. *El Pacto de la Embajada de Mexico.* [Managua: Editorial Centroamericana, 1949.]

Pinaud, José María. *Las verdaderas causas de mi rebeldía frente al Presidente Cortés.* San José: Imprenta La Tribuna, 1940.

Procuraduría General de la República. *Recurso de inconstitucionalidad promovido por el señor Rodolfo Brenes Torres contra los Decretos Leyes No. 41 del 2 de Junio de 1948 y No. 618 del 20 de Julio de 1949.* San José: Imprenta Nacional, 1950.

Sanabria, Víctor M. *Palabra dirigida al venerable clero de la Arquidiócesis de San José.* San José, 1945.

Sancho, Mario. *Costa Rica: Suiza Centroamericana.* San José: Imprenta La Tribuna, 1935.

Tratado Interamericano de Asistencia Recíproca. Washington, D.C.: Unión Panamericana, 1961.

Trejos, Eladio. *Instrucciones para los miembros de las juntas receptoras de votos del partido Unión Nacional.* San José: Partido Unión Nacional, 1948.

Ulate, Otilio. *¿Hacia dónde lleva a Costa Rica el Señor Presidente Figueres?* San José: Imprenta Universal, 1955.

Wolf, Víctor. *Recurso de inconstitucionalidad de los Decretos-Leyes del Tribunal de Intervención establecido por Víctor Wolf Cedeño ante la Corte Suprema de Justicia de Costa Rica.* San José: Imprenta La Nación, 1950.

Zeledón, Marco Tulio. *XVIII Años de vida estudiantil.* San José: Imprenta Nacional, 1959.

————. *Reseña histórica del régimen constitucional de Costa Rica.* San José: Imprenta Nacional, 1941.

ARTICLES

Alexander, Robert Jackson. "The Latin American Aprista Parties." *The Political Quarterly* 20 (1949): 236–247.

"Aplicación de la ley de seguros sociales en Costa Rica." *Revista Internacional de Trabajo* 25 (January, 1942): 103–104.

Arias, Maurilio. "En Tilarán y Cañas si existió segundo frente." *Diario de Costa Rica* (San José), June 14, 1948, p. 2.

Barnhardt, Edward N. "Citizenship and Political Tests in Latin American Republics in World War II." *Hispanic American Historical Review* 42 (1962): 297–332.

Benavides, Héctor. "José Figueres, el hombre de las grandes frases." *La Hora* (San José), February 23, 1949, p. 3.

Blanksten, George I. "Political Groups in Latin America." *The American Political Science Review* 52 (1958): 106–127.

Bonilla, Harold H. "Teodoro Picado y la historia." *Diario de Costa Rica* (San José), July 19, 1960, pp. 2–5.

Brenes Ibarra, Dr. Abelardo. "Prisioneros políticos de un régimen desaparecido." *La Prensa Libre* (San José), June 8, 1948, p. 5.

Cañas, Alberto. "La nueva Costa Rica se descubrirá ante los héroes." *La Hora* (San José), April 24, 1948, p. 13.

———. "Sangre, sudor y lágrimas." *La República* (San José), March 11, 1951, pp. 17–28.

Castro Vargas, Gonzalo. "Jorge Zeledón Castro." *Diario de Costa Rica* (San José), May 18, 1948, p. 5.

Ceciliano, Nathan. "Mi actuación como soldado del Ejército de Liberación Nacional." *El Social Demócrata* (San José), November 27, 1948, p. 7.

Chacón Jinesta, Alvaro. "Operaciones en el frente norte," *Diario de Costa Rica* (San José), May 1, 1948, p. 3.

Chaves, Nicasio. "Diario de un cartaginés," *La Prensa Libre* (San José), April 23, 1948, p. 4.

Child, Irvin L. "The Background of Public Opinion in Costa Rica." *Public Opinion Quarterly* 7 (1943): 242–257.

Cordero Croceri, José R. "El General Miguel A. Ramírez." *La República* (San José), March 11, 1951, p. 5.

———. "Historia del civismo estudiantil." *La Prensa Libre* (San José), July 29, 1948–October 8, 1948, p. 5.

Esquivel Guier, Max. "El contrato petrolero: Historia en comprimidos." *La Nación* (San José), June 8, 1949, p. 4.

Facio, Alvaro. "Forty-Million-Dollar Lesson." *The Inter-American* 3 (March, 1944): 10–12.

Facio, Gonzalo J. "Los golpes de estado, la solidaridad democrática y la no intervención." *Panoramas* 1 (January, 1963): 7–58.

Fallas Monge, Otto. "El trabajo en el proyecto de constitución política." *El Social Demócrata* (San José), January 29, 1949–March 5, 1949, p. 4.

Fernández Durán, Gerardo. "Las cañas huecas." *La República* (San José), March 11, 1951, p. 2.

Figueres Ferrer, José. "Enemigos de nuestra producción." *Acción Demócrata* (San José), December 23, 1944, p. 2.

———. "Nuestra contribución a la victoria." *Acción Demócrata* (San José), December 9, 1944, p. 2.

————. "Tres años después." *La República* (San José), March 11, 1951, p. 2.

Garro, Joaquín, "Peligrosa incursión a la Sierra." *La Prensa Libre* (San José), July 19, 1948, p. 8.

Griffin, K. B. "Reflections on Latin American Development." *Oxford Economic Papers* 18 (April, 1966), 16–24.

Güell, Roberto. "La Batalla de Santa Elena." *El Social Demócrata* (San José), May 5, 1948, p. 7.

Guier, Enrique. "La antigua corte de justicia." In *La tragedia de Costa Rica*, by José Albertazzi Avendaño, pp. 177–185. Mexico City. 1951.

————. "Carta a Diario de Costa Rica." *Diario de Costa Rica* (San José), May 11, 1948, p. 2.

Gunther, John. "Costa Rica: A True Democracy." *Current History*, 52 (December 24, 1940): 11–12.

Gutiérrez, Carlos José. "Santa María, la de los revolucionarios." *El Social Demócrata* (San José), October 9, 1948, p. 8.

————. "El Sargento de la ametralladora." *El Social Demócrata* (San José), April 9, 1949, p. 7.

Guzmán, Juan Rafael. "Datos estadísticos sobre las elecciones habidas en Costa Rica desde Noviembre de 1889 hasta el 2 de Octubre de 1949." *Diario de Costa Rica* (San José), July 24, 1953, p. 17.

Hafter, Rudolph P. "Costa Rica y Honduras: Una excepción y un peligro." *Cuadernos* 67 (December, 1962): 79–84.

"La Historia de la prensa clandestina." *La Hora* (San José), June 5–22, 1948, p. 3.

Jiménez, Carlos María. "Como nació y para que fin fué destinada la Legión Caribe." *La Prensa Libre* (San José), April 30, 1948, p. 3.

————. "Y así llegamos a Santa María de Dota." *La Prensa Libre* (San José), June 12–22, 1948, p. 7.

————. "Y la Legión Caribe cumplió su cometido." *La República* (San José), March 11, 1951, p. 11.

Jiménez, Manuel F. "Coffee in Costa Rica." *Bulletin of the Pan American Union* 79 (February, 1945): 88–89.

Junta Fundadora de la Segunda República. "La revolución en marcha." *La Prensa Libre* (San José), June 10–30, 1948, p. 3.

Kantor, Harry. "Agrarismo y tierra en Latinoamérica." *Combate*, no. 14 (January–February, 1961), 14.

————. "También hay democracia en el Caribe." *Combate*, no. 9 (March–April, 1960), 56–57.

Martén, Alberto. "Control de las intermitencias naturales." *Diario de Costa Rica*, July 3, 1948, p. 1.

————. "El crédito gratuito." *La Prensa Libre* (San José), July 17, 1948, p. 3.

————. "La defensa del valor humano." *La Prensa Libre* (San José), July 22, 1948, p. 3.

————. "Democracia política y democracia económica." *Diario de Costa Rica* (San José), July 11, 1948, p. 1.

————. "Democracia política y democracia social." *La Prensa Libre* (San José), July 8, 1948, p. 3.

————. "Desarticulación monetaria de la relación producto-consumidor." *La Prensa Libre* (San José), July 9, 1948, p. 5.

————. "El hombre y la masa." *Diario de Costa Rica* (San José), July 14, 1948, p. 1.

————. "Sensibilidad revolucionaria." *La Prensa Libre* (San José), July 19, 1948, p. 3.

Martin, Lawrence and Sylvia. "Five Wise Men of Costa Rica." *Christian Science Monitor Monthly Magazine*, October, 1942, p. 5.

————. "Four Strongmen and a President." *Harper's* 185 (September, 1942): 418–427.

Monge de Camacho, Rosita. "Recuerdos de la revolución de 1948 en nuestra querida Costa Rica." *Diario de Costa Rica* (San José), May 14, 1948, p. 5.

Murkland, Harry B. "Costa Rica: Fortunate Society," *Current History* 22 (March, 1952): 141–144.

Núñez V., Guillermo. "En las crónicas de la revolución se ha hecho lamentable olvido de quienes construyeron los tanques." *La Nación* (San José), October 8, 1948, p. 13.

Núñez, Santiago. "El movimiento cooperativista en Costa Rica." *Combate* 18 (September–October, 1961): 53–58.

Oduber, Daniel. "Tarea inaplazable de los costarricenses." *La Nación* (San José), March 31, 1965, p. 12.

————, and Monge, Luis Alberto. "Dictaduras, Imperialismo y Democracia." *Combate* 9 (March–April, 1960): 12–20.

París, Luis A. "Sobre el mártir Alvaro París." *La República* (San José), March 10, 1951, p. 7.

Petersen, Juan Andrés. "Somoza versus the Americas." *The Nation*, January 15, 1949, pp. 63–66.

Ramírez, Miguel A. "La Batalla de el Empalme fué decisiva en la suerta de la revolución." *Diario de Costa Rica* (San José), May 16, 1948, p. 10.

————. "La Batalla de San Isidro del General." *Diario de Costa Rica* (San José), May 4, 1948, p. 1; May 5, 1948, p. 1; and May 9, 1948, p. 5.

Ramos, Guillermo. "Historia del Batallón Simón Bolívar." *El Social Demócrata* (San José), November 13, 1948, p. 6.

Ramos, Lilia. "El tico es apacible, fisgador, indisciplinado." *La República* (San José), March 11, 1951, p. 11.

Ramos Valverde, Rogelio. "El Sr. Oduber no puede alzar una bandera en la que jamás ha creído." *La Nación* (San José), January 21, 1965, p. 20.

Rechnitz, Carlos. "Historia oficial de la guerra civil." *Diario de Costa Rica* (San José), June 1, 1948, p. 5.

Rex (Alberto Cañas). "Hace cuatro años." *La República* (San José), December 20, 1952–January 8, 1953.

Ribas Montes, Jorge. "La batalla por la toma de Cartago." *Diario de Costa Rica* (San José), May 1, 1948, p. 1.

Rodríguez Poorras, Armando. "¿Hubo revolución en Costa Rica?" *Diario de Costa Rica* (San José), April 22, 1949, p. 5.

Rodríguez Vega, Eugenio. "Un frente ignorado." *El Social Demócrata* (San José), September 11, 1948, p. 3.

Sánchez, Francisco, and Alfredo Mejía Lara. "Las gloriosas batallas que abrieron rutas de victoria al ejército de la Liberación Nacional." *Diario de Costa Rica* (San José), May 7, 1948, p. 1.

Sancho G., Belfort. "El Radio Nacional y la guerra de liberación." *Diario de Costa Rica* (San José), October 9, 1949, p. 5.

Thiel, Bernardo Augusto. "Monografía de la población de la república de Costa Rica en el siglo XIX." *Revista de Costa Rica en el siglo XIX* (San José) 1902, pp. 1–52.

Trejos Escalante, Fernando. "¿Cuales conquistas sociales posteriores a 1948 son más importantes que las anteriores a ese año? *La Nación* José), January 18, 1965, p. 17.

BOOKS

Alba, Víctor. *Historia de movimiento obrero en América Latina*. Mexico: Libreros Mexicanos Unidos, 1964.

———. *Parásitos, mitos y sordomudos*. Mexico: Centro de Estudios y Documentación Sociales, 1951.

Albertazzi Avendaño, José. *La tragedia de Costa Rica*. [Mexico: by the author], 1951.

Alexander, Robert Jackson. *Communism in Latin America*. New Brunswick, N.J.: Rutgers University Press, 1957.

———. *Prophets of the Revolution: Profiles of Latin American Leaders*. New York: The Macmillan Company, 1962.

———. *The Struggle for Democracy in Latin America*. New York: The Macmillan Company, 1961.

Anderson, Charles W. *Politics and Economic Change in Latin America.* Princeton: D. Van Nostrand Co., Inc., 1967.

Arciniegas, Germán. *Entre la libertad y el miedo.* Mexico City: Editora Zarco, 1955.

Argüello, Dr. Rosendo. *La verdad en marcha.* Mexico City: Imprenta Nonpareil, 1950.

Argüello, Dr. Rosendo, hijo. *Quienes y como nos traicionaron.* [Mexico City: By the Author], 1954.

Barck, Oscar T., Jr. *A History of the United States since 1945.* New York: Dell Publishing Co., Inc., 1965.

Bayo, Alberto. *Tempestad en el Caribe.* [Mexico City: By the Author], 1950.

Berle, Adolf A. *Latin America: Diplomacy and Reality.* New York: Harper and Row, Publishers, 1962.

Biesanz, John and Mavis. *Costa Rican Life.* New York: Columbia University Press, 1944.

Blanco Segura, Ricardo. *Monseñor Sanabria.* San José: Editorial Costa Rica, 1962.

Brinton, Crane. *The Anatomy of Revolution.* New York: Random House, Vintage Books, 1962.

Brogan, Denis W. *The Price of Revolution.* New York: Grosset and Dunlap, Inc., 1951.

Cañas, Alberto. *Los ocho años.* San José: Editorial Liberación Nacional, 1955.

Castro Esquivel, Arturo. *José Figueres Ferrer.* San José: Imprenta Tormo, 1955.

Chacón Jinesta, Oscar. *Laureles Cívicos: Don León Cortés Castro.* [San José: By the Author], 1947.

Cordero Rojas, Oscar. *Diario: Ecos de una revolución.* San José: Imprenta Española, 1948.

Dobles, Fabián. *Los leños vivientes.* San José: Imprenta Elena, 1962.

Duggan, Lawrence. *The Americas: The Search for Hemisphere Security.* New York: Henry Holt and Company, 1949.

Dulles, John Foster. *War or Peace.* New York: The Macmillan Company, 1950.

Eisenhower, Milton S. *The Wine Is Bitter.* Garden City: Doubleday & Company, Inc., 1963.

Fallas, Carlos Luis. *Mamita Yunai.* San José: Editorial Soley y Valverde, 1941.

Fernández Guardia, Ricardo. *Cartilla histórica de Costa Rica.* San José: Imprenta Atenea, 1964.

Figueres Ferrer, José. *Cartas a un ciudadano*. San José: Imprenta Nacional, 1956.

Fluharty, Vernon L. *The Dance of the Millions: Military Rule and the Social Revolution in Colombia*. Pittsburgh: University of Pittsburgh Press, 1957.

Gibson, Charles. *Spain in America*. New York: Harper and Row, Publishers, 1966.

Hernández Poveda, Rubén. *Desde la barra*. San José: Imprenta Borrasé, 1953.

Herring, Hubert. *A History of Latin America*. New York: Alfred A. Knopf, 1961.

Hilton, Ronald, *Who's Who in Latin America*. Stanford, Stanford University Press, 1945.

Humphreys, Robin A. *The Evolution of Modern Latin America*. New York: Oxford University Press, 1946.

Hyde, H. Montgomery. *Room 3603*. New York: Farrar, Straus, and Co., 1963.

James, Preston. *Latin America*. London: Cassell and Company, 1959.

Jiménez, Carlos María. *Historia de la aviación en Costa Rica*. San José: Imprenta Elena, 1962.

———. *La legión Caribe*. San José: Imprenta Borrasé, 1948.

Johnson, Chalmers. *Revolution and the Social System*. Stanford: The Hoover Institution on War, Revolution, & Peace, 1964.

Jones, Chester Lloyd. *Costa Rica and Civilization in the Caribbean*. Madison: University of Wisconsin Press, 1935.

Karnes, Thomas L. *The Failure of Union: Central America, 1824–1960*. Chapel Hill: University of North Carolina Press, 1961.

Koberg, Maximiliano. *El verdadero orden social*. San José: Imprenta Trejos Hermanos, 1944.

Marshall, Bruce. *The White Rabbit*. London: Evans Brothers Limited, 1952.

Martin, Percy Alvin. *Who's Who in Latin America*. Stanford: Stanford University Press, 1940.

Martínez, Fernando. *El Presidente Cortés a través de su correspondencia*. San José: Imprenta Nacional, 1939.

Martz, John D. *Central America: The Crisis and the Challenge*. Chapel Hill: University of North Carolina Press, 1959.

Mason, Bruce B. (ed.). *The Political-Military Defense of Latin America*. Tempe: Arizona State University Press, 1963.

May, Stacy. *Costa Rica: A Study in Economic Development*. New York: Twentieth Century Fund, 1952.

Michels, Robert. *Political Parties*. New York: The Macmillan Company, 1966.

Ministerio de Gobernación. *Constitución Política de Costa Rica*. San José: Imprenta Nacional, 1950.

Miranda, Jorge. *Expedicionarios audaces o el ocaso del tirano Somoza*. San José: By the Author, 1948.

Monge Alfaro, Carlos. *Geografía social y humana de Costa Rica*. San José: Imprenta Universitaria, 1943.

————. *Historia de Costa Rica*. San José: Imprenta Trejos Hermanos, 1962.

Myrdal, Gunnar. *Economic Theory and Underdeveloped Regions*. London: Duckworth, 1957.

Nacionalización bancaria en Costa Rica. San José: Imprenta La Española, 1951.

Navarro Bolandi, Hugo. *La generación del 48*. Mexico: Ediciones Humanismo, 1957.

————. *José Figueres en la evolución de Costa Rica*. Mexico: Imprenta Quirós, 1953.

La Obra social del Presidente Calderón Guardia. San José: Imprenta Nacional, 1944.

Obregón Loría, Rafael. *Conflictos militares y políticos de Costa Rica*. San José: Imprenta La Nación, 1951.

Ortuño Sobrado, Fernando. *El monopolio estatal de la banca en Costa Rica*. San José: Imprenta Trejos Hermanos, 1963.

Parker, Franklin D. *The Central American Republics*. London: Oxford University Press, 1965.

Poblete Troncoso, Moisés. *El movimiento obrero latino-americano*, Mexico: Fondo de Cultura Económica, 1946.

República de Costa Rica. *Código Electoral*. San José: Imprenta Nacional, 1947.

Reyes H., Alfonso. *Así es Costa Rica*. [San José: By the Author], 1945.

Rodríguez Vega, Eugenio. *Apuntes para una sociología costarricense*. San José: Editorial Universitaria, 1953.

Rojas Suárez, Juan. *Costa Rica en la Segunda Guerra Mundial*. San José: Imprenta Nacional, 1943.

Sancho, Mario. *Memorias*. San José: Editorial Costa Rica, 1961.

Schlesinger, Arthur M., Jr. *A Thousand Days*. New York: Fawcett World Library, 1967.

Schurz, William Lytle. *Latin America*. New York: E. P. Dutton & Co., 1964.

Secretaría de Gobernación. *Constitución política de la República de Costa Rica*. San José: Imprenta Nacional, 1944.

Secretaría de Trabajo y Previsión Social. *Código de Trabajo*. San José: Imprenta Nacional, 1943.

Stephens, John Lloyd. *Incidents of Travel in Central America, Chiapas, and Yucatán*. 2 vols. New Brunswick, N.J.: Rutgers University Press, 1949.

Stokes, William S. *Latin American Politics*. New York: Thomas Y. Crowell, 1959.

Tannenbaum, Frank. *Ten Keys to Latin America*. New York: Alfred A. Knopf, 1962.

Teichert, Pedro C. M. *Revolución económica e industrialización en América Latina*. Mexico: Fondo de Cultura Económica, 1961.

Trejos, Juan. *Geografía ilustrada de Costa Rica*. San José: Imprenta Trejos Hermanos, 1964.

Unión Democrática Centroamericana. *Por qué lucha Centro América*. Mexico City: Gráfica Panamericana, 1943.

U.S. Department of State, *Foreign Relations of the United States, Vol. VI, 1942*. Washington, D.C.: Government Printing Office, 1963.

Valle, Rafael Heliodoro. *Historia de las ideas contemporáneas en Centro América*. Mexico City: Fondo de Cultura Ecónomica, 1960.

Welles, Sumner. *An Intelligent American's Guide to the Peace*. New York: The Dryden Press, 1945.

Wilson, Charles M. *Middle America*. New York: W. W. Norton and Company, 1944.

Zelaya, Antonio. *La inflación y sus consecuencias en la economía costarricense*. San José: Imprenta Nacional, 1944.

Zeledón, Marco Tulio. *Lecciones de ciencias constitucionales y constitución política de la República de Costa Rica*. San José: Imprenta Nacional, 1945.

———. *Historia constitucional de Costa Rica en el bienio 1948–1949*. San José: Imprenta La Nación, 1950.

PERIODICALS

Bulletin of the Pan American Union. Vols. 74–82. 1940–1948.

The Inter-American. Vols. 3–4. 1944–1945.

International Labour Review. Vols. 46–57. 1942–1947.

Newsweek. October 1944–February 1949.

Time. February 1944–December 1949.

Surco (San José), 1942–1944.

NEWSPAPERS

Acción Demócrata (San José), February 1944–May 1947.

Diario de Costa Rica (San José), January 1940–January 1950.

Eco Católico (San José), January 1947–March 1948.
El Social Demócrata (San José), May 1947–January 1950.
La Gaceta (San José), January 1948–January 1952.
La Hora (San José), January 1940–January 1950.
La Nación (San José), October 1946–January 1950.
La Prensa Libre (San José), January 1936–December 1950.
La Tribuna (San José), January 1936–April 1948.
La Última Hora (San José), January 1944–March 1948.
New York Times, January 1946–January 1949.
Trabajo (San José), January 1940–March 1948.

Acción Demócrata: opposes *caldero-nista* programs, 34; merges with Centro, 36, 84–86, 113; as independent party, 36, 112; criticizes fiscal corruption, 62–63, 67; envisions Second Republic, 82, 84; party philosophy of, 84–85; and Figueres, 86; Figueres helps establish, 92; newspaper of, lauds Figueres, 93. See also Social Democratic party

Acción Demócrata: established, 36; on Communists, 43 n., 50–51, 52; on fiscal corruption, 68–69; Social Democrats' philosophy represented in, 86, 95 n.; adopts title "La Lucha sin Fin," 93; Figueres' ideology in, 94; editorializes against Caribbean dictatorships, 94; commends electoral reforms, 116

agriculture: development of, relieves economic strain, 75

Aguilar, Mr. ———: and armaments for liberation army, 144 n.

Alajuela: skirmishes near, 139

Albertazzi Avendaño, José: on Calderón Guardia, 29 n.; on Congressional annullment of elections, 128; on planes for Figueres, 150 n.

Alemán, Miguel: and Costa Rican revolution, 141 n.

Alianza Democrática: Mora joins with, 15

Alma Tica (radio station): and rebellion. 97

"Almaticazo," the: revolt as, 75; as first attempt at insurrection, 96–97

Altamira: revolutionary troops at, 142

Amerindians: poverty among, 20; law for social progress of, 33

Arana, Colonel Francisco: and armaments for Opposition, 104, 136

Arbenz Guzmán, Colonel Jacobo: and arms shipments to Costa Rica, 136

Arévalo Bermejo, Juan José: and social security system, 30 n.; and armaments for Opposition, 104–105, 133, 136

Argüello, Rosendo, hijo: as ally of Figueres, 98, 99; and arms for Opposition, 102, 105, 133; on Alexander Murray, 132 n.; on atrocities by revolutionaries, 148 n.

aristocracy: in Costa Rica, 5. See also oligarchy

armaments: National Police receive, 60–61; Opposition acquires, 98; and "Plan Sunday," 98–99; shipment of, seized in Mexico, 99; Figueres requests from Argüello, 102; transportation of, 133, 136; for army, 140–141

army: buildup of, during World War II, 109; size of, 114; suffers from inexperience, against Figueres' forces, 140; disorganization in, 140; armaments for, 140–141; dissolved, 160 bananas: and landholdings, 6; conditions in zones of, 24–25

bankers: in economic elite, 7

banks: Picado government requests loans from, 73; employees of, in strike, 102, 103; government forces to reopen, 102; nationalized, 159, 160. SEE ALSO National Bank

Barahona, Oscar: authors social security law, 30 n.

Barrio Escalante: construction of, brings accusations of fiscal corruption, 67

barrios: housing problems in, 21–22

Beeche, Octavio: Cortés Castro opposes, 12, 111 n.; on Electoral Tribunal, 121

beneficios: coffee producers control, 6

Biesanz, John and Mavis: on social question, 19 n.

Blanco Cervantes, Raúl: in post-revolution government, 157 n.

Bloque de la Victoria: formed from alliance of Vanguardia Popular and National Republicans, 111; Picado as candidate of, 111

Bloque de Obreros y Campesinos: works for reform, 11, 34, 43; opposition to, 11, 12, 13; organizes strike, 12; popularity of, grows in 1940's, 15; aligns with National Republicans, 16; and *calderonista* social reform program, 27; changes name to Vanguardia Popular, 34; dissolution of, 43; tactics to limit influence of, 47–48; support of, in 1942 election, 110; as leader of labor movement. 110–111. SEE ALSO Vanguardia Popular

Bogotazo: 149

Bonilla, Alvaro: tax proposal of, 77 n.

Braden, Spruille: on non-democratic governments, 115

Brenes Gutiérrez, Miguel: 151

"Brigada Canta Rana": organized by Opposition, 100

brigades, neighborhood: organized by Opposition, 100; promote violent confrontations, 100; assaults by, 101

Brogan, Denis W.: on Cold War, 56

budget: traditional balance in, 65; *calderonista* government overspends, 65, 72; law concerning, 74

business: and fiscal corruption of government, 66; and strikes, 102–103. SEE ALSO industry

Caja Costarricense del Seguro Social: encourages investment in housing, 32

caldero-comunismo: as label for government, 53

Calderón Guardia, Francisco: and compromise with Opposition, 117–118

Calderón Guardia, Rafael Angel: enacts "Ley de parásitos," 8 n.; advocates reform, 14; in 1940 election, 15; popularity of, 16; elected President, 16; program of, 16–18, 27–28; concentrates on social problems, 18; on social question, 19 n.; avoids government control of economic activity, 28; laws of, regarding housing, 28; encourages creation of new industries, 29; on land distribution, 29; creates social security system, 29; program of, for children's shoes, 29; favors small farm to solve agrarian problem, 29; encourages fishing industry, 32; principles of, 33; resistance to programs of, 33; linked by oligarchy to Communists, 33; Figueres criticizes, 37; collaborates with Communists, 42; pragmatism of, in accepting support of Communists, 44; and second term as President, 45; retains party leadership, 45 n.; Opposition portrays as Communist, 57; Communist leanings denied, 57–58; criticizes Ulate, 58; opposes U.S. intervention in national affairs, 58; attempt to assassinate, 58 n., 104; *Diario* criticizes, 60; popularity of, hurt by financial mismanagement, 62; complacency of, 66; and government corruption, 67; administrative abilities of, 69–70; misuses executive power, 73; opposition to reforms of, justifies revolution. 82;

and expulsion of Figueres, 89, 90; linked to Caribbean dictators, 98; promises electoral reform, 108; and suppression of Germans, 109–110; and leadership of labor movement, 110-111; opponents seek to discredit, 112–113, 116–117; replaces Vanguardia as threat to oligarchy, 112; in New York, 113; as 1948 presidential candidate, 120; and outcome of 1948 election, 124, 126, 128; claim of, to presidency, 130; charges Opposition with fraud, 133; and control of Vanguardia Popular, 141; opposition to reform program of, transferred to revolutionary junta, 159, 160; mentioned, 22, 146

calderonistas: focus program on social reform, 18; principles of, 33; and capitalism, 33; terrorist tactics of, 45; and U.S. anti-Communist policies, 56–57; and fiscal corruption, 63, 80; as "civil oligarchy," 64; intention of, to maintain power, 130; nullify 1948 election, 134–135; face armed force of Opposition, 135

Canal Zone. SEE Panama Canal Zone

Cañas Escalante, Alberto: on *mariachis*, 25; on Centro-Acción Demócrata alliance, 85; on Figueres, 90

capital, foreign: and economic elite, 7; in enterprises, 8

capital, private: encouraged by Calderón Guardia, 28; used in housing, 31–32

capitalism: favored by Acción Demócrata, 84, 85

Cardona Quirós, Edgar: in post-revolution government, 156 n.

Caribbean Legion: aids National Liberation army, 137–138; numbers of, increase during revolution, 138; Somoza threatened by, 147; Figueres obligated to, 155–156

Cartago: low-cost housing in, 32 n.; Figueres' plantation near, 87; workers' strike in, 99, 101, 102; violence in, 99–100, 101–102; liberation army occupies, 143, 147, 150

Casamata: government troops defend, 140, 143, 148

Castro Cervantes, Fernando: organizes Almaticazo, 97; and compromise between government and Opposition, 117–118, 120; as presidential candidate, 119; contributes to Figueres' organization, 132

Castro Esquivel, Arturo: on Figueres, 87, 145 n.

Catholic church: and program of social change, 16; fights poverty, 27; and Communist reform program, 43; communism threatens, 47; Figueres conflicts with, 87

caudillo civil: Calderón Guardia as, 107; in Costa Rica, 107 n.; Cortés as, 108; Figueres as, 155

Centoz, Luigi: negotiates with revolutionaries, 145

Central America: feudalism during colonial era in, 5; Figueres seeks freedom for nations in, 95

Central American Union: Figueres seeks to aid reestablishment of, 95; arsenal for, 105

Centro para el Estudio de los Problemas Nacionales (Centro): advocates social and economic reform, 14; membership of, 14, 36; student strength in, 14–15; on housing shortage, 22; opposes *calderonista* programs, 34, 37–38; as non-political group until 1945, 34; involvement of, in politics, 34–35, 36; studies by, of Costa Rican problems, 35; socialist programs proposed by, 35; refers to self as Generation of Forty-eight, 35; forms nucleus of Social Democratic party, 36; epithets applied to, by opponents, 36 n.; guides programs of Social Democrats, 37, 83, 84; attacks social security law, 37–38; opposes government's creation of La Victoria, 38; criticizes fiscal corruption, 62, 67; theoretical framework of, justifies revolution, 81; envisions Second Republic, 82–83, 84; merges with Acción Demócrata, 84–86, 113; and Figueres, 86; and 1944 election, 111; success of, 161. SEE ALSO Generation of Forty-eight; Social Democratic party

Cerdas, Jaime: in Communist party, 49 n.

church. SEE Catholic church

cities: middle class emerges in, 9, 10; voting patterns in, 10; housing shortage in, 21–23

Ciudad Quesada: Nicaraguan troops in, 142 n.

"civil oligarchy": as phenomenon, 64 n.

Civil Registry: electoral fraud at, 122

coffee: and landholder aristocracy, 5–6; production of, and national wealth, 7; effect of, on economy, 73

Cold War, the: effect of, in Costa Rica, 45–47, 55; obscures merits of political factions, 61; Figueres' position in, 149

Comintern: Vanguardia Popular declares adherence to, 59

communism: effect of, on 1948 revolution, 41; internationalism of, 43; as threat to nations, 45; produces U.S.-Soviet Union break, 45–46; *La Nación* on, 58–59; merits of, obscured by politics, 61

comunismo criollo: indigenous communism as, 11–12; political attack on, 12–13; domestic aspect of, blurred by international propaganda, 50; development of, 50; policies of, 50–51; changed by Cold War, 55

Communist party. SEE Bloque de Obreros y Campesinos; Vanguardia Popular

Communists, Costa Rican: and United Fruit Company, 24; collaborate with Calderón Guardia, 42–43, 44; support government's reform program, 42; respectability of, 43; in anti-Fascist demonstrations, 43; suffer from alliance with government, 44; and change in international views of communism, 45–46; portrayed as threat, 47; development of indigenous party of, 48–49, 50; Mora as respected leader of, 49–50; suffer from identification with international communism, 50; defense by, of human rights, 50–51; as Popular Front, 51; make false claims of

power, 55; criticize government's fiscal corruption, 63; Figueres links government to, 88; assaulted by brigades, 101; strength of, declines in 1946 elections, 116; resist revolutionary forces, 116; Figueres appeals to U.S. attitude toward, 149; U.S. threatens intervention against, 150

compromise, political: impossibility of, after 1948 election, 134–135; revolutionary forces negotiate with diplomatic corps, 145; Picado favors, to end conflict, 148–149; ends conflict, 150–151

comptroller: office of, created, 74

Congress: Communist deputies in, 58, 60; boycotted by Opposition, 117; and electoral fraud, 125, 128; annulls 1948 election, 128. SEE ALSO government, Costa Rican

Constituent Assembly: enacts constitution for Second Republic, 156; discards draft of constitution, 159–160; strengthens adherence to governmental processes, 161

constitution: tradition of adherence to, 3–4, 161; amendments to, on social guarantees, 30–31; social function of property in, 30; on presidential terms, 44; for Second Republic, 156, 159–160; of 1871, abrogated, 156 n.

cooperatives: investment in, encouraged, 31–32

Cordero Croceri, José R.: on Opposition brigades, 101

Corrigan, Frank P.: Ulate charges as pro-Communist, 61

corruption. SEE fiscal corruption

Cortés Castro, León: opposes Communists, 12, 13; tactics of, in elections, 15, 44–45, 111; authoritarianism of, 15; opposition to, 15–16; leaves National Republican party, 28; founds Democratic party, 34, 108–109; party of, in Opposition, 37 n.; threat of, to *calderonista* reforms, 44; and government's fiscal corruption, 63; and income tax, 76; as *caudillo civil*, 108; reactionary politics of, 109; government campaign against, 112;

attempts to ease tensions, 113; proposes compromise to Picado, 117; death of, 117; mentioned, 119

Cortés Fernández, Otto: criticizes Picado, 60

Costa Rica: tradition of stability in, 3–4; and other Hispanic American countries, 4–5; society in, modernizes, 4; Spanish colonists in, 5; colonial agrarian democracy in, 5; coffee production in, 5–6, 7; landholding in, 6; economic elite in, 7–8; growth of middle class in, 9; bases for disequilibrium in, 17–18; poverty in, 19–20; population growth in, 20–21; housing shortage in, 21–23; U.S. citizens in, 22; ineffective use of land in, 23; malnutrition in, 24; effects of World War II on, 26, 66–67, 71, 109–110; Communists in, collaborate with government, 41–43; effect on, of U.S. anti-Communist policy, 45–46; anti-Communist campaigns in, 47; wartime economy of, 66–67, 71; foreign trade of, 71–72, 73; and Pan American Highway, 72–74; external debt of, 73; programs to solve economic problems of, 74–75; ideologies in, justify revolution, 81; Second Republic in, 82–83, 154–160; Figueres plans liberation of, 105; army buildup in, 109; U.S. military personnel in, 109; Germans in, suppressed, 109–110; attempts to pacify, 113; electoral crisis in, 124–128; insurrection begins in, 128–129; armaments to rebels in, 133; negotiations in, for peace, 145, 150–151; foreign intervention in, 146–147, 149–150; effect in, of revolution, 161; National Liberation's power in, 161; improvement of conditions in, 161

Costa Rica: Suiza Centroamericana: rural life described in, 22–23

Costa Rican Labor Federation: Fallas as leader of, 49

Court of Immediate Sanctions: as "special court," 158 n.

courts: independence of, from government control, 114; justice in "special courts," 158 n.

credit: rural system of, 27

customs duties: furnish income, 72

David, Panama: arms shipment to, 133

Davis, Nathaniel P.: as U.S. ambassador to Costa Rica, 54; negotiates with revolutionaries, 145

decree laws: abrogate 1871 constitution, 156 n.; proscribe Vanguardia Popular, 158; require contributions to government, 159; nationalize banks, 159; reaction to, 159

democracy: tradition of, 3; agrarian aspect of, 5; implications of, 9; and participation in political decisions, 9–10

Democratc party: Cortés Castro forms, 28, 34, 108–109; in coalition of the Opposition, 37 n.; Castro Cervantes represents, 117–118, 119 n.

Desamparados (canton): government defense in, 140

Diario de Costa Rica: study in, on housing shortage, 21–22; Centro on national problems in, 34; anti-Communist articles in, 52; anti-Calderón Guardia campaign in, 57; Calderón Guardia in, on fiscal corruption, 63 n.; Figueres' speech from building of, 92; and 1944 election, 111

dictatorships, in Caribbean region: resistance to, 10; collaboration with exiles from, 98; plots to overthrow, 105, 132 .

diplomatic corps: negotiates with revolutionary forces, 145

Dobles, Fabián: in Communist party, 49 n.

Dominical: armaments for Opposition at, 98–99, 133; government troops at, 140

Dominican Republic: exiles plan attack on, 104

Donnelly, Walter J.: as U.S. ambassador to Costa Rica, 54; denounces communism, 54; activities of, 54 n.

dysfunction: as cause of revolution, 4; and landholding, 6–7; communism's ability to remedy, 41

Eco Católico: favors tax reform, 78
economy: imbalances in, bring increased government activity, 71
education: and wealth, 7; expansion of, produces middle class, 10; esteem for, 77; and taxation, 77–78
Eisenhower, Milton: on Donnelly, 54 n.
elections: participation in, encouraged, 10; women petition for, 103; guaranteed by pact between government and Opposition, 103–104; tensions concerning, 106–107; precipitate crisis of 1948, 107; opponents charge obstruction of, 107; tradition of exalting, 108; in 1944, 111–112; government fraud in, 112; bring cohesion to Opposition, 113–114; Opposition candidate for, 118–119; Ulate wins, 122–123; voting discrepancies during, 123, 124–127; annulled by Congress, 128; Figueres fears compromise after, 134
electoral code: Vanguardia Popular demands, 115; Picado produces, 116; used in 1964 elections, 116; Opposition seeks maintenance of, 118; adhered to, in 1948 elections, 121, 123; ignored by *calderonistas*, 130
electoral issue: and fraud, 107; chronology of, 107–108; Opposition consolidated by suffrage issue in, 113–114; and demands for free elections, 115; electoral code in, 115–116
Electoral Registry: denounced by *calderonistas* as Opposition-dominated, 122; implements electoral laws, 122
Electoral Tribunal: established by electoral code, 121; as hope for fair elections, 121; insists on free elections, 121; discovers fraud by National Republicans, 122; and voting discrepancies, 123; verdict of, on elections, 124–128; faces electoral crisis, 124–127; agitation at offices of, 125, 127; accused of favoring Opposition, 134; permanence of, 161

electric power companies: nationalization of, 85; terrorism against, 99
elite. SEE oligarchy
El Salvador: students in, praised by *Acción Demócrata*, 94
Empalme, El: battle at, 140
entrepreneurs: break isolationist tradition, 7
Escalante, Carlos Manuel: 69
exiles: in Costa Rica, after revolution, 159
Export Import Bank: loans by, to Costa Rica, 71, 72, 74, 75

Facio, Alvaro: on Pan American Highway, 73 n.
Facio Segreda, Gonzalo: anti-Communist activities of, 53; and Figueres conspiracy, 98 n.; in post-revolution government, 157 n.
Facio, Rodrigo: asserts apolitical concerns of Centro, 34
Fallas, Carlos Luis, as labor leader, 49; in Communist party, 49, 50; on election fraud, 108 n.; leads government troops, 140
farmers: and land redistribution, 8 n.
Fernández Durán, Roberto: on housing deficiencies, 23
Fernández Guardia, Ricardo: on 1924 election, 11 n.; on fiscal corruption, 70; on Picado's economic program, 75; on government-Opposition compromise, 117
Ferreto, Arnoldo: in Communist party, 49 n.; mentioned, 51
Figueres Ferrer, José: Acción Demócrata supports, 37, 85, 86; criticizes Calderón Guardia, 37, 86, 88; speech of, brings exile, 37, 88–89, 114; on government corruption, 67; personifies rebel, 86, 92; biographical notes on, 87–88; accused of traitorous activity, 88–89; writes on Costa Rican politics, 89–90, 92; envisions Second Republic, 90, 93; ideology of, transcends national politics, 91; mystique of, 92; returns to Costa Rica, 92; speeches of, 92–94; and formation of Social Democratic party, 94–95, 96; as conspirator, 95; organizes

ally with, 41–44; fiscal corruption of, 62; expands financial expenditures to implement social reform, 64–65; bureaucracy of, 65–66; complacency in, 66; wartime economy of, opposes frugal traditions, 66; exploited by industrialists, 66–67; opponents seek to reveal dishonest practices of, 67; exiles Figueres, 88–89; Figueres outlines plans for operation of, 92; discredited in Opposition propaganda, 98, 114–115; terrorism against, 99, 104; violence used by, against opponents, 100, 103; and workers' strike, 102–103; pact of, with Opposition, guarantees elections, 103–104; and compromise with Opposition, 117–118, 120; negotiations over form of, 145; lack of coordination among troops of, 148; adherence to processes of, after revolution, 161

Gran Hotel Costa Rica: election ballots counted at, 126

Grecia: sugar refinery cooperative at, 32

Griffin, K. B.: on social classes, 9 n.

Guanacaste: poverty in, 20; social reform program focuses on, 27; Figueres' speeches in, 93; political prisoners in, 151

Guatemala: workers' strike in, 102; Dominican exiles' arsenal in, 104; Figueres secures arms from, 105, 133, 136, 137

Gunther, John: on Costa Rica, 3 n.

Guzmán, Gerardo: on Electoral Tribunal, 121; discovers fraud, 122

health: in *barrios*, 21–22
Heredia: housing in, 32 n.
Hora, La: Centro on national problems, in, 34
housing: inadequacies of, 19, 21–23; and middle class, 22; program of, proposed by Calderón Guardia, 27; laws on, 28; rents for, frozen, 28; low-cost cooperatives created, 28; construction of, 28; institution for, 28, 32 n.

huelga de brazos caídos: in Cartago, 101, 102. SEE ALSO strike, workers'

Ideario Costarricense: Figueres outlines national plan in, 92
immigration: and business enterprises, 8; and population growth, 20–21; origins of, 21 n.
Incidents of Travel in Central America, Chiapas, and Yucatán: Costa Rican society described in, 5
income tax: advocated, 75; attempts to institute, 76. SEE ALSO taxes
Indians. SEE Amerindians
industry: cattle, and landholding, 6; private, encouraged, 28, 29; fishing, 32; and government's fiscal corruption, 66; and wartime economy, 66; leaders in, exploit government, 66–67
inflation: complicates economic problems, 72
Instituto Nacional de Vivienda y Urbanismo: encourages low-cost housing. 32 n. SEE ALSO housing
insurrection: follows annulment of 1948 election, 128–129. 133. SEE ALSO revolution of 1948; strike, workers'

Jiménez Oreamuno, Ricardo: in Generation of 1889, 9 n.; Volio supports, 11; combats Communist influence, 13; in 1940 election, 15; proposes income tax, 76; presidential term of, 116
Johnson, Howlett: as U.S. ambassador to Costa Rica, 54
Jones, Chester Lloyd: on Costa Rica, 3 n.; on population, 21 n.
Jones, Colonel R. E.; in anti-Fascist demonstrations, 43 n.
Junta Nacional de la Habitación: on housing shortage, 22. SEE ALSO housing
Junta, Revolutionary: "special courts" of, 63 n.–64 n. 158 n.; governs Second Republic, 156, 158; dissolves Pact of the Mexican Embassy, 158; resistance to, 159; failure of, 160;

revolution, 96, 144; power of, strengthened by Almaticazo, 97; acquires armaments, 99, 102; terrorist organization of, 99; and strike, 102, 104; seeks international support, 104–105; pact of, with Caribbean exiles, 105; criticizes efforts at compromise, 118; considered as presidential candidate, 119; appointed campaign manager for Ulate, 120; and violence at Valverde house, 129; on necessity of force to overcome *calderonistas*, 130; Pact of Caribbean supports own organization, 131; organizes insurrection, 131–132; fears compromise after election nulled, 134; armed forces prepare at farm of, 135; moves headquarters to Santa Maria de Dota, 137; and Caribbean Legion, 138; leads troops to occupy Cartago, 143; advocates civil disobedience, 144; negotiates with diplomatic corps, 145, 148; warns of attack on capital, 149; appeals to U.S. attitude toward Communists, 149; in San José, after peace negotiated, ·152; speech of, on organization of Second Republic, 152; in interim government, 154 n.; success of, 155; as *caudillo*, 155; and Caribbean Legion, 155–156; pact of, with Ulate, guarantees revolutionary goals, 156; as president of Second Republic founding junta, 156; transfers authority to Ulate, 160; fails to transform nation, 160; strengthens adherence to governmental processes, 161

Figuls, Fernando: in Figueres conspiracy, 98 n.; and armaments for Opposition, 105

finances: government's mismanagement of, 62; and fiscal corruption, 64–65; tradition of frugality in, overturned, 65–66; and foreign trade, 71–72, 73; from taxes, 72; from liquor monopoly, 72; for Pan American Highway, 72–73; laws concerning, 74; and need of revenue, 74–75

fiscal corruption: as issue in re\ tion, 62, 79–80; criticized government's opponents, 63; ministries, 63; and nation's financ. problems, 64–65; results from ove turning tradition of frugality, 65 66; and wartime industrialization. 66–67; practices of, revealed by Opposition, 67

fishing industry: encouraged by Calderón Guardia, 32

Fluharty, Vernon L.: on Bogotazo, 149 n.

Formoso, Manuel: attempt to assassinate, 58 n.; home of, destroyed by terrorists, 104

Frailes: government troops defend, 140, 143

fraud: Calderón Guardia accused of. 113; as issue consolidating Opposition. 113. SEE ALSO elections

Gámez Solano, Uladislao: in postrevolution government, 156 n.

Garro, Joaquín: leads Opposition brigade, 100, 102

Generation of 1889: establishes reforms, 7; on implications of democracy, 9; politics of, as goal of revolution, 82

Generation of Forty-eight: Centro refers to self as, 35; after revolution, 155; success of programs of, 161. SEE ALSO Centro para el Estudio de los Problemas Nacionales; Social Democratic party

geography: and Costa Rica's isolation from neighbors, 4

Germans: suppressed in Costa Rica, 109–110

Germany: oligarchy in, 64 n.

Golfito: government troops at, 140

González Flores, Alfredo: overthrown, 4, 11; and income tax, 76

González Víquez, Cleto: in Generation of 1889, 9 n.

government, Costa Rican: activity by, during World War II, 26, 66, 71; fights poverty, 27; Calderón Guardia avoids participation of, in economic activity, 27–28; Communists

strengthens adherence to governmental processes, 161
justice. SEE courts

Kekicht, Thomas: studies Costa Rican economy, 74
Koberg Bolandi, Maximiliano: on electoral question, 121, 125 n.

Labor Code: enactment of, 29, 30, 31; establishes labor ministry and courts, 31; as support for collective bargaining, 31; opposition to, 38; strike violates, 103; brings support to Calderón Guardia, 111
labor movement: fights poverty, 27. SEE ALSO workers
landholding: type of, in Costa Rica, 6; and land industries, 6–7; and economic elite, 8; and uncultivated land, 8, 23; and "Ley de los parásitos," 8 n., 29; constitution on, 29
Land Law. SEE "Ley de los parásitos"
Lara, Fernando: 120
Law for New Industries: Calderón Guardia government sponsors, 29
Law for the Protection of the Indian: enactment of, 33
Leo XIII, Pope: and social guarantees of constitution, 30
León Herrera, Santos: salary of, 68; designated as President, 145; pact provides interim term of, 150–151
"Ley de los parásitos": enacted to encourage land redistribution, 8 n., 29
Ley Orgánica de la Controlaría General: creates comptroller's office, 74
Ley Orgánica de la Tesorería Nacional: supervises government revenues, 74
Ley Orgánica de Presupuesto: organizes budget, 74
Liberación Nacional. SEE National Liberation movement; National Liberation party
liquor monopoly: furnishes income, 72
literacy: high rate of, 3
Llano Grande: Figueres speeches in, 93
Lombardo Toledano, Vicente: 60

López Masegosa, Julio: manufactures bombs, 142; activities of, 142 n.
Lucha sin Fin, La: as name of Figueres' plantation, 87; name adopted for political crusade by *Acción Demócrata*, 93; Figueres forces organize at, 135
Lyra, Carmen: on Communist party, 49 n.; on González' overthrow, 76 n.

Managua, Nicaragua: 146
mariachis: described, 25; progovernment workers as, 103 n.; in army, 141; as victims of conflict, 152
Martén, Alberto: directs *Acción Demócrata*, 36–37; receives special funds, 68–69; and fiscal corruption, 68–69; on tax reform, 77; seeks national power, 87, 88; on Figueres' writings, 91; helps create mystique of Figueres, 92; in Figueres conspiracy, 98 n.; in post-revolution government, 154 n., 157 n.
Martén Carranza, Ernesto: receives government funds, 69
Martínez, Hernández: and strikes in El Salvador, 102
Masís Dibiassi, Bruce: aids Opposition brigades, 100–101; in post-revolution government, 157 n.
medical service: for Indians, 33; and social security system, 38 n.
meseta central: population pressure on, 8 n., 21; Communists' influence in, 11; poverty in, 20; and banana zone, 25; and fish diet, 32; revolutionaries reach, 148–149
Mexico: social security program in, 27; Costa Rican embassy in, 79; Figueres in, 89 n., 90, 91; political exiles in, 91
Michels, Robert: on oligarchies, 64 n.
middle class: emerges in cities, 9; composition of, 9; in national life, 10; resists reform, 33, 39; opposes Calderón Guardia, 40; in government bureaucracy, 66
Mills, C. Wright: on oligarchies, 64 n.
Minister of the Interior: accused of fiscal corruption, 71
Ministry of Development: fiscal corruption in, 63, 70

Ministry of Public Works: fiscal corruption in, 63

Moín: battle at, 143

Monge Alfaro, Carlos: on Costa Rica, 3 n.; on revolution, 96

Morales, Aureo: Picado orders arrested, 151

Mora Valverde, Manuel: establishes Bloque de Obreros y Campesinos, 11; and 1935–1936 campaign, 13; gains support for Communists, 13; elected to Congress, 13; opposes Cortés Castro's presidency, 15; collaborates with Calderón Guardia, 42; dissolves Bloque, 43; forms Vanguardia Popular, 43–44; and international communism, 44, 59, 61; opposition to, 47–48; as *caudillo*, 49; prestige of, 49–50; opposes violent revolution, 51; effect on, of Cold War, 54; loses prestige, 55; Calderón Guardia on, 57–58; attempt to assassinate, 58; foresees social revolution, 82; terrorist activities against, 99, 104; on Congress' annullment of 1948 election, 128; and compromise between Calderón Guardia and Ulate, 135; strengthens position, 141; combats revolutionary forces, 146, 150; and Nicaraguan intervention, 147; influence of, in negotiated peace, 151

Mosca, Gaetano: on oligarchies, 64 n.

Murray, Alexander: aids Figueres in planning revolution, 132; military experience of, 132–133; operates intelligence network, 138, 140, 144; spreads rumors to confuse government forces, 144; advises Figueres, 145; on Communist resistance, 146 n.

Myrdal, Gunnar: on economic processes, 6 n.

Nación, La: on Costa Rican communism, 55; Opposition's anti-Communist manifesto in, 58; impartiality of, 58; on attempt to assassinate Mora, 58–59; on *Acción Demócrata*, 86 n.

National Bank: and rural credit, 27; and social security system, 30; extends operations into rural areas, 31–32; encourages investment in housing, 32; sponsors La Victoria, 32

National Liberation, Army of: arms for, 136; ambushes government troops near La Lucha, 136; along La Sierra highway, 136; and Caribbean Legion, 137–138; U.S. assists, 142; in April offensive, 142–143; in San José, 145, 152; in Cartago, 147, 149, 150; Somoza's forces threaten, 150

National Liberation movement: books on, 3 n.; Centro in literature of, 85, 86; war of, begun, 135; armaments for, 136; and Caribbean Legion, 137–138; effect of, on Picado, 143–144; use of propaganda in, 144; press portrays as rightist movement, 144; goal of, to found Second Republic, 144, 152, 154; military success of, 152; ideology of, 153, 160; moves to right politically, 158

National Liberation party: establishes institution for housing, 28 n., 32 n.; in power since 1948, 161; success of programs of, 161

National Library: director's position criticized, 79

National Police: receive arms, 60–61; and workers' strike, 103; inspect Opposition leader's house, 129

National Republican party: wins 1924 election, 11; opposes communism, 12; segment of, advocates reform, 14; aligns with Bloque de Obreros y Campesinos, 16, 41, 42; social reform program of, 34, 41, 42; composition of, 39; Cortés Castro alleges Communists lead, 44–45; suffers from alliance with Vanguardia Popular, 48; alliance officially severed, 58; effect on, of Vanguardia's adherence to international communism, 59; opponents charge with fiscal corruption, 64; seeks tax legislation to implement programs, 75, 76, 78; fraud by, in elections, 107, 122; voting trend away from, 116; convention of, acclaims Calderón Guardia, 120; accuses Opposition of electoral fraud, 124, 125, 126; leaders of, leave San José, 146; unprepared for revolution, 152–153

National Union party: in coalition of the Opposition, 37 n.; as Ulate's party, 57; suggests Communist control of government, 60; Ulate represents, 119 n.

Navarro Bolandi, Hugo: on Costa Rica, 3 n.; on Generation of 1889, 9 n.; on election of 1924, 11; on Gonzalez' overthrow, 76 n.; on Centro-Acción Demócrata alliance, 85

newspapers: declarations in, on tax reform, 78

Nicaragua: Acción Demócrata praises students in, 94; Figueres promises liberation of, 105; intervention by, in Costa Rica, 146–147, 149–150; fortifies frontier against invasion, 149

Niehaus family: sugar refinery of, expropriated, 32; position of, 110 n.

Nuñez, Father Benjamin: organizes labor group, 111; negotiates with diplomats, 145; political activity of, 146 n.; in post-revolution government, 156 n.–157 n.

nutrition: deficiencies of, 23–24; and fishing industry, 32

Obregón Loria. Rafael: on banana strike, 12 n.

Ochomogo: liberation army at, 143

Odio, Benjamín: directs Electoral Registry, 122; joins Figueres forces, 125; and electoral fraud, 125–126

Oduber, Daniel: on social reform, 18 n.; in Figueres conspiracy, 98 n.

oligarchy: as heirs of Generation of 1889, 7; support maintenance of status quo, 7–8; and economic department, 8; supports democratic tradition, 10; fears Communist party, 11; links Calderón Guardia to Communists, 33; challenged by *calderonista* reforms, 39; allies with middle class to oppose Calderón Guardia. 40; and fiscal corruption, 64; as phenomenon, 64 n.; Calderón Guardia threatens, 112, 113

Opposition, the: formed in 1945, 37; Social Democrats known as, 37; as coalition of anti-*calderonista* forces, 37 n.; benefits from U.S. anti-communist party policy, 45–46; resistance of, to Picado administration, 45; terrorist organization of, 45; anti-Communist propaganda of, 45, 48, 61; labels Calderón Guardia as Communist, 48, 57; *Acción Demócrata* on, 52; on Vanguardia Popular, 61; joined by corrupt officials, 63 n.–64 n.; criticizes fiscal corruption, 64, 69, 75; opposes taxes, 76–77, 78; on Calderón Guardia's campaign activities, 79–80; adopts ideology justifying revolution, 94; Social Democrats work for cohesion within, 96; Figueres orients toward revolution, 97–98; and violence in Cartago, 99–100; brigades of, 100–102; supports strike, 102–103; pact of, with government, guarantees elections, 103–104; accuses pro-government forces of electoral fraud, 107; propagandizes against *calderonista* regimes, 114; boycotts Congress, 117; Picado seeks compromise with, 117; attempts at compromise, bring criticism from within. 118, 120; convention of, chooses 1948 presidential candidate, 118–119; unity in, 119–120; and fraud in 1948 elections, 124–125, 126, 128; supports Ulate's claim to presidency, 130; Electoral Tribunal accused of favoring, 134; U.S. assists, during revolution, 142; and Second Republic, 158, 159

Orlich, Cornelio: and Figueres conspiracy, 98 n.

Orlich, Francisco: joins Figueres in seeking national power, 87, 88; elected to Congress, 88; helps create mystique for Figueres, 92; and Figueres conspiracy, 98 n.; leads revolutionary troops, 139

Ornes, Horacio: leads liberation army offensive, 142–143

Ortega y Gasset, José: 35

Ovares, Julio César: as first designate to presidency, 135

Pacheco Tinoco, Rigoberto: investigates Figueres' organization, 136; killed, 136

"Pacto del honor, El": Opposition and government negotiate, 103; guarantees elections, 103–104

Pact of the Caribbean: exiles sign, to overthrow dictatorships in Caribbean region, 105; and Second Republic, 131; armaments obtained through, 133

Pact of the Mexican Embassy: ends conflict, 150–151; provisions of, 157; as obstacle to Second Republic, 157–158; dissolved, 158

Palabras gastadas: Figueres' political philosophy in, 89–90, 91–92

Panama: Costa Rica ships goods to, 26

Panama Canal Zone: Pan American Highway as U.S.'s link to, 72; foreign threats to, 74; Figueres obtains plane in, 142 n.; U.S. troops in, prepare for intervention, 150

Pan American Highway: construction of, 26; cost of, increases budget deficit, 72–73, 74; armaments along, 99; Figueres troops at, 136, 140

parasites: farm laborers as, 8; squatters known as, 23; cultivate new lands, 23. SEE ALSO "Ley de los parásitos"

Pareto, Vilfredo: on oligarchies, 64 n.

Pasaje Racia: housing conditions in, 22

patrón: and workers, 10, 82

Peña Chavarría, Dr. Antonio: 15

personalismo: of political parties, 10

Picado, Alfredo: in Communist party, 49 n.

Picado, René: on 1948 election, 122–123, 124

Picado, Teodoro: Oduber on, 18 n.; as candidate of National Republicans, 44; support of, by Vanguardia Popular, 44, 55; in 1944 election, 45, 112; *Acción Demócrata* criticizes, 53; and Vanguardia's support of international communism, 59–60; and fiscal problems, 73, 74–75, 76; tax reform program of, 76–78; criticism of administration of, 78, 98; and

Almaticazo, 97; linked to Caribbean dictators, 98; reaction of, to strike, 103; and women's petition for elections, 103; attempts by, to ease tensions, 113; and compromise with Opposition, 117–118; supports free elections, 121; response of, to insurrection, 139; on anti-government propaganda, 139 n.; and control of Vanguardia Popular, 141; on U.S. assistance to Opposition, 142 n.; distressed by revolution's effects, 143–144; appoints León Herrera as president, 145; and Nicaraguan intervention, 146 n.–147 n., 147; favors compromise to end conflict, 148–149, 150; negotiates pact, 150–151; leadership qualities of, 151–152

Pinochet, Tancredo: on poverty, 20

Pius XI, Pope: and social guarantees, 30

"Plan Sunday": and revolutionary operations, 98–99

police. SEE National Police

population: growth of, causes social problems, 20–21

poverty: in Costa Rica, 19–20; ignored by elite, 20; as political issue, 20

Powers, Joshua (agency): 60

Prensa Libre, La: reports Cartago violence, 101, 102 n.; negotiations summarized in, 151 n.

press: freedom of, 10, 114

prison: political enemies of government in, 144

propaganda: used by revolutionaries, 98, 144

Public Works Administration, U.S.: loan of, to Costa Rica, 72

Puerto Limón: voting in, 125 n.; liberation army seizes, 142–143

Puntarenas: fishing industry in, 32; Figueres speeches in, 93; voting in, 125 n.

Quirós, Arturo: organizes Almaticazo, 97

railroads: furnish income, 72; terrorism against, 99; liberation army controls, 143

Ramírez, Miguel Angel: as chief of staff, liberation army, 137; defeats government forces, 137

rebellion: defined, 4 n.

reform: various groups advocate, 26–27; as issue, 112–113. See also social reform; taxes

Reform party: expresses desire for social change, 11

Reimers, Federico: Figueres accused of collaborating with, 89; property of, 89 n., 110 n.

"resistance," the: Opposition's neighborhood brigades as, 100; in Cartago, 100–102

Rerum Novarum: labor organization as, 111

revolution: defined, 4 n.

revolution of 1948: breaks stable tradition, 4; communism as issue in, 41, 53–61; fiscal corruption as issue in, 62; rationalizations for, 81, 94; Figueres as prime mover of, 86; and formation of Social Democratic party, 94–95; election tensions precipitate, 107; Caribbean Legion in, 137–138; Figueres explains in speeches, 144; negotiations to end, 145; Pact of Mexican Embassy brings peace in, 150–151; Figueres' success in, 155; Second Republic the result of, 155–156; effect of, 161; bitterness engendered by, 161

Revolutionary Junta. See Junta, Revolutionary

ricos progresistas: implement social reform, 28

riot (1942): Figueres blames government for, 88

roads: for Indian regions, 33; priorities misdirected in construction of, 72–73; to frontier, 72; and Pan American Highway, 72–73

Rodríguez, General Juan: provides armaments for Figueres, 136

Rodríguez Vega, Eugenio: on Costa Rica, 3 n.; on wealthy class, 7; on education, 7; on social question, 19 n.

Rojas Suárez, Juan: on Calderón Guardia, 29 n.

Sáenz, Carlos Luis: elected to Congress, 13; in Communist party, 49 n.

Sanabria Martínez, Archbishop Victor Manuel: and reform program, 17, 43; proposes compromise between *calderonistas* and Opposition, 129

San Carlos: skirmishes at, 139

Sancho, Mario: on Costa Rican society, 5; on reforms, 7; on rural life, 22–23; on foreign capital, 23; on education of workers, 49

San Isidro del General: and armaments for liberation army, 99, 137; Figueres troops capture, 136; battle at, 140

San José: housing in, 21–22, 32 n.; anti-Fascist demonstrations in, 43 n.; 1942 riots in, 88; seizure of, as goal of Almaticazo, 97; and violence in Cartago, 101; strike in, 102–103; violence in, 103; transfer of authority in, 145; *vanguardistas* prepare for combat in, 146, 149, 150; Figueres warns of attack on, 149

San José, province of: 13

San Pablo: sinking of, and riot. 88

San Ramón: Figueres born in, 87; Figueres speeches in, 93; revolutionaries capture. 139

Santa María de Dota: revolutionary headquarters at, 137, 139

Schlesinger, Arthur M., Jr.: on Kennedy's principles, 33

Scott, Edward "Ted": cooperates with Murray, 144

Scotten, Robert M.: on fiscal corruption, 70–71; recommends financial aid to Costa Rica, 71

Second Republic: Centro and Acción Demócrata develop idea of. 82, 84; justifies revolution, 83; Figueres seeks to erect, 90, 93; and Pact of Caribbean, 105, 131; Murray's contribution to, 133; founded after revolution, 152; junta of, 154, 156 n.–157 n.; Ulate as first President of, 156; constitution for, 156; Pact of Mexican Embassy as obstacle to, 157–158; failure of, 159–160

Sierra, La (highway): revolutionary army along, 136

social class: farm laborers as, 8; divisions of, based on wealth, 8–9

Social Demócrata, El: anti-Communist stories in, 51, 53

Social Democratic party: opposes *calderonista* programs, 33–34, 37; Centro as nucleus of, 36, 37, 83, 84, 95; as part of Opposition, 37, 37 n.; terrorist tactics of, 45; ideological opposition of, to Vanguardia Popular, 46; anti-Communist campaign of, 53; and U.S. approval, 53, 55–56; as spokesmen of attack on fiscal corruption, 64, 79; and tax program, 77; philosophy of, in *Acción Demócrata*, 86; ideology of, justifies revolution, 94; formation of, as key event of revolution, 94–95; manifesto of, 95–96; prepares for revolution, 96; role of, within Opposition, 96; and Almaticazo, 97; and workers' strike, 99; brigades organized by, 100; propaganda of, against government, 114–115; demands free elections, 115; opposes compromise with government, 118, 120; conflicts with Figueres plan to overthrow Caribbean dictatorships, 132; threat of, to *calderonistas*, 135; international support for, 142; after revolution, 155; in Second Republic, 156 n., 158; advocates broad program of modernization, 160

"Social Guarantees": amendments on, to constitution, 30; and U.S. Bill of Rights, 30–31; rights implicit in, 31

socialism: Centro supports, 35; of National Liberation regime, 144–145, 153; in Second Republic, 158, 160

social issue: *calderonista* program identified with, 39

social reform: *calderonista* programs for, 44; discredited by fiscal corruption, 70; finances for, 72, 109; revolutionary junta fails in, 160

social security system: creation of, 27, 29, 30; insurance program of, 30; Figueres criticizes, 88

Soley Güell, Thomas: 15

Somoza, Anastasio: Opposition propagandizes against, 98; *calderonista* regime compared to, 114; and armaments for government, 141; intervention of, in Costa Rica, 142 n., 146–147, 149–150; fears Caribbean Legion, 147

South America: social security programs in, 27

Soviet Union: during World War II, 43; post-war antagonism toward U.S., 46; Vanguardia Popular declares adherence to, 59

Spain: colonists from, in Costa Rica, 5

"Special Courts": and former government officials, 63 n.–64 n.; dispense revolutionary justice, 158 n.

Spencer, Herbert: 87

Stephens, John Lloyd: on Costa Rican society, 5

strike, workers': in Cartago, 99, 101, 102; effect of, in other countries, 102; violence in, 102–103; government's reaction to, 103

students: in Centro, 14–15; in Opposition brigades, 101

suffrage. SEE electoral issue.

Surco: as publication of Centro, 34; creation of La Victoria attacked in, 38

Talamanca area: poverty in, 20

Tavio, Juan José: leads confrontation at Opposition leader's home, 129, 135; pro-*calderonista* activity of, 129 n.

taxes: Calderón Guardia's reforms for, 27, 73, 76; furnish income, 72; advocated to relieve economic strain, 75; opposed by commercial sectors, 76; linked with education for passage, 77–78; non-political groups express opinions on, 78; Opposition attacks as wasteful, 78. SEE ALSO income tax

teachers: pay raises of, linked to tax program, 77–78

Tejar, El: battle at, 148

terrorism: Opposition employs, to resist Picado regime, 45; used by Vanguardia Popular, 45; Figueres directs, 95, 98; extent of, 99; intensifies after strikes, 104

Thiel, Bernardo Augusto: on population, 21 n.

Tijerino, General Toribio: leads government troops, 140; killed, 140

Tinoco, General Roberto: defends Cartago barracks, 148, 149

Tinoco Granados, Federico: overthrows Gonzales Flores, 4

Torres, Edelberto: as ally of Figueres, 98, 99

towns, rural: poverty in, 26 n.–27 n.

Trabajo: Communist articles in, 46; terrorism reported in, 99 n.

trade, foreign: effect on, of World War II, 71; decline in volume of, decreases revenue, 73

transportation: deficiencies of, 19

Transportes Aéreos Centro Americanos: airplanes of, used by Figueres troops, 136

treasury, public: depletion of, 65

Tribuna, La: terrorism reported in, 99 n.; bombed, 104

Tribunal of Probity: as "special court," 158 n.

Trujillo, Rafael: *calderonista* regime compared to, 114

Ubico, Jorge: and strikes in Guatemala, 102

Ulate, Otilio: and 1940 election, 15; political party of, 37 n.; defends indigenous communism, 50; views of, in *Diario de Costa Rica*, 57; as Opposition candidate, 57, 118–119; criticizes government alliance with Communists, 60; on Cartago violence, 101; and 1944 election, 111; on suffrage, 114; and compromise of government with Opposition, 118, 120; campaign manager for, 120; criticizes electoral code, 121; and results of 1948 election, 122–123, 126–127, 128, 133; and violence at Valverde house, 129; imprisoned, 129; in hiding, 129; claim of, to presidency, 130; and U.S. assistance to Opposition, 142 n.: Figueres pledges to honor election of, 144; pact of, with Figueres, on revolutionary goals, 156; receives authority, 160

Unión Nacional. SEE National Union party

United Fruit Company: power of, 24–25; and regional development, 27; antipathy toward, 47

United States: Populist party in, 11; citizens of, in Costa Rica, 22; and Costa Rican Communists, 43, 54; communism appears as threat to, 45; antagonism toward Soviet Union, 45–46, 47; effect of anticommunism in, on Costa Rica, 45–46; gives approval to Social Democrats, 56; and anti-Communist policies of other nations, 56–57; and Costa Rica's economic situation, 71, 72; and Pan American Highway, 72–73, 74; Figueres in, 87; troops of, to Costa Rica, 109; and armaments for Costa Rican government, 141, 142 n.; assists Opposition, 142; Figueres appeals to anti-Communist policy of, 149; threatens intervention in Costa Rica, 150

university: Calderón Guardia proposes founding of, 27; formed, 33

urbanization. SEE cities

Vaglio, Victor: defeats "resistance" in Cartago, 101

Valverde, Carlos Luis: home of, inspected by police, 129, 135; killed, 129, 135

Valverde, Fernando: and 1940 election, 15; and Figueres, 92, 98 n.; organizes Almaticazo, 97; in postrevolution government, 154 n., 156 n.

Vanguardia Popular: Bloque de Obreros y Campesinos changes name to, 34; supports Labor Code, 38; power of, 41, 55, 116; collaborates with National Republicans, 41, 42, 55; terrorist tactics of, 45; identified with international communism by Opposition, 46, 51–52, 61; alliance with government hurts National Republicans, 48; programs of, 48; Acción Demócrata criticizes, 53; influence of, on national programs, 55; declares adherence to international communism, 59; petition to outlaw, 59; Opposition propagandizes against, 61; ideology of, 82,

153; and Cartago violence, 99–100; Calderón Guardia replaces, as threat to oligarchy, 112; calls for electoral code, 115; weakened by 1946 election, 116; denounces Electoral Registry, 122; seeks to strengthen position, 141–142; and attack by revolutionary forces, 146, 149, 150; opposes Nicaraguan intervention, 147; U.S. threatens to intervene against, 150; unprepared for revolution, 152–153; proscribed, 158. SEE ALSO Bloque de Obreros y Campesinos; Mora Valverde, Manuel

Vargas, Fernando: petition to outlaw Vanguardia, 59

Vargas, José María: on Electoral Tribunal, 121

Vicenzi, Moisés: position of, attacked by Social Democrats, 79

Victoria, La (cooperative): sponsored by National Bank, 32; sugar refinery at, 32; Centro opposes creation of, 38

Villa Quesada: Nicaraguan forces occupy, 149–150

violence: in Cartago, 99–100; of neighborhood brigades, 100; by government, 100; by Opposition, 100–101

Volio, General Jorge: leads reform party, 11; movement of, as basis of

comunismo criollo, 50

Volio Mata, Alfredo: and fiscal corruption of Development Ministry, 70 n.; aids Opposition brigades, 70 n., 100–101

Volio Sancho, Fernando: aids Opposition brigades, 100–101

Wallberg, Enrique: in government forces, 141

"War of National Liberation, The." SEE National Liberation movement

Welles, Sumner: on population growth, 21 n.; on Costa Rica's foreign trade, 71 n.

women: petition free election, 103

workers: types of, in middle class, 9; Communists seek reforms for, 42, 43; Communists organize, 49; educational work of, 49; strike by, in Cartago, 99, 101, 102; in pro-government forces, 103; in militia, 139; guarantees of, negotiated, 151

World War II: social problems intensify during, 26, 28; causes change in Costa Rican economy, 26, 66; and fiscal corruption, 66; causes suppression of Germans in Central America, 109–110

youth: in Social Democrats, 86; Figueres appeals to, 94